REV. ARIE ELSHOUT
1923–1991

Minister of the Gospel of the (Netherlands) Reformed Congregations*

---

*Throughout this book, the *Reformed Congregations* in Holland (*Gereformeerde Gemeenten*) are designated as (*Netherlands*) *Reformed Congregations*. The parenthetical inclusion of the word "Netherlands" serves to highlight the full correspondence relationship between the *Reformed Congregations* in the Netherlands (*Gereformeerde Gemeenten*) and its sister denomination, the *Netherlands Reformed Congregations of North America*. Rev. Elshout served churches in both federations. The word "Netherlands" will not be in parentheses when these North American congregations are referenced.

A Word in Season

The Life and Ministry of Rev. Arie Elshout

Adriaan F. Van Toor

Translated by Bartel Elshout

REFORMATION HERITAGE BOOKS
Grand Rapids, Michigan

Reformation Heritage Books
2965 Leonard St. NE
Grand Rapids, MI 49525
616-977-0889 / Fax 616-285-3246
orders@heritagebooks.org
www.heritagebooks.org

Printed in the United States of America
19 20 21 22 23 24/10 9 8 7 6 5 4 3 2 1

ISBN 978-1-60178-694-4

Originally published as
Aan Armen Uit Genâ
© 2008 Den Hertog B.V., Houten

For additional Reformed literature, request a free book list from Reformation Heritage Books at the above regular or e-mail address.

Table of Contents

Preface

I became acquainted with Arie Elshout as a twenty-nine-year-old young man, when, as a candidate for the ministry, I had accepted the call of the (Netherlands) Reformed Congregation of Utrecht (1961). A year earlier, Rev. Elshout had departed from this congregation of eight hundred souls. Since I was to become his successor, he took the initiative to visit me shortly after my ordination in order to engage in a discreet and confidential conversation about the congregation. He wanted to communicate some matters of importance to me. His primary objective was to shield me from certain pitfalls. This intent typifies at once who Arie Elshout was. He was always concerned about others. This pastoral concern would be confirmed subsequently in the two books he authored, entitled *A Helping Hand* and *Overcoming Spiritual Depression*.

We had a very profitable conversation that focused on the Lord's gracious operations. As a result, an intimate bond of friendship was forged between us, a bond that always remained intact.

Rev. Elshout was open and honest. He presented himself as he truly was. In the company of others and also at ecclesiastical gatherings, he always succeeded in steering the conversation in a positive direction. He had the gift of knowing how to address certain issues in a conversation. In so doing, he abhorred all forms of pretended piety and legalism. Frequently, with delight, he would speak of Christ and what was to be found in this Christ for an unworthy and guilty sinner. Not only was he pastorally gifted in private conversations but also in his sermons. He sought to comfort concerned souls. He would always direct them to seek salvation outside of themselves in Christ. This feature was prominent in his sermons.

For so long, he had sought for something within himself, and he knew that this was a dead-end street. He knew how liberating it was to find salvation entirely outside of himself in Jesus Christ, and it was his desire to proclaim this truth to others. In that process, we must relinquish our tears, our impressions, and our repentance as a foundation for our hope, and we must learn that "by the works of the law shall no flesh be justified" (Gal. 2:16). How sharp he could be in exposing this tendency, pointing out the deficiency of all religious emotionalism as a ground for eternity! This sharpness was not always appreciated, and he had to encounter rather significant opposition. In the midst of all this opposition, he remained faithful to his Master, however, by preaching nothing else but Jesus Christ and Him crucified.

Although he had a cheerful nature, he also knew of times of intense strife about his spiritual state and the execution of his office. During the decade of the 1970s, while ministering in America, he came into such depths for himself that he no longer was able to do his work. During that period, he and his wife visited us for several weeks in Franklin Lakes. These were difficult weeks—first of all for himself, and secondarily for his wife. But they were also difficult weeks for me personally. Arie was plagued by haunting questions and doubts; time and again he would speak to me about them. However, this greatly strengthened the bond of our friendship.

The Lord delivered him out of these depths and set his feet "upon a rock" (Psa. 40:2). In hindsight, we may know that there was a purpose for these ways. I believe that they equipped him later to write books about depression and spiritual conflict. At his funeral, it was therefore my desire to speak about 2 Corinthians 1:4, "Who comforteth us in all our tribulation, that we may be able to comfort them which are in any trouble, by the comfort wherewith we ourselves are comforted of God."

It is my wish that this biography would yield comfort for struggling souls—comfort proceeding from the same God and Savior who comforted Arie Elshout in all his trials and tribulations.

Rev. Cor Harinck
Emeritus Minister of the (Netherlands) Reformed Congregations
Kapelle-Biezelinge, the Netherlands

Translator's Preface

It has been an extraordinary and unforgettable privilege for me to translate this biography of my father (and mother!). For obvious reasons, it was a task in which I was also engaged emotionally. My intense and extended interaction with the text of this biography have only reaffirmed what my siblings and I have known since we were children: the life story of our parents is the story of God's remarkable and gracious dealings with two sinners.

When our parents celebrated their fortieth wedding anniversary in 1985, we asked our father to commit to writing—also for the benefit of our children and grandchildren—the many stories our parents had told us. Our father agreed to do that, and during the six remaining years of his life, he faithfully recorded his memoirs for us—memoirs written strictly for the benefit of our extended family.

All of this changed, however, when our mother was approached by the author of this biography, Adriaan Van Toor, informing her of his desire to publish the story of the pilgrim's journey of our beloved parents. After careful and prayerful consideration, our mother agreed to fully cooperate with this proposed publishing venture.

When Mr. Van Toor approached our mother, he had no knowledge of the existence of our father's written memoirs. How astonished and pleased he was when our mother handed him these memoirs! This provided him at once with the complete framework of the life story of our parents. With this valuable documentation in hand, he then engaged in his own independent research of every aspect of this story.

And thus the moment arrived in 2008 that this biography was published in the Netherlands, having as its title *Aan Armen uit Genâ* (for poor sinners, merely of grace). These words, taken from the rhymed rendition of Psalm 72:12,[1] were graven upon his heart by the Holy Spirit as the message he would be called to proclaim as a minister of the gospel.

Since, however, an exact translation of this phrase is difficult to achieve, we have opted for *A Word in Season* (Isa. 50:4), a title that accurately summarizes our father's ministry as well—especially in light of the context in which these words are found. God gave him a special gift to speak a word in season to the weary, and to comfort the feebleminded (1 Thess. 5:14). Not only was this gift evident in every aspect of his pastoral ministry, but also in the three books he has written—books that have been, and continue to be, a "word in season" for many.[2]

It never occurred to our father that his life story would be published. In his own words, he viewed himself as one of God's sparrows rather than an eloquent nightingale. Yet, God's sovereign purpose was otherwise! It has been a humbling and encouraging experience for our late mother, and our family, that this biography has been so well received in the Netherlands.

Since our father served two North American congregations (1967-1974), it was our late mother's express desire that our father's biography be made available in English as well. We are hopeful that many in the English-speaking world will be edified by the account of God's remarkable dealings in the lives of our parents.

Finally, a heartfelt thanks to all who have assisted me in the translation, editing, and publishing of this biography: my brothers Frits and Arie who checked the accuracy of the translation, my brother Frits who translated the appended sermons, my dear friend and English mentor, Jacqueline Markus, for her valuable editorial review of the translation, another dear friend, Samuel Van Grouw, for his design and typesetting work, the staff of Reformation Heritage Books for preparing this translation for publication, and our family friend, Rev. C. Harinck, for writing a fitting preface. Also a word of thanks to the author, Adriaan Van Toor, and the publishers of the Dutch original, Den Hertog Publishers (Houten, the Netherlands), for their gracious permission and cooperation.[3]

Let me conclude by emphasizing that the story of our parents is ultimately not about them, but rather, about a faithful, covenant-keeping God who, for Christ's sake, was (is!) also their God. Therefore, to Him alone be all the glory!

On behalf of the Elshout family,
Bartel Elshout
Translator

---

[1] "He [Christ] shall deliver the needy when he crieth; the poor also, and him that hath no helper."

[2] I have translated these books into English, and they have also been published by Reformation Heritage Books. Two of the books, *A Helping Hand* and *Overcoming Spiritual Depression*, minister to those who are afflicted with depression and/or burnout, and his third book, *This Do in Remembrance of Me*, provides pastoral guidance for a proper and fruitful partaking of the Lord's Supper.

[3] In consultation with the author, Adriaan Van Toor, the original publication has been enhanced by making a number of corrections, including some relevant information, and the addition of some photographs.

Introduction

Arie Elshout would become a professional soccer player. Everyone was certain that he would reach his goal. He was gifted in handling the leather ball, was proficient in the technical aspect of the game, knew how to outmaneuver his opponent, and was the top scorer of his team. There was no doubt about it. This boy would become a success on the soccer field.

~

Arie Elshout would become a member of the management team of *Van Ommeren*, a prominent shipping firm in Rotterdam. Mr. Kroeze was certain of that. The young Elshout was unquestionably a suitable replacement for him. This trustworthy employee would be highly successful in the company and would contribute to its continued growth.

~

Arie Elshout was destined to become a minister of the gospel. However, no one except the Lord knew this fact. His will and counsel would be accomplished, and no mere human would be able to alter His purpose. Indeed, Arie Elshout did become a minister of the gospel. This came to pass in ways that were incomprehensible, ways that were characterized by valleys, depths, and even things that seemed impossible. That which is impossible with man is possible with God, however. He arranged all circumstances according to His will, thereby affirming that all things *must* work together for good.

~

The lives of Arie Elshout and his wife testify of the wondrous leadings of an almighty God who in joy and in trials, in happiness and in sorrow, always remains the Faithful One. Arie Elshout wrote of this wonder to his children: "Thus it is my desire to pass on to the following generations that the LORD truly is who He declares Himself to be in His Word, and that for His name's sake and the sake of His Son, He truly is a Rewarder of those who seek Him…so that children, grandchildren, and friends might also magnify and fear God…the great God who has done wondrous things, whose mighty hand and Spirit, by grace and for Jesus's sake, has given us grace for grace out of His fullness."

The final three words of his personal notations summarize the lives of both Pastor Elshout and his wife: *soli Deo gloria*. And for all who humbly fear His Name, this same faithful God will be what He was for these redeemed sinners—Arie Elshout and his wife.

CHAPTER 1

Peculiar Folk

They were peculiar folk. The language they spoke was weighty, had a low pitch, and was somewhat intimidating, while their eyebrows extended significantly beyond their eyes. Even when these strangers laughed, the citizens of the village of Elshout, who were normally rather spontaneous, were on their guard.

No one knew exactly what their place of origin was. Of course, stories abounded. One person claimed that they had migrated across the Balkans, and another demonstratively pointed in the direction of Poland. Another person maintained that they were gypsies, and yet another, that they were Jews. The truth, however, was carefully concealed within the resolute privacy of the group.

One thing was certain: they were craftsmen. These migrants were able to work with leather as no one else could in the village of Elshout. Their hands transformed rough animal skins into ornate horse saddles that were reinforced with copper, and even with silver. People came from far and near with sufficient gold in their wallets to select the most beautiful saddles. In fact, members of the nobility came to Elshout in person or would send their estate manager if there were no other options.

A saddle maker at work in the village of Elshout

(Picture acquired from the Shoe & Leather Museum in Waalwijk)

These saddle makers prospered and were able to establish themselves in the *Langstraat* region of the province of North-Brabant. The children quickly learned to express themselves in an intelligible way, a mixture of the colloquial dialect of North-Brabant and gibberish. For the older ones, it was more difficult to speak the Dutch language. When it came to doing business, however, one needed only half a word. They bought homes and acquired carriages, and after a generation, everyone assumed they belonged to the community. The village was known throughout the region for its leather craftsmen, and the people of Elshout spoke about "our" saddles.

Would it be to anyone's surprise that these strangers adopted a Dutch family name? What else would it be but "Elshout"? They adopted the name of the village in which they had found a home!

Entering the village of Elshout

The village of Elshout was small. The original farming community resided in close proximity to the *Onze Lieve Vrouwe Kerk* (The Church of Our Dear Lady). According to legend, this church was originally a chapel that had been built on the location where a great miracle had taken place. The village consisted only of a few streets where the small farmers' homes were situated in a rather disorderly fashion. Among these homes were some larger homes for the leather craftsmen. It really did not amount to very much. For many of its citizens, the town of Elshout was too small. They migrated to Den Bosch or Waalwijk, cities where there was work, and therefore also a future. There they would at least find sufficient provision for many small mouths and large stomachs. Some, however, moved even further away; they moved westward, in the direction of Rotterdam. Consequently, the Elshout clan began to expand as a puddle of water upon dry ground.

Take, for instance, Arij Jacobszn, his son Arij, and his son Barthel, the metal worker. They were hard workers and yet as easygoing as the people of North-Brabant. Life itself had made them serious, however. Barthel, born in 1837, was optimistic when at the age of twenty-two he moved to Heenvliet to start a family with Arendje Elderkamp. They were blessed with thirteen children.

Yet their life became an accumulation of adversity and sorrow. Seven of the thirteen children were stillborn, and four of them died at a very young age. There were two survivors: Jan and Hendrika. Finally, in 1880, Barthel stood at the grave of his wife whom he loved so very much and with whom he had experienced much. Left behind were Barthel and two children, of whom the oldest one was only eleven years of age.

Seven years later, Barthel married again—this time to Jannetje van Kempen. This marriage lasted only one year, and there were no children born.

His next marriage with Pleuntje Visser also resulted in much adversity. There were nine children, of whom four were stillborn. The way to the grave was frequently traveled by Barthel Elshout. Fifteen times he buried a child, and twice he buried a wife. Though a man may not readily shed tears, Barthel would not have had sufficient supply to drown his sorrow.

Jan Elshout had heard about the saddle makers, but it must have been something of a distant past. Jan was born in 1869 in Heenvliet on the

Jan Elshout (left) was employed by the Water Department of Rotterdam.

Marriage Certificate of Jan Elshout and Catharina Bol Raap

island of Voorne-Putten, where there was very little prosperity, and it was difficult to find work. The Water Works of Rotterdam, however, hired him as a boiler man, and twenty-one-year old Jan moved to the port city. Employment opportunities abounded in Rotterdam. Jan assisted in the building of the water tower and helped with the initial installation of the city's drinking water network.

His departure to Rotterdam proved to be a good decision. In the way of God's providence, Jan became affiliated with the *Vereniging tot Verbreiding der Waarheid* (The Society for the Proliferation of the Truth). Worship services were conducted each Sunday in the facilities of *De Driehoek* (The Triangle), located on *Eleonorastraat*. These services were conducted by Pleun Kleijn. He would read a sermon and then add his own application to it. Kleijn became Jan's

Katrien (Catharina) Elshout had five children before she died of tuberculosis.

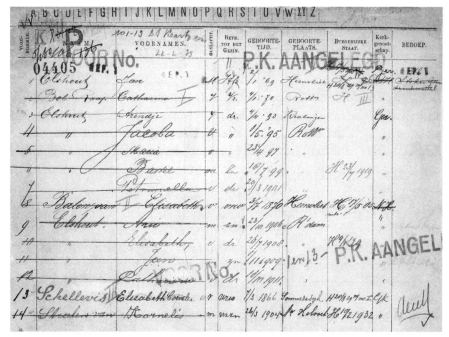

The civil record of Jan Elshout's family—It indicates that he was widowed twice and married three times. First marriage to Catharina Bol Raap—children: Arendje, Jacoba, Marie, Bartel, and Petronella. Second marriage to Elizabeth van Balen—children: Arie, Elizabeth, Jan, and Catherina. Third marriage to Elizabeth Schellevis—children: none (one step-son Kornelis Schellevis).

spiritual friend, and the sermons he read became a blessing for Jan. Pleun soon appointed him to be the lead singer and the reader of Scripture. Jan would not miss these services for anything. They were as ointment for his soul, as bread for the hungry, and as a fountain of water for him that is athirst.

As the father of nine children, Jan considered himself a blessed man. Yet, his life was not free of sorrow. How happy Jan was with his Katrien Bol Raap, the wife of his youth! They were so fond of each other, and in 1892 they were united in marriage. She gave birth to five children. God's thoughts, however, were higher than his, for Jan had to let go of his Katrien after her body succumbed to tuberculosis.

Jan, with his five children, walked to the grave. Little Petronella did not realize that she would never see her mother again, and Jan therefore left the little girl at home. Poor little Bartel was only six years old, however. With a sad and serious look, he followed behind the coffin, his hand clinging to his father's. The girls followed: Arendje, Jacoba, and Maria. The way to the grave was so very difficult, for Jan could not share his sorrow with others. Oh, there was sympathy enough, and his bosom friend, Pleun Kleijn, spoke words of comfort. But it was his Katrien who was being buried, and he would now be without her—permanently. God's way is in the sea and His path in the great waters. Quietly, he prayed for strength and for grace to be able to follow, in whatever way that might be.

A few years later Jan became acquainted with Elisabeth van Balen, and in 1905 he married her. Happily, his children received a mother again. Arendje, the oldest child, was twelve years old at the time. They received more children, however: two brothers and two sisters. Yet, there continued to be cause for concern.

Deep in thought, Jan walked up and down in the living room of the home on *Zwartjanstraat*. There was a frown upon his forehead, and there was concern in his eyes. What would become of Bartel? His boy had been well-trained and was a skilled metal worker. The *Jacobs Company* at *Het Gorzepad* was very pleased with him. Effortlessly and flawlessly, he repaired the copper couplings on the oil barges. He was also talkative and not afraid of anyone. Regardless of whether Bartel was speaking to a mate or to the captain, he would always be able to strike up a conver-

Opa (Arie) and Oma (Sijgje) Hennink—The parents of Neeltje Hennink
Arie Elshout was named after his maternal grandfather, Arie Hennink.

sation. Whether they spoke English or Russian, Bartel was able to make contact. There was no problem in that sense.

Church was the problem. Bartel had bidden the church farewell, for he no longer wanted to have anything to do with it. To him, it was nothing but a depressing and narrow-minded environment. He wanted to live to be free and to enjoy life.

It did not help matters that he had met the daughter of Hennink. That thought brought a brief smile to Jan's face. It was so typical of Bartel. He and his friend Nol had taken two girls out on a date. They both were interested in the same girl, however. Bartel immediately took action and whispered in Nol's ear, "Don't think that you will get her. Neeltje is for me." Nol had little choice but to be satisfied with the other girl.

Bartel and Neeltje Elshout (age: ±50)

Neeltje Hennink's father had a haulage firm on *Pijnackerstraat*, and he transported goods in and around the harbor. Consequently, he made a very good living. Neeltje's parents were without question decent folks, but they were unchurched and hostile toward religion. Yet, there would have to be a wedding, for Neeltje was pregnant. Bartel did not beat around the bush: he very much wanted to marry her. Neeltje hesitated, however, for she did not really know whether she truly wanted Bartel as her husband. She had not yet had the courage to tell her parents about the secret that was slowly but surely manifesting itself within her. "It must, however, be done," Jan said to Bartel.

He brushed it off, saying, "Dad, it will all work out. I already have come up with a plan."

~

A barrel organ was parked on the corner of *Zwartjanstraat* and *Pijnacker-straat*. Its melodies resounded loudly throughout the street. Various people came outside or pushed the curtains aside to see what all the noise was. Someone rang the bell at the Hennink residence. With his cap cocked on his head, a little fellow asked for Neeltje. Surprised, she came to the door. "Can you come along for a minute? Bartel Elshout is waiting for you."

Neeltje slipped on her shoes, quickly straightened out her dark curly hair, and followed the boy to the barrel organ.

Bartel mischievously looked into the eyes of Neeltje. "My girl," he said, "you must now tell your father and mother, and if you don't, then I will do it—with the barrel organ."

Neeltje was really shaken up, but she knew of no other solution than to go quickly to her parents and tell them the entire story of Bartel, who was in love with her, of her relationship with him, and of her pregnancy.

After Father and Mother Hennink had recovered from the initial shock, they reacted in a levelheaded and decisive manner. Bartel and Neeltje would get married on July 23, 1919, and, after having briefly lived with Bartel's father, they would live on *17 Korenaarstraat*. Less than four months later, a daughter, Katrien, entered the world. Three years later, having moved to *91b Hooglandstraat*, Arie and Sija were born. From there, the family moved to 56a Vinkenstraat, where the next four children were born: Aagje, Nellie, Jan, and Bart. Since moving frequently was not uncommon prior to World War II, the Elshout family moved again on June 21, 1935—to *18b Davidstraat*. Here the last two children, Bep, and Sjaak, were born

It was after the birth of Arie in 1923 that the effects of the economic depression became a reality. Bartel lost his job, and poverty began to have its effects. He took to the streets and knocked on the door of businesses everywhere in order to secure a job, but it was all in vain. His brother-in-law, Jan Beije, knew of a solution: America was the land of great promise. Jan finally persuaded Bartel, and Bartel left his wife and children behind to earn money in America.

Upon arriving in New York, Jan and Bartel had to stand in line. The city was swamped with seekers of good fortune. Bartel wanted to accept anything that would be available. Via the speakers, an announcement was made that painters were needed, and he immediately raised his hand. He stepped out of line and went to the counter. Very convincingly, he told them that his name was Rembrandt, while boasting of having

To earn money, Bartel departed
for America

Neeltje Elshout with Catherine & Arie
(1925)

Arie as a young toddler

many years of experience as a painter. He got the job! Bartel's father Jan reflected on all these doings with raised eyebrows. He did not understand how one could leave a wife and two children behind. As father and "opa", Jan considered himself responsible, so he therefore took Neeltje and the children under his wings. Opa Elshout availed himself of every opportunity to tell his daughter-in-law, as well as little Katrien and Arie, how good it is to serve the Lord.

After a year, Bartel returned—one illusion less, and one experience gained. The great promises and dreams regarding America had not become reality for him. Furthermore, he missed his wife and children, and so he rejoined them.

A little more than a year later, Sija was born. This occasion was a good opportunity for Grandfather Jan to have a serious talk with his son Bartel, for it really troubled him that his three grandchildren had never been baptized. His concern appeared to make an impression on Bartel, and he acquiesced in the baptism of his wife and children. It was an impressive moment in the Old Reformed Church of Bolnes, when Rev. L. Boone sprinkled the baptismal water upon the heads of Neeltje and her three children. Little Arie was three years old at that time.

Bartel, however, still did not attend church services. The only religious practice of the family was the praying before and after the meal—nothing more than that. Bartel did not like any of the fuss. Although he wanted to live a respectable life, Sunday was for things other than going to church. During the week, there also had to be some fun, such as dancing and frequenting the theater.

Bartel took good care of his family, although he did have a temper. No, it was not that he would beat up his children, but in his temper he occasionally would hit the door with his fist. Somewhat surprised and embarrassed, he would then look at the crack in the door, and it would quickly calm him down. Indeed, Bartel was very strong. Working as a fitter for the *Rotterdamse Droogdok Maatschappij*, he needed a lot of muscular strength. When, however, he used a broomstick to open up a clogged drain, he did indeed solve the problem, but the neighbor lady downstairs began to see large brown spots appear on her ceiling.

~

Then, from one day to the next, the life of Bartel changed radically. This change probably occurred around December of 1939. The family was now living in Rotterdam-West, at 18b Davidstraat. As was customary, Father Bartel still dressed up as Santa Claus on December 5.

When a few weeks later, however, the children wanted to bring the Christmas decorations from the attic and came home with pine branches, Father expressed his disapproval. He no longer wanted to go along with this custom, for he could no longer go along with worldly customs. The children were surprised and confused when they had to put everything away again.

What was it that caused Bartel to reconsider? Was it due to the political tensions, or was it the threat of war? Or, was it the death of his half-brother Jan that affected him so much? When repairing an elevator, it came down on Jan with its full weight and crushed him. Who knows what could have been the cause? One thing was certain, however, Bartel began to order his life according to God's precepts. Sometimes he went beyond that, but Mother Neeltje resisted this change. She wanted to

An elementary school class picture—
Little Arie is in the middle of the picture standing next to his desk.

cooperate with her husband, accompany him to church, and live according to God's law, but she did not want to submit to human precepts.

Since the location where the services of Pleun Kleijn were held was too far away, the family decided to seek affiliation with the (Netherlands) Reformed Congregation at the Boezemsingel. Rev. G.H. Kersten was the pastor there, and he was a good friend of Kleijn. Bartel and Neeltje first enrolled in the confession of faith class, and in 1940, both parents with five of their children, stood in the front of the church. Upon the affirmative answer of both parents, all obstacles for the administration of baptism had been removed. You could hear a pin drop in the congregation when the solemn words resounded, "Arendje, I baptize you in the Name of the Father, and of the Son, and of the Holy Ghost; Nellie..., Bartel..., Jan..., Elisabeth Cornelia...I baptize you...."[4]

There was joy in the heart of Father Bartel. There was peace in the heart of Mother Neeltje. This is how it should be! "But as for me and my house, we will serve the LORD" (Josh. 24:15).

Yet, there were matters that tempered the joy of Father Bartel. Katrien was married. She, along with her husband, had become members of the *Gereformeerde Kerk* (the Reformed church of Dr. Kuyper). What would become of that?

---

[4] The first four children had been baptized on an earlier occasion.

What was even worse, however, was that a team of horses would not succeed in getting Arie to church. This boy was sixteen years old, and he had no intention whatsoever of changing his life. Why should he? Formerly, he did not have to go to church, did he? Since, in his estimation, his father and mother were not religious, then why did everything suddenly have to be different? He wanted no part of this change. He was a talented soccer player, and the Rotterdam Soccer Club thought the world of him. He was a boy who liked adventure and having fun.

Father Bartel sighed.

Arie Elshout as a high school student
This picture was taken on his fourteenth birthday, January 20, 1937.

CHAPTER 2

A Change in Direction

Two men, dressed in dark clothing, were exiting Davidstraat. It was late, already after ten o'clock. They were reflecting on the visitation they had conducted with the Elshout family. They agreed that it was a good visit—although an unusual one as well. These were people who desired to fear the Lord, a couple whose lives the Lord had directed in incomprehensible ways. By virtue of his upbringing, the husband knew so well how things ought to be, for he had come from a solid home. He was a son of Elshout from Eleonorastraat. He attended church services there, was a reader, and also the lead-singer. He even taught catechism when Pleun Kleijn was absent. His son Bartel, however, had enough of all this religion, and he had escaped to America. But the Lord knew how to find this man there and bring him under His Word. What a wonder it is when the Lord prevails in the life of a person! Brothers Klop and Van Kranenburg were in full agreement about this wonder.

Elder A. Van Kranenburg   Elder Christian Klop

Nevertheless, tonight there had been a confrontation with the oldest son, Arie. What an unusual discussion! Arie did not go to church and also did not want to stay for family visitation. He was, however, polite enough first to shake hands with the office-bearers before retiring to his room.

Yet Elder Klop could not remain silent. He addressed Arie in a friendly and warm manner, saying, "The Lord is so worthy to be served, also by young people. A life without God can never amount to anything."

The boy was feisty in his response: "Why don't you look at your own people? On Sunday they sit in church as such decent people, but during the week they are either dishonest businessmen or do other things that are questionable."

Elder Klop replied, "That is true; you are right. There are such people. But if you have such keen insight into this situation, then you certainly ought to do better than that."

The boy replied, "If I ever change my life, then I will do better than that, rather than living so inconsistently and hypocritically as they do."

At least a conversation had started. Father and Mother Elshout held their breath. They had never seen Arie behave in this way. They were familiar with his intensity, but the questions that the boy asked were new to them.

Behind the façade of the boy's belligerence, there were unanswered questions and riddles with which he had been struggling for some time already. Arie considered himself too young for all this religion. Why should he concern himself with death and eternity when he was only seventeen years old? That is something for older people. Just listen to these older folk when they speak of their strife and doubt. What concerns and troubles they encounter! No, Arie wanted no part of these experiences.

At the same time, however, there was the small voice within which always made him uncomfortable: "You will encounter death, will you not? And then what? If God truly exists (and in the depth of your heart you are convinced of this truth), would it not be a good thing to serve Him?" Arie voiced his questions to these brothers, and gradually the evening turned into an unforgettable family visitation for these brothers, as well as for Arie.

∼

At the Mathenesserplaza, the elders boarded the streetcar, which noisily drove away. Through the window, they caught just a glimpse of Arie, who was running toward them. And then the boy vanished.

He stopped and was panting. He had wanted to continue his conversation with the elders. He was hoping that they would have missed the streetcar, for then he would have asked them additional questions. When Arie walked back to his home, his mind was in turmoil. "It is true, the Lord has never wronged me, and I have done nothing but evil."

Suddenly he stood still. *Had the Lord ever done anything that should prompt me neither to fear nor obey Him?* This question arose in his heart and would not leave him alone. It was as if the Lord Himself were asking him this question. Arie detected a sorrow he had never felt before. He was ashamed before the Lord regarding his life and his misbehavior. In contrast, he thought about how extraordinary God's goodness was in sparing him. His inner resistance was now broken. Something had changed in his life that would never be reversed. He no longer could live as he had done until now, neither did he desire to do so. In childlike fashion, he said, "Lord, I will never sin again, and from now on I will do whatever my mother tells me to do." He was resolved that he would devote his life to the Lord, and this determination filled him with joy.

On Sunday morning, his father and mother were sitting at the breakfast table with the children. The little ones were quite surprised when Arie took his place at the table as well. He never did that. They wanted to comment, but Mother silenced them by saying, "Let's first eat, children, or else we will be late for church." From behind their plates, the children looked stealthily at Arie, who somewhat self-consciously was eating his breakfast and trying to act as if nothing was unusual.

As the family was making its way to church, Arie followed them from a distance. In the morning, he had begged and asked the Lord to grant him His help and assistance. He had promised that he would follow the Lord, which was his desire. For the remainder of his life, he would never again leave his place empty in God's house.

Young Arie really went to work. He had said to the elders that he would live a better and more consistent life. Well, he would do his utmost to fulfill this resolution. It was his intention never to sin again. Initially, he was inclined to believe that by going to church regularly he had accomplished a great deal, but then he learned that sin was much more deeply rooted than that. With sadness, he stared ahead of himself. On the sleeve of his jacket he detected a hair, and he took a good look at it. What is one hair? He had thousands of them, perhaps even a million. His transgressions, however, were more than the hairs on his head. He had indeed heard this statement in sermons, but now its truth became increasingly real to him. The preached Word increasingly impacted his life. On the one hand, he felt that he could not live unto the Lord as he should. His heart was so corrupt, and his iniquities had the upper hand in his life. Yet, he simultaneously experienced such a heartfelt love for the Lord who had never ill-treated him, who, instead, had done nothing but good to him. Oh, how reasonable the Lord would be if He were to abandon him! At the same time, however, he prayed intensely that the Lord would not forsake him but instead would be mindful of him.

It seemed rather remarkable to him that whenever he was in church, regardless of who was preaching, the minister seemed to know exactly what was going on in his heart. He heard about his guilt before God and the impossibility of ever resolving it. He knew that this was entirely true. He heard that his guilt was daily increasing because he was not able to live as the Lord required of him. It dawned on him that this was true as well. He also heard, however, that God glorifies His grace in men, and it was his intense desire that this grace would become his portion. He even believed and embraced this truth…but then as it applied to others.

It was a summer afternoon. A few clouds were drifting as feathers high in the sky, quickly evaporating into the warm atmosphere. The little ferry was making its regular rounds between the shores of the Maas River. It was Saturday, and many people were returning from the market with their goods. Most of them were seated on the upper deck with their heads tilted upward so that the rays of the sun would shine on their faces.

Below deck, unnoticed, Arie was on his knees. An indefinable fear had taken hold of him. Just imagine if this boat were to sink! Then he would die, and he would have to appear before God. "Oh, God," he prayed, "be merciful to me the sinner." And indeed, Arie then experienced that the Lord was gracious. The ferry did not sink, which amazed him. None of the people on the ferry noticed that this young man had left the ferry and then joined them again.

It had not occurred to anyone else that the ferry could have sunk. The weather was so gorgeous! Arie then rode his bike into the south side of Rotterdam. His thoughts were meandering through the Scriptures, and he saw Psalm 119 before his eyes:

> *How blest are they who make His Word their treasure,*
> *Who keep His testimonies and display*
> *Their love for Him whose goodness none can measure.*

Yes, that was it! This text was exactly what occupied his mind. This gave him courage, for it said, "How blest are they…." The Lord knew the yearnings of his heart. For the first time in his life, he was glad that the

Lord knows and sees all things—not only his sins, but also his sighs and concerns.

~

Arie would attend church not only on the Lord's Day but also during the week. When Rev. W.C. Lamain would preach in Portugaal, he would quietly sit in the back. The minister not only addressed sin and the necessity of the new birth, but he also pointed to the only way of salvation, Jesus Christ. Obviously, Arie had heard of this only Name many times before, but now it was different. The Spirit Himself was speaking by means of the words of the minister who displayed Christ in all His suitability and willingness as Savior. For this quiet young man seated in the back of the church, light arose for the first time, for he saw something of the glory of this Person. It was like the sun breaking through the clouds on a cloudy day. The heart of Arie was filled with joy and amazement. There *was* a way of salvation! It was also possible for him. The minister said, "If there is anyone here who would part with the entire world in order to possess this blessed Jesus, let him wait for me after the service."

Arie did not wait, however. The light that had dawned in his soul had faded, and it was a sad young man who rode his bike through the streets of Portugaal. He thought that all he had heard had not been true, and that he had deceived himself. But no sorrow would ever be able to erase from his memory what had happened. The seed of love had been planted in his heart, a love that yearned for Him who said, "Come unto me, all ye that labor and are heavy laden, and I will give you rest."

The direction of Arie's life had definitively been changed. In vain his soccer friends called upon him to train with them, play a game, or watch an important match. He would no longer join them—not on Sunday, but also not during the week. Such involvement was no

Rev. W.C. Lamain, pastor of the (Netherlands) Reformed Congregation of Rotterdam-Zuid (South) – 1932–1943

longer possible, and it was no longer his desire. His heart had been set too much on playing soccer; it had become idolatry for him. It was wrong, and thus he had put a radical stop to it.

~

At the business college, the exams for Dutch and English business correspondence were handed out. Arie had worked very hard to prepare himself for this moment. Ahead of time, however, he had first bowed his knees and asked whether the Lord would help him. The first three segments were rather easy. Swiftly and almost without hesitation, he filled in the blanks. He felt that failure was almost impossible at this point, and he turned in the test papers.

The fourth segment, a translation from English into Dutch, followed. As he quickly glanced over the material, he was overcome with a feeling of panic. Many words were unknown to him, and therefore the meaning of many sentences was not clear to him. Quietly he besought the Lord to help him. He was indeed mighty to do so. On the day of Pentecost, He had enabled men, by His Spirit, to speak languages that they had never learned before. Nothing happened, however, and the clock was ticking. Seconds became minutes, and Arie saw the hands of the clock come ever closer to the time when he must turn in his paper. "Lord," he prayed, "wouldst Thou put into my thoughts that which I do not know—not because I am worthy, but for Thy great Name's sake?" He began to write and recorded what came into his mind. When he put down his pen, the time had expired. He no longer had the opportunity of reviewing his work.

Outside in the hallway, those who had taken the exam stood in small groups and compared their work. When Arie compared the fourth segment of the exam with those of the others, he lost all courage. There was no way he could have passed.

Prior to his departure to Germany, twenty-year-old Arie had his picture taken.

But wasn't God mighty to help him? Perhaps He was not willing to do so. Arie was buffeted by intense strife, for if the first would not be true, then he feared that the rest of what the Lord had done in his life would also not be true. Upon returning home, he quietly slipped upstairs. He fell upon his knees before his bed and told the Lord all that was on his mind, including his sense of despair. He sat down upon his bed and stared ahead.

Suddenly he had an idea. He jumped up from his bed and walked to his bookshelf. He took the dictionary and started paging in it. He was utterly amazed. Look at this! He had correctly translated the first unknown verb. He quickly continued to flip the pages. The second word had been translated correctly, as well as the third. Tears began to fill his eyes, and he did not dare to turn any other pages. The Lord did hear and help him after all. He again fell upon his knees.

Nineteen-year-old Arie was biking to his work at Van Ommeren. Fortunately, he knew the way like the back of his hand, for he was not focused on the traffic. He was thinking about what he had read that morning in Ezekiel 16:22, "And I will establish my covenant with thee; and thou shalt know that I am the LORD." It was as if he could breathe again, and he was set at liberty. A quiet joy took hold of him, for the Lord will establish His covenant. The forgiveness of sins was also possible for him. At the same time, he was praying, "But Lord, how canst Thou forgive, considering that Thou art holy and righteous? Do not the demands of Thy holiness have to be met? I cannot meet those demands!"

Almost immediately a text from Hebrews was impressed upon him, "For by one offering he hath perfected for ever them that are sanctified" (Heb. 10:14).

"Also for me," was the rejoicing of Arie's heart. How inexpressible was his joy! The efficacy of Christ's sacrifice was opened up and applied to him. He knew that he also could be saved through His work without having to add anything of his own. Nothing needed to be added. Nothing could be remedied by his own works, for this was not necessary. If it were not for the fact that Arie was riding his bike, he would have been jumping for joy. So intensely joyful he was, and so amazed he was about God's goodness! It was true what Paul wrote, "I, the chief of sinners, obtained mercy." After arriving at his work, Arie first sought a quiet place to thank, adore, and praise the Lord for His grace.

CHAPTER 3

In Exile

No one in Rotterdam, even if he were to become one hundred years of age, would be able to forget the bombing of the city on May 10, 1940. The fear, the deafening noise, the explosions, the screaming, the fires, the clouds of dust! All who found themselves in the midst of this inferno and experienced its terror were hardly able to talk about it. Those who lived in areas of Rotterdam not affected by the bombing were eye-witnesses of all this destruction and encountered its wretched consequences. Who in the city did not have close or distant relatives, acquaintances, or friends who suffered personal loss? Bartel Elshout and his family lived only a few miles away from the affected inner city. On that day, all members of his family had returned home safely.

Not a single resident of Rotterdam will forget the bombing of May 10, 1940.

As of May 10, Rotterdam knew what it meant to be at war, and its citizens experienced its terrors. Yet many gradually resumed their daily routines. Everyone had to return to his job. The shopkeepers again sold their merchandise, employees returned to their offices, and government officials went to city hall. Construction workers began the removal of the debris.

The churches opened their doors on the Lord's Day. A careful observer would note that church attendance increased slightly during the initial weeks after the bombing, but before long it declined.

The presence of the Germans hardly caused a problem, and resistance toward them was only minimal. Consequently, for the average citizen of Rotterdam, the initial year of the war transpired with minimal repression by the occupier.

Arie Elshout also daily pedaled on his bike to Van Ommeren. He enjoyed his work there, and his boss, Mr. Kroeze, was pleased with him. At night, he attended class at a business school where he either continued his studies to acquire a diploma for English business correspondence or was snooping in books.

One could not but notice, however, that he was reading his Bible with inner delight, for he highly esteemed God's Word. When attending church on Sunday, he listened with relish to the sermons of Rev. Kersten. There was a tender love toward God in his heart. Daily he received a morsel of grace as a confirmation of the words of Psalm 16:7: "My reins also instruct me in the night seasons."

His heart yearned after Christ and His righteousness. It seemed to him as if he had received a new Bible and as if he were reading things that were all fresh to him. He would read of Christ's work, His suitability, His willingness, and His faithfulness upon every page of God's Word. With liberty and joy, he would repeatedly entrust himself to Him, and upon all this,

Rev. G.H. Kersten, pastor of the (Netherlands) Reformed Congregation of Rotterdam-Centrum – 1926–1948

he experienced God's approbation. Gradually, he began to understand the truth of these words: "But to him that worketh not, but believeth on him that justifieth the ungodly, his faith is counted for righteousness" (Rom. 5:4). It was a blessed time for his soul.

One afternoon he was meditating on John 3:16. Stirred by love for Him who had first loved him, he felt a strong desire to address this God of full salvation as Christ had taught his disciples, "Our Father which art in heaven." Never before had he addressed God as Father! He had never dared to do so. Yet, at this moment, he could not refrain himself. Trusting in the mediatorial work of Christ, he uttered the *Father name*.

It was a moving moment, for it was as though the Lord Himself responded to him, *"My child."* It was as if he had never committed nor known any sin. As the prodigal son was kissed by the father, so he was privileged to experience restoration into God's favor. For Christ's sake, he was adopted as God's child. After a time of seeking, a time of finding became reality for him.

The war became increasingly oppressive. The Germans were increasingly flexing their muscles by issuing a multitude of ordinances. Although these ordinances benefited the enemy, they were detrimental for the citizens of Rotterdam. It also became increasingly obvious that there no longer was room for any Jews in the country.[5]

Conscripted laborers and German soldiers mingling near the train station
"Delftse Poort" located in Rotterdam

---

[5] A family member forwarded the following anecdotal incident, involving Arie's grandfather, Jan Elshout: "Jan Elshout lived near Wilgenstraat. When he observed that his Jewish neighbors were being taken from their homes, he asked the Dutch SS officer whether he would be permitted to pray with these people. He then proceeded to do so in the middle of the street. Jan Elshout spoke to them about the God of Abraham, Isaac, and Jacob, and of Him who is the Hope of Israel, saying, 'When all doors will now be closed for you, never forget that the door to God's throne of grace, in the Messiah of Israel, will always remain open!' The residents of the Wilgenstraat were deeply impressed by this" (F. Van Holten, *Ziende den Onzienlijke*, [Kampen, the Netherlands: De Groot Goudriaan, 1999], 64).

Germany was in great need of laborers to keep its war machine operational. Furthermore, the Germans who had been sent to the frontlines needed to be replaced at home to keep the "regular economy" going. Germany resolved this dilemma by "drafting" people from occupied territories for forced labor in Germany. To sustain the influx of new laborers, the Germans continually lowered the minimum age for this service. The day therefore came when twenty-year-olds became eligible. In July, 1943, a summons for Arie to report was deposited in the mailbox of the Elshout family.

This summons did not come as a surprise to Arie, for the Lord had used words from Jeremiah 46 to convince him that he would have to go to Germany. The Lord promised Arie, however, that His presence would also go before him there.

When Rev. Kersten heard this news, he shook his head. Why would a twenty-year-old young man like Arie have to go to Germany? He said to Arie, "Let us go talk to Van Dijk, a member of our congregation. He might be able to help you." Van Dijk had a prominent position in city hall, and he occasionally succeeded in arranging matters so that young men could remain in Holland. Mr. Van Dijk frowned, however, and shook his head. He could not think of a way in which he could help Arie. This young man would have to go.

Bartel traveled with Arie until they reached the border. In the train, father and son did not say much to each other. They were both preoccupied with their own thoughts. Having asked the Lord to give him the grace of submission, Arie was at peace, even though he had no idea how things would turn out.

Braunschweig would be his assigned destination. What would life be like there? Initially, he had been happy when he heard that he would have to go to Rheinland. That was not so far from home. Shortly thereafter, however, his destination was changed to Braunschweig. He would be much further from home, at least 350 miles. The time to say good-bye at the border was short. Arie's father had to return immediately, and he therefore embraced his son. It was not certain whether they would ever see each other again. Working in Germany was a dangerous undertaking, for the Allies tried to destroy all industrial enterprises with their bombs. These bombing raids resulted in many casualties, also among the forced laborers imported from occupied territories.

As his father tried to hold back his tears, Arie sought to encourage him, saying, "Dad, I will return. I am certain of this, for the Lord has promised this to me. He said to me, 'I will not make a full end of thee, but correct thee in measure; yet will I not leave thee wholly unpunished' (Jer. 46:28). Although I must go because of my own sins, the Lord will go with me."

The trip was long as the train continued in the direction of Osnabrück and Hanover, and there were frequent stops. There were also other Dutchmen in Arie's train compartment. Some sat with sullen looks on their faces. Their minds were either on their girlfriends or on their wives and children. Others were ecstatic and cocky. For them it was some sort of an adventure. Seated on a wooden bench, Arie crawled into a corner. His mind was also on home, but more than that, his heart was crying out to the living God. All that mattered to him was to know that He would abide there with him.

No sooner did the train come to a standstill in Braunschweig before men were already dragging their suitcases behind them as they exited the train. German soldiers were patrolling the platform with guns slung over their shoulders, and some held the leash of a trained dog. Men in civilian clothing had lists in their hands. Boisterously, they called out names, and the men had to line up in various groups.

Arie's group was obviously complete, for the group began to move forward. After having ambled along for several miles, the men could discern a few barracks in the distance. Inside, there were only some bunkbeds and some shelves for storage. Everyone tried to secure the best possible spot, and for Arie this meant that he wanted a spot toward the rear. He wanted to be left alone. He placed his suitcase under his bed and tucked his Bible under his pillow. When he looked around a bit, however, and saw all these men mingling together, he felt miserable and sighed, "Lord, do not forsake me."

This German camp consisted of a few barracks. The men had to wash themselves outside. There was also a kitchen. With a bit of imagination, one could call the communal area a lunchroom. The meals were rather basic, but they were not that bad. When Arie heard about conditions in other camps, he had no reason to complain. Everyone daily performed clerical duties for the Louis Fricke Transport Company

Although Arie worked diligently, he noticed that others were looking at him askance. His colleagues thought, "What sort of a fellow is he? He prays before he eats, gives thanks afterwards, and then reads his Bible. We had better keep our distance from him." Arie sensed the coolness with which he was treated. He felt hurt by it, but he continued to pray, give thanks, and read his Bible.

When the company celebrated its seventy-fifth anniversary, it was time for a party. Arie had already heard about it. His colleagues were ready to have a good time by partying in the movie theater. No exceptions were made, and the foreign employees therefore would be included as well. Arie knew what was coming. What should he do? Declining the invitation would result in even greater hostility, and they would mock him all the more. He therefore decided to accept the invitation. The Lord would surely understand—so he reasoned. The contrary was true, however. Was this consistent with being a witness for Christ? Was his intended course of action all that was left of all the lofty promises he had made to the Lord? No, he could not proceed in this way, and therefore he could not accept this invitation. Consequently, he declined. His colleagues were furious. Dreadful curses were heaped upon his head. Someone even said, "If bombs are ever dropped upon Braunschweig, we hope that they will end up on your head."

Louis Fricke continued his business venture after the war.

Things turned out differently, however. English bombers did indeed arrive, dropping their lethal cargo upon Braunschweig. The warehouses of the Louis Fricke Company were destroyed. When that occurred, however, Arie was hospitalized due to a bout of pneumonia. There he was safe when the bombs fell, for he was protected by his God.

He was comforted by His Word, "If the world hate you, ye know that it hated me before it hated you. If ye were of the world, the world would love his own: but because ye are not of the world, but I have chosen you out of the world, therefore the world hateth you. Remember the word that I said unto you, The servant is not greater than his lord. If they have persecuted me, they will also persecute you; if they have kept my saying, they will keep yours also. But all these things will they do unto you for my name's sake, because they know not him that sent me" (John 15:18-21).

These words strengthened Arie and gave him joy as well. His colleagues could rage against him as much as they wished, but he knew he was safe. He then did what only grace will enable us to do. He prayed for those who were hostile toward him.

~

The food in this camp was quite tolerable. A woman had been appointed to cook the meals, and she used the available ration coupons to produce reasonable meals for these men. It could have been different! Arie had heard that there were camps where the cooks kept some of the ration coupons for themselves and served stingy meals.

His relationship with his fellow countrymen remained very strained. Although he was treated as an outsider, it did not trouble him. Could it be any different? Or, should he participate after all? These men would visit the brothels as often as they could. They had found an efficient way to secure some money. Some of these men were drivers who would deliver merchandise during the day. At night, it was very simple to return and pick up the same merchandise, and thus steal it. The stolen goods would be sold, and they would then share the proceeds.

Arie, however, wanted no part of this activity. Behind his back, these men were whispering about him. By refusing to take his share, Arie would also not be an accomplice. He could pose a danger for them. They had better beware of this pious fellow.

They would leave him alone as far as their nightly escapades were concerned, but they continued to make him the focal point of their ridicule. Whenever possible, they would make a fool of him—except when the air raid sirens would howl, and the English bombers would be flying overhead. Since lights could not be turned on during raids, complete darkness would prevail in the barracks. Occasionally, beams of light from anti-aircraft artillery would shine through the windows, and a sinister glow would then move across their fearful faces. Many would gravitate toward Arie, for they reasoned that this fanatic must have his own special guardian angel protecting him. Therefore, the closer they would sit to him, the less chance there would be that they would be hit if a bomb were to fall. As soon as the "all clear" signal was given, however, they would quickly forget their anxiety, and they would begin to pester him afresh.

~

One day, Arie noticed that something was afoot. The men were snickering behind his back. When they walked past him, they looked at him with a mocking grin. Something was brewing. At nightfall, one of the men entered the camp. He had a visitor with him, a young woman. Arie was aghast, for the woman wore heavy make-up, was dressed very provocatively, and looked around arrogantly. Arie did not know what to make of it when the men were pointing in his direction. Then the woman approached him and began to taunt him. Arie backed away. What did they want from him, and why was this young woman here?

Arie could not believe what was happening, and he looked everywhere to see if there was a way of escape. The men, however, had formed a circle around him and the woman. They started jeering, and Arie felt cornered. The woman then reached for him.

"Lord, help me," he stammered. There seemed to be no way out for him. But Arie in no way wanted to participate in this charade. Never! Although Arie was not tall, he was as quick as a cornered cat, and he lunged forward, landing upon one of the beds. Above this bed, an ornamental sword was attached to the wall. He ripped it from the wall and was brandishing it furiously. "If you make one more move, I'll cut off your head," he cried out.

Now it was the woman's turn to back off. This situation could prove to be dangerous for her, for she could tell that Arie meant business. She no longer wanted to participate. She had been asked to participate in playing this joke. The men would pay her well, and she was accustomed to seducing men. This prank, however, in her opinion, went too far. She put on her coat and disappeared.

The men grinned rather sheepishly. Their money was gone, and they did not get what they were looking for. "We'll get you next time," they growled at Arie.

One of the men, a big fellow, witnessed all this commotion and shook his head. It was neither right nor fair that they collectively were pestering this young fellow. When Arie was about to become their target again, he stood up for him, and said, "If anyone so much as lays a finger on Arie, he'll have to deal with me." That did it. The men had a great deal of respect for him, and no one would even entertain the notion of getting entangled with him. He was a skilled fighter—something he had learned during the Spanish Civil War. They had better leave Arie alone for now. They would surely get another chance.

Their moment never came, however. During a night when Arie was absent, sleeping by a family that had befriended him, there were intense bombing raids. The barracks were hit by Allied bombs, and nothing but scorched soil was left.

CHAPTER 4

Anxiety and Stress

When the bike swayed somewhat to the left, Elfriede's little head nodded to the right, and when her mother steered in a different direction, her little head again nodded in the opposite direction. She hardly knew how to remain seated on the luggage carrier. It was getting rather dark, and it was also cold. It would take quite some time before they would be home.

In church, it had been so nice and warm. The round stove filled the entire room with warmth. Dressed in a heavy coat and pressed closely against her mother, Elfriede's eyes fell shut automatically. The deep voice of the minister faded away and became softer and softer. Her mother allowed her to doze, for if you were five years old, you were not expected to listen to the entire sermon.

Dad and Mom Melzian—Elfriede is sitting on the front fender, Irmgard on the cross bar, and little Werner on his mother's lap. The train station of Heßlingen (later called Wolfsburg) is in the background.

It was a long bike trip of two hours from the church in Brome to their home in Heßlingen. Elfriede was a bit jealous of little Werner, who was only a few months old. Mother had constructed a little wooden box on the bicycle for him and had fastened it to the handle. Covered by a blanket, Werner was sound asleep in this box. Irmgard, who was only three years old, rode in a homemade bicycle seat on the back of her father's bike. She was also asleep.

Elfriede's grandparents, Opa and Oma Melzian, had eight children.
The oldest son, Willie, perished in World War I. The second person standing
from the right is Friedrich, who would later become Elfriede's father.
At the far left is Herman who would perish in World War II.

Elfriede mused that there was still one seat left on the bike, obviously for Fritz. He was no longer alive, however. They had put him also into a wooden box, but not one made for a bicycle. Instead, the little coffin had been buried. Although Elfriede had been told by her mother that she was present when the burial occurred, she did not remember this event very well. Fritz was only three years old when he had become ill. The doctor said that he had diphtheria. He appeared to be on the mend, but then died suddenly. Rather than attributing his death to diphtheria, the doctor concluded that his little heart had given out. Elfriede therefore became the oldest child.

The Lord's Day was a pleasant day, but also a long day. Early in the morning, Dad and Mom Melzian would travel to Brome by bicycle to worship with the local Baptists. There was no such congregation in Wolfsburg. Of course, there was a Lutheran church, but Father Melzian did not approve of this church. He claimed that he found no food for his soul there, and he preferred to make this long trip by bike. Between services, the family would visit relatives, enabling them to attend the afternoon service as well. Following that service, they would again return home.

Upon their arrival, Mother would help the children remove their coats, and they would then snuggle up to each other on the couch. As he did every evening, Father conducted family worship. He would read a portion of Scripture, followed by everyone kneeling in front of his or her chair. Father would then thank the Lord for all the blessings of that day, pray that all the sins they had committed would be forgiven, and ask that they be kept during the night. After the prayer, the children were put to bed and were sound asleep within five minutes.

Opa and Oma Bischkopf had five children. In the middle of the picture are Friedrich and Meta, the parents of Elfriede who sits on the floor in front of them.

Elfriede knew no better, for that was the way the day went. From the moment she could think and talk, religion had played an important role in her life. Her father was a deacon in the church. There was also an elder who functioned simultaneously as the leader of the congregation. In the absence of a pastor, he or one of the members conducted the service.

In 1929, just prior to the birth of Günter, Dad and Mom Melzian decided to move to Braunschweig. The church was much closer, and there was a congregation there consisting of at least three hundred members.

Elfriede attended the local public school, the simple reason being that there was no Christian school. There was a Roman Catholic girl in her classroom. Although both girls were teased at times, they were incorporated into the group.

The girls would chatter a great deal among themselves. These ten-year-old girls could participate in any conversation—also about the new chancellor, for example. The feeble Hindenburg had resigned, and the new chancellor, Hitler, had come to power. Everyone at school was saying that he was a remarkable individual. This president loved children, and he was opposed to smoking and the drinking of alcohol. He really wanted to exert himself on behalf of large families. All of this appeared to be commendable.

At home, however, Elfriede heard her father speak with his friends, and they were not at all of this opinion. She detected concern in their voices, especially after the "Kristallnacht" (1938) when so many Jews were murdered. Her father had said that this action marked the end. This

Friedericke and Wilhelm Bischkopf, who would become the grandparents of Elfriede Melzian—This picture was taken during World War I. Wilhelm was home for a short furlough.

The wedding picture of Elfriede's parents, Fritz and Meta Melzian

At the end of her first school day, Elfriede's mother was waiting to give her daughter her "Ostertüte" (Easter Candy Cone). Elfriede's Easter picture was then taken.

persecution would have serious consequences, for if Hitler laid his hands on God's chosen people, he would have God against him.

Common, daily, and familiar things were changing. For example, school attendance on Saturday was declining. All who belonged either to the Hitler Youth or the Alliance of German Girls were not required to attend school on that day. After a while, the classroom was so empty that it no longer made any sense to have class on Saturday. In fact, by then the government had determined that it was mandatory to be a member of this alliance. Participation was rather enjoyable, for there were lots of sports, and you learned how to interact with each other. Standing in a circle, the girls would sing patriotic songs. Father Melzian was not all that concerned about such activities on Saturday—that is, as long as it did not interfere with the observance of the Lord's Day. Personally, he did not participate, and he certainly did not join the Nazi Party (NSDAP). It was not all that difficult for him to keep his distance from the party, for his boss belonged to the same denomination and would not make matters difficult for him.

At school, Elfriede often felt so alone. Her classmates thought it strange that she was a Christian. What was the purpose of praying to and thanking God for your meals? She would not attend school parties. Although she was accepted by her classmates, they looked at her warily.

She loved it when she could again attend Sunday School, have catechism instruction, meet with the youth group, attend the weekly Bible Class, and join in choir practice. All week long there were activities in the church, and Elfriede would be present.

When she asked her father whether she could be baptized, he replied, "My daughter, you are only eleven years old."

"That is true," Elfriede responded, "but it is my wholehearted desire to serve the Lord, and I want everyone to know that I desire to belong to Him."

A segment of Elfriede's class on a nature outing—Instruction could not be given since the other segment of the class were attending a "Jungmädel" session (a Girl's Club). Later, everyone would be required to attend such sessions. Elfriede is the girl with the pigtails and wearing a hat. She is standing behind the little girl wearing the white coat.

Her father discussed this question with the consistory, and it was also addressed at a members' meeting. Elfriede spoke freely and candidly of her desire to profess her faith and be baptized. She spoke not only of being conscious of her own sinfulness but also of her only hope in the atoning work of Jesus. Upon hearing this confession, the membership had no objection. Elfriede's walk was exemplary to many, and she appeared to be assured of her convictions. Young Elfriede was therefore baptized by immersion.

~

The local congregation and her parental home were safe havens for Elfriede. Hers was a tightly knit family, and her father was a true father. Even

Elfriede Melzian as the young girl who desired to profess her faith and be baptized

though he could be very strict, demanding that everyone ultimately yield to his will, he also took great interest in everything and was cheerful. He loved to tell stories and share all the interesting things that occurred while at work. As a salesman of farm supplies, he met all sorts of people, especially farmers. It was so cozy at home when he would describe these encounters.

Elfriede's six-year old brother, Günter, in 1936 after his first school day—Her brother would die a few months later.

Mother Melzian was also a true mother who was always available for her children. Because of her steadfast trust in the Lord, she, more than anyone else, made her imprint upon the family. That trust had certainly been challenged, particularly when Günter became ill. The doctor's diagnosis was diphtheria. The heart of his mother was filled with fear. "No, Lord, not again! Please help and preserve my boy," she sighed. Day and night the parents were watching at the bedside of their boy who was wrestling with death. Although they could indeed pray for him, they could do no more than that. God's ways were incomprehensible and past finding out, and the Melzian family was deeply affected when six-year-old Günter died. His mother's heart was breaking.

Elfriede was fourteen years old, and quietly she stared ahead. She could not comprehend this loss. Her father tried to comfort her by saying, "Günter is in heaven, for he was still so young." Elfriede reflected that if she were to die, she would also go to heaven, for she had been baptized.

Although Elfriede did not say anything contrary to this statement, her heart was in turmoil. Was it really true that she would indeed go to heaven? She felt an inner emptiness. No, she was not yet prepared to die. More needed to happen. Beginning with that day, Elfriede sought to fill this void, not realizing that it was the Holy Ghost who was causing her to feel this sense of emptiness. He was teaching her that by nature she was separated from God, even though her religious life was externally beyond reproach. It was the Spirit who was actively convicting her of sin and righteousness, making room for the work of another, namely, Christ. The Spirit did so according to His own time frame, however.

Elfriede was very involved in church activities. Here she is with her Sunday School class, flanked on the right by her youngest sister Sigrid.

Elfriede was nearly seventeen years old when she graduated from high school. During her evening hours, she earned diplomas in stenography and typing. The moment arrived, however, that she too, as well as all German youths, had to complete a "Pflichtjahr," a year of public service. It was mandatory to devote one year of your life to the service of others by working either in a factory, in a family, or on a farm. Her father had a customer who lived twenty miles from Braunschweig. He had a large farm and could use some help. His business was officially recognized by the government, for it was managed according to government regulations. Elfriede became an intern there and received fifteen marks a month as spending money. This amount was three marks more than the required twelve marks—an illegal bonus given to her by the farmer.

Elfriede regularly sent letters home in which she gave an account of how things were going. She wrote:

> The days here are long, and we must work hard. Everything is well organized, however, and the meals are very good. During the afternoon, I am allowed to rest for an hour, and my evenings are my own.
>
> Our day begins with milking cows at five o'clock in the morning. When it is cold, it feels so good to snuggle up against the warm

bodies of the cows. It is no wonder that you increasingly begin to consider these animals as your friends.

The situation here is much better than in Knesebeck where I worked prior to this assignment. There I had to work from four in the morning until ten o'clock at night. Worse than that, I could not go to church. You have always taught me that God's Word was not faithfully preached in the Evangelical Lutheran Church. The farmer did not understand this concern at all. He said to me, "You are so religious, and yet you never go to church." I could not get across to him that the sermons preached in that church were not sound. It was because of my convictions that I could not attend there.

Seventeen-year-old Elfriede at work during her "Pflichtjahr"—This was a year of compulsory employment, first in Knesebeck.

When the war erupted during that year, Elfriede was hardly aware of it. It seemed that she was safe on this farm until she woke up one night from the noise and screaming she heard. The farmer was removed from his bed by soldiers, hardly had time to say good-bye to his family, and was placed in transit to the front. He was replaced by a few Polish laborers who took over his work on the farm.

War means, however, having to live always to some extent with fear and anxiety. One would hear of people being betrayed, and the Nazis increasingly oppressing even the German population. One would hear

The interior of the sanctuary of Elfriede's church in Braunschweig, a building
that was subsequently severely damaged during the war—
In the circle near the top is written: "One Lord, one faith, one baptism."

of either colleagues or acquaintances from the congregation losing their
lives at the frontlines or as a result of cities being bombed. Since Braunschweig was an industrial city, the English would regularly make it a
target of their bombing raids. When the air raid sirens sounded, everyone would look for a safe spot and wait anxiously for the all-clear signal.

Elfriede had secured an office job at the Agricultural Training Center
where farmers received their education. Several buildings were located
on the school premises, one of which was an air raid shelter. When the
sirens howled, everyone on those premises would take refuge there. The
sirens would howl often, for Braunschweig was a prime target for the
Allied Forces. Many factories that were important to the "war-machine"
were located there: the Bussing truck factory, as well as the Zeiss and
Voigtländer factories that manufactured precision lenses. The bombers
would almost always target these factories. The school premises were
therefore outside of the danger zone. The people used to run to the air
raid shelter as fast as they could, but later they took a bit more time and
would first try to finish some of their work. In order to do some more
work, Elfriede would frequently carry her typewriter under her arm
when she went to the air raid shelter where there were designated corners for people to work.

"Come on, Elfriede," said one of her colleagues, "They are coming toward Braunschweig." Elfriede, however, hesitated a bit. She wanted to finish something, so she grabbed her typewriter and walked toward the air raid shelter. She had just arrived at the stairway when all the windows exploded with a tremendous bang. Everything was darkened by a cloud of dust and debris, and part of the building had been blasted away. In a daze, Elfriede looked around her and then ran to the shelter. It was a wonder that she survived this bombing. One of her colleagues was less fortunate. He had taken a look outside at the moment that the bomb fell exactly between the buildings. As a result of the flying debris, one of his legs was torn off.

At home it was not much safer, for the air raid shelter was much further away. When a person emerged from such a shelter after a bombing, he or she would always have to wait to see if one's house were still standing. At one point, the Melzian backyard had been transformed into a huge bomb crater. The house was still standing, however.

On another occasion, the house had been hit by fire bombs that remained lodged in the roof structure. Father Melzian ran upstairs, climbed onto the roof, dislodged the bombs before they ignited, and threw them down into the yard. The window panes were broken several times as a result of air raids, and new window panes were no longer available. Planks had to be used to close the gaping holes. If these were to be blown out of their casings, they would be fairly simple to repair.

The prevailing tension of war meant for Elfriede that she also could trust no one. The Gestapo had been informed that many people frequently visited the Melzian home. Consequently, the Gestapo wanted to know what was going on, and policemen came to search the home. They asked, "That organ over there, what is it for? Are you conducting secret meetings? How about that typewriter? Do you need that for your work? And, you don't even know how to type? Oh, your daughter is doing this typing." It all turned out well, but the family always had to be careful.

When eleven-year-old Sigrid, along with her entire class, was evacuated to a location outside of the city, everyone was rather relieved. A lack of food and relentless tension caused her to languish at home. It would be good for her if she lived in the country for a while. Sigrid herself, however, did not like this change at all. She was homesick and wanted to be with her father, mother, sisters, and Werner. That would be too dangerous, however, thus Sigrid was not permitted to return home. Elfriede and Irmgard therefore tried to visit her regularly. It would normally take an hour by train to get there, but circumstances were not normal. It now took hours.

On one such trip, due to an air raid, they suddenly had to exit the train, run from it, hide behind bushes, and lie flat on their stomachs! Once the air attack ceased, Elfriede was permitted to return to the train. What she encountered there caused her to shiver. Some older people had been unwilling to leave the train. They believed that things wouldn't be all that bad. But it did turn out badly. Shot to death and seriously disfigured, they were still sitting in their seats. One man was still holding his train ticket as if he wanted to prove that he

Elfriede (left) and her sister Irmgard

had a reservation for this seat. Beneath their seats, the puddle of blood grew larger.

～

Since there was no more food, Werner and Elfriede foraged beyond the city limits. All the shops were empty, and all supplies had been depleted. Perhaps some of Father's clients would be willing to give them something. Most of them were willing to do so, but then they would have to pay for it, and sometimes heftily—not with money but with valuables. Astonished and angry, Elfriede and Werner went from one place to the next, using their father's list of addresses. Upon returning home, they were disappointed. "I would rather die from hunger than hit the road again," Elfriede said.

When her mother had to undergo a stomach operation, however, and needed special food, Elfriede left home again and went to the farmer where she served her "Pflichtjahr"—her year of duty. She asked for apple juice, for that would make her mother stronger. Without any ado, she obtained a few bottles and had to promise that she would come back if she needed more. Elfriede was amazed. There had been so many Christian farmers on whose doors she had knocked in vain. Yet this man, who was only a nominal Lutheran, had received her warmly, and she was even permitted to come back. Although she did not understand what motivated him to be so kind, she was grateful.

CHAPTER 5

Destined for Each Other

Braunschweig was a sizeable city with a population of approximately 100,000 people. Many of the young men were absent; they were at the frontlines. Their positions in the labor force had been assumed by men pressed into forced labor—not only Dutchmen, Belgians, and Frenchmen, but also Poles and Slovakians. Thus it was a busy city in which industry was thriving, and there were also many large office buildings. On Sunday morning, however, there would not be a trace of activity, for no one was working, and many would sleep in. Occasionally, one would find open church doors.

Arie had already visited many churches and participated in many services. Occasionally, he would derive some comfort, for the Word of God is effectual everywhere, even in this distant country of Germany. He was not happy with the preaching, however. Frequently the exposition of the Bible would be Arminian, and people would be called upon to make a free-will decision for God. Several times already, he had returned home a disappointed man. He therefore felt that it would be better to take his Bible and seek seclusion.

During a short furlough in Rotterdam, he told others about what he had encountered church-wise in Braunschweig, telling them that he now worshipped at home. He expected nothing less than sympathy for his predicament. Yet it turned out differently than he expected. A God-fearing woman admonished him that it was his duty to involve himself with a local church, for the Belgic Confession teaches that it is not good to isolate one's self.

During this furlough, Rev. Kersten asked him to stop by for a visit. Arie then shared with him what life was like in Germany, and how dangerous it could be for the men pressed into forced labor. He also spoke about the temptations they encountered, as well as his spiritual struggles and the encouragements he had received. Rev. Kersten listened with a sympathetic ear, for he proved to be well informed as to what "his" boys were encountering in Germany. Upon leaving, the pastor gave him a folder of printed material. It was a preliminary draft of *A Treatise of the Compendium*.[6]

---

[6] *The Compendium* is an abridged version of the Heidelberg Catechism. Kersten prepared a brief exposition of this Compendium for young people preparing themselves to make public confession of faith. This exposition of *The Compendium* was published after World War II.

After walking a short distance from the office of the Fricke Company, Arie came upon a church building that was somewhat hidden from view. A sign on the wall informed him that these were the premises of the *Evangelische Freikirchkliche Gemeinde* (Evangelical Free Church). He decided to worship there the following Sunday. Although it was a congregation of Baptistic persuasion, Arie heard things that resonated with him. He had never heard anything like it in Braunschweig.

Various pastors conducted the worship services, but Arie felt the most kinship with Pastor Mosalkow. He was a German who hailed from Russia and had been converted in a remarkable manner. Thus the young Dutchman was welcomed with open arms by this congregation.

Other pastors also preached in the congregation. These were not Calvinists, for they were more closely allied with those of Arminian persuasion. Arie could not be silent about this preaching, and he condemned it passionately. Indeed, such free will preachers were guilty of degrading the Lord Jesus by making Him to be a Savior restricted by the exercise of man's free will.

Some members in the congregation agreed with him, whereas others were as passionate as he was in their disagreement. Consequently, he decided that he would no longer attend the worship services.

Arie was perplexed about what was happening to him. He would diligently read God's Word and would faithfully meditate upon what he had read. Yet something was lacking. Its appeal was gone, and there was no stirring of his soul. He lacked a sense of the Lord's favor. Something was gnawing at his heart, and he knew that he himself was the cause of it. He had deserted the congregation to which the Lord had directed him. There he had been privileged to sit under sound preaching, but now he had arrogantly turned his back upon it. It was wrong of him to have done so. Arie recognized his error and confessed it before the Lord. He should have continued to worship there. It would have been better to discuss these doctrinal errors rather than walking away from them. That was the way of least resistance. Such a response could not possibly be right. On his knees, Arie asked the Lord whether He would lead him back and whether he might be of some benefit for this congregation of the Evangelical Free Church. The Lord answered that prayer—but in a different way than Arie had expected.

While walking, he literally bumped into a woman. When he wanted to apologize and then continue on his way, he suddenly recognized her as one of the deaconesses[7] of the congregation. She asked him, "Why are you no longer worshiping with us?"

Not only did Arie give an honest answer, but he also confessed that his conduct had been wrong. This response resulted in a long conversation,

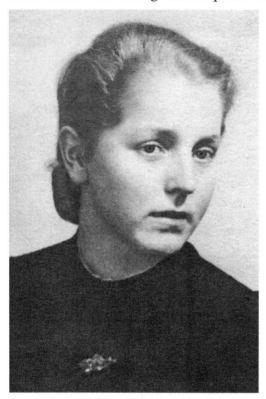

Elfriede Melzian—The girl with whom
Arie Elshout fell in love

and they warmly bade each other well—Arie giving his promise that he would again attend the services.

When shortly thereafter Arie was asked to become the leader of the youth group, he viewed it as the Lord's answer to his prayer. As he sought to instruct the young people from the Word of God, he was also guided by Rev. Kersten's *Treatise of the Compendium* and his old catechism booklet written by Rev. Abraham Hellenbroek.

The young Dutchman connected well with the members of the youth group—especially with Elfriede Melzian. She was his age, had light blond hair, and a pretty face. Initially, Arie did not particularly notice her features. He simply enjoyed talking with her. They understood each other and were of one mind regarding the sermons they heard. After the youth group sessions, they would walk together with a group of young people. Even though the way to the barracks did not lead past the home of the Melzians on *Dillingerstrasse*, Arie did not mind making a detour so that he could spend a little more time with the group and could be in Elfriede's company a bit longer. When Werner, Elfriede's brother, invited Arie into their home, he readily accepted his invitation. He enjoyed being with the Melzians in Lehndorf, for it was a meeting place for young and old. Sometimes the living room would be filled with young people, and together they would sing while

---

[7]Although these women were referred to as deaconesses, they were not ordained office-bearers. They were employed by the church as full-time social workers.

gathered around the organ. "The voice of rejoicing and salvation is in the tabernacles of the righteous" (Psa. 118:15). Elfriede looked quietly in Arie's direction, and out of the corner of his eye, Arie would look at Elfriede. When either one of them would be asked to select a hymn, it would always be hymn #333:

> *Wunderanfang, herrlich's Ende*
> *Wo die wunderweisen Hände*
> *Gottes führen ein und aus!*
> *Wunderweislich ist sein Raten,*
> *Wunderherrlich seine Taten;*
> *Und du sprichst*
> *Wo will's hinaus?*[8]

On evenings when it would get rather late, there would always be a bed ready for Arie, and he would thus be permitted to spend the night at the Melzian residence. What a treat this was for him! He was able to spend the night in a normal bed rather than upon a bunkbed among twenty men who made no attempt to hide their aversion for him and his lifestyle.

The neighbors watched all these young people enter the Melzian home, and they heard them singing. They assumed that something suspicious was going on; they were probably making anti-Nazi propaganda. After all, this Melzian fellow was not a member of the party, was he? Once more they reported them to the NSDAP, and the family was consequently harassed. Father Melzian had to come to the police station to explain the intent and purpose of these gatherings. They were under surveillance, and several times the Melzian home was inspected.

Dad and Mom Melzian were very fond of this Dutchman who attended their worship services and contributed to the cozy atmosphere at home. Nevertheless, their attitude changed when they noticed that a romantic relationship was developing between Arie and Elfriede.

It was also a revelation for Arie and Elfriede when they discovered that their genuine friendship was moving beyond that stage. A mutual fondness for each other was emerging. Arie did not understand what was going on, and he honestly bared his heart before the Lord. Such an arrangement could never materialize: a Dutchman and a German who would be hated in his country. There were enough girls in the Netherlands, and he knew of several who would love to have him. There was an additional stumbling block: a Calvinist and a Baptist—one in favor of infant baptism, and the other opposing it.

---

[8] Wonderful beginning, glorious ending; wherever the wondrously wise hands of God are leading! Most wondrous is His counsel, and most glorious are His deeds; When Thou dost speak, who will hinder?

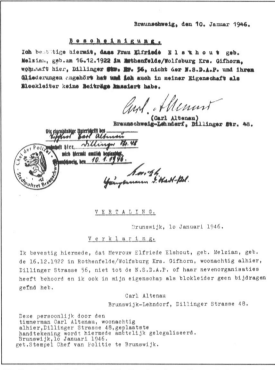

Braunschweig, den 10. Januar 1946.

B e s c h e i n i g u n g.

Ich bestätige hiermit, dass Frau Elfriede E l s t h o u t geb.
Melzian, geb.am 16.12.1922 in Rothenfelde/Wolfsburg Krs. Gifhorn,
wohnhaft hier, Dillinger Str. Nr. 56, nicht der N.S.D.A.P. und ihren
Gliederungen angehört hat und ich auch in meiner Eigenschaft als
Blockleiter keine Beiträge kassiert habe.

Carl Altenau
(Carl Altenau)
Braunschweig-Lehndorf, Dillinger Str. 48.

V E R T A L I N G.

Brunswijk, lo Januari 1946.

V e r k l a r i n g.

Ik bevestig hiermede, dat Mevrouw Elfriede Elshout, geb. Melzian, geb.
de 16.12.1922 in Rothenfelde/Wolfsburg Krs. Gifhorn, woonachtig alhier,
Dillinger Strasse 56, niet tot de N.S.D.A.P. of haar nevenorganisaties
heeft behoord en ik ook in mijn eigenschap als blokleider geen bijdragen
gefnd heb.

Carl Altenau
Brunswijk-Lehndorf, Dillinger Strasse 48.

Deze persoonlijk door den
timmerman Carl Altenau, woonachtig
alhier,Dillinger Strasse 48,geplaatste
handtekening wordt hiermede ambtelijk gelegaliseerd.
Brunswijk,lo Januari 1946.
get.Stempel Chef van Politie te Brunswijk.

To be admitted to the Netherlands, a formal declaration was needed verifying that Elfriede had never been a member of the NSDAP, and that she had never made a contribution to the Nazi party.

Arie could not suppress the sentiments of his heart, however. He could not squelch the feelings he had for Elfriede, and he told her that he loved her. She responded that she loved him as well. Their courtship was not problem-free, however. Father Melzian was furious! How shameful it was that his daughter had a relationship with a foreigner! This relationship could jeopardize his social status, and he could lose his social connections. It would render him even more suspect to the Nazis. He made every effort to disengage the relationship between Arie and Elfriede. When, however, the bond of love unites two people, adverse circumstances will strengthen rather than weaken that bond. Both of these young people felt knit to each other with such a bond of love. The Lord Himself had brought them together, and in spite of all that would militate against this union, nothing could annul it.

Happily, Mother Melzian was less fanatic in her judgment. She had seen this relationship developing for quite some time already. Let it be that Arie was not a Baptist. He was certainly a Christian who, in her eyes, lived uprightly.

Matters in the Melzian home became very tense when Elfriede was confronted with an impossible choice by her father. She could arrive at only one realistic conclusion: she must leave her home. With tears in her eyes, she said good-bye to her mother. There was no other choice for her. No matter what would happen, her choice for Arie was irreversible. Elfriede's second cousin, Ilse Wiederbusch, also lived in the same neighborhood. Since her husband was fighting at the front, she had an extra bed for Elfriede.

The ensuing months were difficult for this young couple. The war became increasingly radical in its effects. Braunschweig had been largely destroyed by bombs, including the barracks in which Arie had been residing. Fortunately, he was able to rent a small room from Mrs. Woltersdorf, who lived next to the Melzians. Food had become very scarce, and the mail delivery system was no longer functioning.

As an industrial city, Braunschweig was an important target for the Allied forces.
It was therefore heavily bombed in 1944. There was not a single house left standing
on *Fallersleberstraße*.

Arie and Elfriede were most discouraged, however, by the strained relationship with Father Melzian. Nevertheless, they decided to become engaged to be married, for they wanted everyone to know that the Lord had brought them together, and that they were destined for each other. But how would the situation with Father and Mother Melzian be resolved? Although an attempt to have a discussion at the front door failed, a little note given to one of the other children was received. Father Melzian refused to budge, however. Werner and Irmgard also reacted bitterly. As profoundly happy as Elfriede was with Arie, so deeply she was grieved by her family's rejection of her relationship.

This tension lasted until Mother Melzian became ill. Early in the morning, twelve-year-old Sigrid rang the doorbell at the home of Ilse Wiederbusch. When she stood at the bedside of Elfriede, she asked whether she would come home to help the family. Elfriede responded that she would be more than willing to do so, but only upon one condition: Arie should also be allowed to come home. Father Melzian thought about this a bit, swallowed his resentment, and stated that this arrangement would be all right. Two things were battling for preeminence in his heart. On the one hand, he was worried about what people would say. On the other hand, he observed that these young people loved each other and would never terminate their relationship. Indeed, they were truly compatible. He honestly had nothing against Arie—nothing substantial. In his heart, the German and the Christian were at odds with each other.

When Elfriede entered, Father Melzian had a warm feeling in his heart. How good it was that she was home again! When Arie entered and said, "Good evening," Father Melzian responded by telling Arie that he should not talk so much. In his heart, however, the Christian had prevailed—by grace. His expression was still somewhat stern, but that did not bother Arie and Elfriede. They were only too happy that they were together again. Mother Melzian was no less happy.

It all seemed backwards. The Dutchman Arie was forced to work in Germany, and the German Melzian received a summons to go to the Netherlands. Arie would have loved to have gone to the Netherlands, but he was prohibited from doing so. Father Melzian did not want to go, but he was compelled to do so. He was not absent very long, however, for a few days later, in the middle of the night, he knocked on the door. He had been dismissed because of his weak health. It sounded as music in his ears when he heard, "This man is not fit to build trenches and bunkers. He is of no use to us." Greatly relieved, he returned to his home.

According to Hitler, the war was going well. He boasted of one victory after another. Father Melzian knew better, however. After General Rommel had suffered a decisive defeat at El Alamein, it seemed as if the tide were turning. Contrary to all the pompous words of the Nazi leader, many rumors were abounding that the army was being defeated everywhere. The German population did not fail to notice the landing of the Allied troops in Normandy—not only because of the stories that were circulating, but also because it became painfully noticeable. An increasing number of people were being summoned to go to the frontlines. The age of eligibility for active duty was increasingly extended in both directions, resulting in the conscription of men that were either much younger or much older.

At last, entire school grades were being called to arms, even boys of sixteen or seventeen years. They would be trained for only a few days, and then they were mercilessly placed on a train that would take them to the frontlines. Many girls also were enlisted to engage the anti-aircraft weaponry mounted on rooftops.

Elfriede was choked up when she rode her bike past Werner's school. She saw a group of boys in the schoolyard who were surrounded by soldiers, and she saw army vehicles behind them. Immediately she caught on. She saw Werner standing in the middle of the group, and most of the boys were crying. Although Werner was barely sixteen years old, he had to go fight near Berlin. There the German army was surrounded by the Russians and the Americans. The German empire was in its final death throes, and it was only a few weeks later

Two young German soldiers—
Entire school classes were compelled to enlist in Hitler's army.
The young men, who actually were but children, received training for only a few days—or at best a few weeks.

that Werner was taken prisoner and sent to an American prisoner of war camp. He would be held prisoner there until November 1946.

Elfriede crossed the hospital grounds with a pounding heart. Sigrid had been admitted to the hospital after undergoing an appendectomy. Although the doctors had declared the surgery to have been successful and were confident that she would recover, last night everything had gone completely wrong. After the air raid sirens sounded, everyone hid in the bomb shelters. Elfriede had been quietly praying there: "Lord, please take care of our family and protect us—but wilt Thou also care for Werner and Sigrid?" Elfriede was worried. After the all-clear signal had been given, she emerged from the shelter and could see clouds of smoke hanging above the city.

A rumor began to spread rapidly that the hospital had been bombed. Elfriede ran as fast as she could to the hospital grounds. She found indescribable chaos, and there were also many fatalities. Elfriede had no idea where she should begin her search. She questioned people, but no one had an answer. "Sigrid Melzian? No, we never heard of her." Elfriede was therefore greatly relieved when she heard that Sigrid had been taken to the bomb shelter in a timely fashion, and that she was alive.

The nation was in ruins. Many of the soldiers who fought at the frontlines would never return. Allied airplanes controlled German airspace. What was about to happen was rather obvious. The Melzians were yearning for the end of the war. Halfway into April of 1945, the Canadians and the British entered the city. The Russians had come as close as twenty miles outside the city. Gruesome stories were circulating about the Russian soldiers. They were marauding, stealing, and they could not leave the women alone.

Braunschweig held its breath. There was great relief when the Americans temporarily assumed the administration of the city. They were not exactly saints either, but anyone was better than the Russians. On April 12, Braunschweig surrendered.

Arie would probably be able to return to the Netherlands quite soon, but he did not want to leave Elfriede behind, and she would rather be with Arie. They decided that they should get married as soon as possible so that Elfriede would be able to secure Dutch citizenship. On May 18, 1945, Elfriede Melzian and Arie Elshout exchanged vows before the civil authorities in Braunschweig.

In the midst of the ruins of the city, the chaos in the civil government, the tension about the Russians who were approaching, and the lack of the most basic necessities, there was this young married couple. They looked at each other and knew themselves to be united to each other until death would part them.

On April 12, 1945, a cease-fire went into effect in Braunschweig. Arie had to carry documentation with him that proved his Dutch citizenship.

The pastor of the Baptist congregation was still residing near the Eastern frontline, and he was therefore not able to confirm this marriage. They then turned to Pastor Dupré, for both Elfriede and Arie felt a real kinship with him. This old pastor, however, lived in Platendorf, approximately twenty-five miles from Braunschweig. Bridges and highways had been destroyed, there was no public transportation, and the pastor was therefore not able to officiate.

It was finally Pastor Althof who agreed to officiate at the church ceremony. Although he was a conservative Adventist, he was permitted to speak on behalf of this Baptist congregation.

The pastor expounded Colossians 3:12-17, thereby giving the young couple this portion of Scripture as their wedding text: "Put on therefore, as the elect of God, holy and beloved, bowels of mercies, kindness, humbleness of mind, meekness, longsuffering; forbearing one another, and forgiving one another, if any man have a quarrel against any: even as Christ forgave you, so also do ye. And above all these things put on charity, which is the bond of perfectness. And let the peace of God rule in your hearts, to the which also ye are called in one body; and be ye thankful. Let the word of Christ dwell in you richly in all wisdom; teaching and admonishing one another in psalms and hymns and spiritual songs, singing with grace in your hearts to the Lord. And whatsoever ye do in word or deed, do all in the name of the Lord Jesus, giving thanks to God and the Father by him."

It was a prophetic testimony. The life of Arie and Elfriede would unfold in conformity to these words. God's grace would be glorified in their hearts, regardless of their circumstances.

Not much is needed to celebrate a wedding, and there was but little available. Whatever was there had been gathered from neighbors and family members. Father Melzian, Arie, and the sisters had visited family members in order to secure some extra food, but while they were in transit, they were detained by the Polish. They were not permitted to proceed and had to surrender their bikes. Fortunately,

All cameras had been confiscated during the war. Fortunately, Mrs. Czernecki, a member of the congregation, had retained one camera and took some pictures. This formal wedding picture did not surface until 1990. Having a wedding bouquet was equally extraordinary. Having worked for a grower, Elfriede received this bouquet as a present from him.

Arie was able to prove that he was not a German. As a result, the Polish became a bit less rude, and they permitted them to keep their bikes. Thus, they returned homeward—relieved, but at the same time disappointed that their trip had been in vain.

The interior of the Evangelical Free Church in Braunschweig (taken around 1950)

The wedding guests consisted primarily of ladies and girls. The men and boys had not yet returned from the front lines.

Neighbors each put their best foot forward. Somewhere in their home, they would find whatever could not be purchased. One brought a cup and saucer as a wedding present, another found a new bath towel in the closet, and a third one brought a dish—all items that were scarce and therefore very precious. It was an expression of love.

What about Father Melzian? He proudly received the best wishes expressed to him. He told everyone that he was very glad indeed, for it was a blessing to have such a son-in-law. No, one could hardly find a better one....

The official certificate affirming that Elfriede and Arie
had been united in matrimony on May 18, 1945

CHAPTER 6

Number 742

Triumphantly, Arie held up the letter: "It is really true, Elfriede. We can really go to the Netherlands. It says it right there! Look, here is the proof that we can cross the border. Pack your suitcase. We are going home!"

For a brief moment, Elfriede's face betrayed concern. She was obviously happy that this moment had come at last, but Arie's home was not yet her home. She had no idea what to expect. She did know that she had to bid farewell to her father and mother, as well as Irmgard and Sigrid.

A picture taken upon Werner's return after having been a prisoner of war—
From left to right: Irmgard, Mrs. Melzian, Sigrid, Werner, and Elfriede

She had no idea whether she would ever see Werner again, for he was still a prisoner of war. Werner had bitterly rejected her when she became engaged to Arie. He was, however, still her brother. She did not doubt for a moment that the day would come that they would be reconciled.

Elfriede gave some thought to what she should take along to the Netherlands. Would one suitcase be enough? She was quite certain it would be, for there was not much she could take along—at best some clothing and a few odds and ends. She should also not forget to take some photographs to remind her occasionally of home. How peculiar to speak of "home," for what really is home? It is plainly the place where you live and can be together with your dear husband. Things would therefore also work out in the Netherlands. They were both convinced that the Lord would be with them. He would show them the way. They only needed to follow.

Quite a group had gathered in a public square in Braunschweig waiting for transportation. When a few open trucks entered this square, everyone knew that the journey would begin. Arie and Elfriede climbed on to the rear of the truck and looked for a spot on the floor close to the canvas. There would then not be too much of a draft, for it was still so chilly that the wind even penetrated your coat. They then drove to Lüneburg, and there the group was divided into two. One group would continue its journey by truck. Arie and Elfriede were fortunate, however, for they could travel to Brussels by airplane. When there proved to be no room for all the suitcases on the plane, Arie had a solution. One of Elfriede's aunts lived in Lüneburg, and she would pick up the suitcases and store them.

"Don't worry about these," she said, promising Arie and Elfriede that she would take good care of them.

With just some hand luggage they continued their journey, thinking that they would arrive in the Netherlands in just a few days. They would certainly be able to borrow some items.

There were no seats left in the airplane. Once more Arie and Elfriede had to be satisfied with a spot on the floor against the wall. This spot would enable them to brace themselves during take-off and landing. Soon the plane was completely filled with both refugees and people who had been forced to work in Germany. The atmosphere was tense and joyful at the same time, for they were going home!

After more than an hour the plane landed in Brussels, and the group proceeded to the Dutch consulate. At this point, Elfriede and Arie were separated and interviewed individually.

The Consul looked at Arie and asked, "Are you married?"

"Yes," Arie responded.

"When? On May 18, 1945? Are you not aware of the law that was passed in 1944?"

There was a look of surprise on Arie's face. He asked, "What law? What do you mean?"

The Consul folded Arie and Elfriede's marriage license and said to them, "In November 1944, the exiled government passed a law that Dutch nationals would no longer be able to marry Germans. This means, Mr. Elshout, that your marriage is not legitimate, and thus null and void. You are therefore not married, and your wife, Elfriede Melzian, is not a Dutch national."

Arie turned pale. He could not grasp what was happening. What did all of this mean? Would he have to be married all over again in the Netherlands? Well, that should not be a problem, should it?

The official shook his head, however, and said, "Marriage will not be an option. Your wife will have to return to Germany.

```
Bund evagelisch-freikirchlicher Gemeinden
in Deutschland                    K.d.ö.R.
Gemeinde Braunschweig,Madamenweg 175,
      Fernruf 8541.

                      T r a u s c h e i n.-

Arie E l s h o u t , geb.2o.1.1o23 in Rotterdam, Sohn des Schlosser-
meisters B.Elshout und dessen Ehefrau, beide wohnhaft in Rotterdam,
Davidsstrasse 18, und
Elfriede M e l z i a n, geb. am 16.12.1922 in Rothenfelde, Tochter des
Kaufmanns Friedrich Melzian und dessen Ehefrau Meta Melzian, geborene
Bischkopf, beide wohnhaft in Braunschweig,Dillingerstrasse 56, sind
nach vollzogener standesamtlicher Eheschliessung am 18.5.1945 in
Braunschweig als Eheleute christlich getraut worden, worüber ihnen diese
Urkunde ausgestellt wird.
Trautext:                        Braunschweig, den 18.5.1945
Kolosser 3,12-17.                     Evangelisch freikirchliche Gemeinschaft
                                            w.g. W.Althoff.


                  B e s c h e i n i g u n g.

Hiermit wird bescheinigt, dass der kaufmännische Angestellte
Arie E l s h o u t,reformiert, wohnhaft Dillingerstrasse 57,Braunschweig-
Lehndorf, und die
Elfriede Irmgard Ilse Melzian. baptist, wohnhaft Braunschweig-Lehndorf,
Dillingerstrasse 56, am 18 Mai 1945 vor dem hiesigen Standesamt die Ehe
geschlossen haben.

                              Braunschweig, den 18. Mai 1945
           Stempel Standesamt         Der Standesbeamte
           Braunschweig.              w.g. Kamfeldt.
```

Marriage certificate issued in Germany to Arie and Elfriede

There is no room for her in our country. Don't you understand this after all that has happened?"

Arie did not understand, and his head was spinning. Elfriede had to go back to Germany. If that was how things were, he would also return to Braunschweig. He would not abandon his wife.

The Consul responded and said, "That will not work. You may not return to Germany. Instead, you are to continue your homeward journey as soon as possible."

In a daze, Arie dejectedly collapsed on his chair. The Consul deemed the interview concluded. As Arie walked through the building, it seemed as if he were dreaming. Then he saw Elfriede, and she had just received the same message. Dejectedly, they stood together.

"Ma'am, you are under arrest. Come along!"

Arie tried to persuade the Belgian soldier not to proceed. How could this be? How could this be allowed? It was to no avail, however, and he watched his wife being taken away like a criminal. Once outside the building, she stepped into a truck designed especially for the transport of prisoners. This glimpse of Elfriede was the last he saw of her. A battle was raging within him, including anger, anxiety about his wife, and dejection.

∽

Arie had no idea how he got back to the refugee reception center. How was this possible? His heart cried out, "I am very desolate and brought exceeding low. My griefs of heart abound!" (Psalter 63:1).

∽

The truck rumbled toward the city of Brussels. Elfriede saw that there were other women who were all seated in separate cubicles—as if they were criminals. The truck stopped before the prison gate. The iron gate was securely locked. A small window in the door was opened, and everyone looked curiously through the opening. Slowly, the heavy gate turned on its hinges, and the truck drove on to the prison property—an enclosed area surrounded by high, insurmountable buildings. Little windows were located near the top, and the steel bars gave a grim impression. Brussels guarded its prisoners better than its reputation.

The women had to exit the truck. As they walked through doors with reinforced glass where passing guards were leering shamelessly at them, they were led into the building. Finally, a door swung open, and Elfriede had to enter a cellar. It was a cell for two persons. Elfriede was, however, the fifth woman who was shoved into this small room. She mumbled a few words, and it was as if she were dreaming. Questions were multiply-

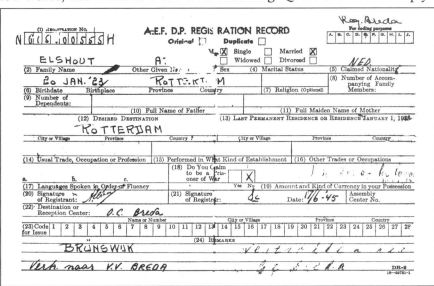

An official declaration confirming that Arie was being transported to the Netherlands by the Allied forces

ing within her. How could this have happened? Where was Arie, and what would happen to him? What was her crime? She loved her husband who was a Dutchman. He loved her, a German. Was that a crime? Was that the reason why she was locked up in a cell?

After nightfall, the women decided they would go to sleep. There were several sacks filled with straw. When they laid them side by side, there was just enough room for them all to lie down. Sanitary facilities were lacking, and there was no light.

Elfriede slept very little. After she finally dozed a little, a few guards were banging on the door. They informed the women that the men were being transported to the Netherlands, and they had to return to Germany. Dejectedly, Elfriede listened to this decision. Did she have to go back home? Was not her home where Arie was? They had promised unconditional fidelity to each other and had asked the Lord to crown this decision with His blessing.

One by one the women were taken elsewhere. They were "cross-examined" by military police upon orders of the Dutch embassy. It was a rough interview. After returning to her cell, Elfriede fell to the floor and sobbed. She could not have imagined that things could be any worse than they already were. One of the women stooped over her and tried to comfort her. Although she lovingly wiped Elfriede's face with a small cloth, Elfriede could not be comforted.

After having been transferred to another cell, Elfriede enjoyed a bit more "luxury." She now had to share a cell that was meant for five women with ten women. At least there was a sanitary container. Every morning a basin with water would be shoved into their cell so that they could wash themselves. The "luxury" of using the container came, however, at a premium. The women would rotate the location where they would lie down so that it would not always be the same person who would sleep next to the sanitary container.

In the morning, they would take turns as to who would first make use of the water that initially would be fairly clean. There was much conversation among the women. They were all in the same boat; therefore, they tried to encourage each other. They were certain that before long they would at least be able to return to Germany.

Elfriede could not comprehend the Lord's ways. "Why did this have to happen to me?" she asked. "Lord, did I not always seek to serve and follow Thee, and now this trial?" She fretted and sought to come up with an explanation. She was not angry with the Lord, but she could not grasp why this was happening to her. She remained in the dark about this incomprehensible way until it pleased the Lord to shed His light upon it. It was as if He asked her, "Did you always love Me? Have you always served Me?"

Elfriede recognized that she had always had herself in view. She wanted to be somebody for the Lord, without the Lord Himself being of any true value to her. Her religion had been nothing more than an external show, and all her righteousnesses were as filthy rags. The words of Isaiah were applicable to her: "Thou hast made me to serve with thy sins, thou hast wearied me with thine iniquities" (Isa. 43:24). The wretchedness of her sinful life became real to her, and she lost all hope. Her prison became a prison in a double sense of the word. It was no longer this small cell that oppressed her, but rather her sinful and ungodly heart.

Her discussions with Arie came back to mind. If only he were here! So often he had said, and so often they had sung at home,

> *Could my tears forever flow, all for sin could not atone;*
> *Thou must save, and Thou alone* (Toplady).

These two lines of poetry had now become an experiential reality for Elfriede. The Lord was shedding His light upon who she was, and she grieved over this revelation. She had been so certain that she loved the Lord, therefore this grief was so unsettling to her. That which she deemed to have been the fear of the Lord proved to be no more than an external form of serving herself. How could the Lord ever be merciful to her? For Elfriede it became reality: "I looked on my right hand, and beheld, but there was no man that would know me: refuge failed me; no man cared for my soul" (Psa. 142:4).

The women around her were talking about home, freedom, and the work that would await them. Elfriede, however, was sighing. Her heart was crying to God out of the depths of her prison cell. Nevertheless, when all hope vanished for Elfriede, the Lord again caused His light to shine upon her. That which was impossible with man, God made possible in His beloved Son, for *"God so loved the world."* Elfriede could believe that it was possible to be saved—also for her, the worst of all sinners. By renewal the Lord used the words of Isaiah to speak to her soul: "I, even I, am he that blotteth out thy transgressions for mine own sake, and will notremember thy sins" (Isa. 43:25).

∽

Although all doors were literally closed for Elfriede, the Lord opened a door for her that was of infinitely greater significance. There was a song in her heart:

But God will save from death and shame
All those who fear and trust His Name,
And they no want shall know (Psalter 87:2).

After several days, however, her hopes for a speedy release were dashed. Elfriede was transferred to Vilvoorde, approximately six miles to the north of Brussels. When the roll was called there, all the women had to undress themselves. She had to surrender all her possessions—all extra clothing and all valuable items that reminded her of home and of Arie. She could keep only the clothes she was wearing. As of this moment, Elfriede was no longer Elfriede. First, they stripped her of her name Elshout by declaring her marriage null and void, and here the Allies even stripped her of her first name. No longer did Elfriede Melzian exist. The woman wearing impoverished and worn-out clothing, who so valiantly tried to retain her self-respect, had been reduced to a number: 742.

At Elfriede's new location there were no cells, but rather, dormitories. Forty women had to share one room. Although they were told repeatedly that this situation would be temporary, the days accumulated and turned into weeks. There was no indication whatsoever that they would be released. At the end of July, however, after having been incarcerated for seven weeks, a rumor was spreading among the women: "We are finally leaving. We will be transported to Germany."

Once more the women had to climb into trucks that transported them to Brussels. In a school building, Elfriede waited for further transportation. It was pleasant here, for she could wander from one room to the next. She had not been able to move about this freely for a long time.

After a few days, the group was on the move again. The women had to walk from the school through *Stoofstraat* to reach the truck. What a wretched sight it was! The women were suffering from dysentery and looked dreadful as a result of having been bitten by lice. Many people were watching this pathetic procession, and they were railing at these "kraut women."[9] A shoe came flying through the air, followed by rocks. The eyes of Number 742 filled with tears. She felt alternately grieved and angry. Was this happening because she was German? Or, did this happen because Christ Himself had said, "If the world hate you, ye know that it hated me before it hated you" (John 15:18). That thought gave her some rest. Holding her head high, she walked to the truck and climbed into the back.

---

[9]A derogatory name for German women.

When the truck made a stop in Münster, the women were permitted to exit. There were no more guards, and no orders were being barked. Nothing! Elfriede was left to fend for herself. The only things she had were the clothes she was wearing.

It was only a short distance to the Dutch border from Münster. If she could cross that border, she would be able to go to Arie. That was her deepest desire, and she decided that she would attempt to get into the Netherlands. This was easier said than done, for she had no money, could not secure food coupons, and did not have a roof over her head. She aimlessly roamed the streets of Münster, not sure of what she was looking for. Perhaps there would be a place where she could sleep or an opportunity to get into the Netherlands.

She walked through street after street, crossed intersection after intersection, and moved from one town square to another. The cathedral was her landmark, for all the houses looked alike, and she had no idea where she was. One house was different, however. There was a flag extended from the window. Instead of being a German flag, it was the Dutch three-colored flag. Perhaps these people could help her. After ringing the bell, she was asked to step in. The man told her that he could not help her to get out of Germany and into the Netherlands. Since, however, he visited the Netherlands frequently, he would be able to take a letter along if Elfriede would write one. If she would then return after four weeks, he would have an answer from her husband. She quickly wrote a short letter.

~

Elfriede finally concluded that there was no other option for her but to return to Braunschweig. This journey would be rather difficult, for passenger trains were not running, and freight trains were running only intermittently. The train station was crowded with people, and they were pushing to get to the front of the line. They were all trying to get a spot on one of the freight cars. Elfriede no longer had the energy to keep trying. She sank to the floor in one of the hallways of the train station. She spent the night there along with hundreds of other people.

The next day some trains were departing, but they all were headed in the wrong direction. When she finally heard the word "Hannover," she jumped up and found herself a spot on one of the train cars—a spot in the open air. This spot did not matter to her—as long as she was moving in the direction of home. In Hannover, the situation was not much better. Finally, she found a spot on a train carrying coal and having Braunschweig as its destination. Gratefully, Elfriede walked the last segment from the train station to her home. She was a sight to behold, for coal dust was even in her ears. At first, Elfriede was too tired to say much about her experience. She was sad, and she was worried about Arie—yet, she was thankful that her life had been spared.

Not everyone was sympathetic toward her, however. A few people could not refrain from rubbing it in by saying to Elfriede: "We told you all along that it would come to nothing with this Dutchman." These reproachful words wounded her deeply.

CHAPTER 7

How Can This Be?

Arie felt out of sorts. There he stood in the midst of the busyness of the refugee reception center in Brussels—all alone. His wife had been taken elsewhere, and there was nothing he could do about it. He had to leave it in the Lord's hands. At least, that was what he would have told others. His circumstances were such, however, that this was not as easy as he had thought.

He decided to look for Elfriede, but wherever he went, he came up empty-handed—whether it was the in the embassy, the military barracks, or the prison. Dejectedly, he returned and was told that he should travel to the Netherlands as soon as possible. He was also told that his wife had returned to Germany long ago.

He had no money, and his papers would only permit him to cross the Dutch border. Other borders, particularly the one with Germany, were sealed completely. He traveled with a group of Dutchmen who were in the mood to celebrate. Arie could hardly conceal his resentment.

He had to show his documents at the border. The customs agent looked at him and said, "Why didn't you just marry a Dutch girl?"

Arie bit back and said, "Why didn't you just marry your neighbor girl?"

The customs agent looked at him somewhat puzzled. "Is he ever touchy," he thought, and he returned the documents to Arie, saying, "You had better head for home, and I wish you the best."

Dad and Mom Elshout embraced their son joyfully. They had been so concerned about his living all by himself in Germany. The little bit of news that had trickled their way had only increased their concerns. All of Germany had been bombed. The big cities had been leveled, and the death toll was very high.

There would be a brief moment of relief when they occasionally received a letter, for that meant that he was still alive. They realized that some letters simply never arrived. At times Arie would refer to what he had written earlier, and his parents then had to guess what this could have been.

A few days earlier two letters had arrived simultaneously, and they were quite shocked. Mother Elshout was bedridden with a rather serious throat infection, and she had lost her voice. They opened the first letter together. To their utter amazement, they read that Arie was married—married without their knowing about it. He was married to a German woman named Elfriede. She had to be of a different faith. It was incomprehensible to them how Arie, of whom they had such high hopes when he left them, could have acted in this way. They had been so hopeful that he had been on the right path, and they had believed that the Lord Himself had been dealing with Arie. Now look at this shocking news: Arie married to a German woman! "How is this possible?", Mother asked Dad. In saying these words, it surprised her that her voice had come back. How did that happen?

The second letter proved to be of an earlier date, and Arie wrote that he was engaged to Elfriede Melzian. He told them about this woman and the family from which she hailed. He also wrote about the spiritual bond that united them. He told them about the bond of love between them, the church to which Elfriede belonged, and the precious faith that was also experiential reality in Germany and among its people.

Father and Mother Elshout could hardly get a handle on this news, for if this were true, their son had not acted in a frivolous manner. Instead, he had asked the Lord for direction. It was He who had opened doors for this young couple. Then all had to be well.

And yet, here is Arie—all by himself. Where was his bride? His father and mother had spoken so much about her, and they each had their own idea what their daughter-in-law would look like. Now it appeared that it would take some time before they would see her.

Arie told his story, and he had great difficulty in hiding his disappointment and grief. The spiritual liberty he so often was privileged to enjoy in Germany was gone. Dullness and barrenness now seemed to prevail. Inwardly, he felt shaken, for both unbelief and rebellion were agitating within him. Just think of how many men with German wives he had met! They all had been able to cross the border without the least trouble. Why not him?

Mother Elshout let her son get everything off his chest. All would certainly work out in the end, for when the Lord begins something, He will also finish it. He would not forsake her son. If she had understood things well, He would also not forsake his young wife.

Father Elshout finished a corner in the attic so that Arie could have his own private spot. In the midst of the busyness of the family, he would then have a place of solitude.

The headquarters of the Van Ommeren Shipping Company—Arie's employer
prior to and after the war. This picture was taken at a later date,
as is evident from the helicopter pad on the roof.

Arie was comforted by one thing: No one had said a bad word about
his German wife. They all had to get used to the situation. His father,
mother, and the children bombarded him with questions—about Elfriede,
her parents, her family, and about what the war had been like in Germany.
Arie readily responded to these questions, but he rather would have talked
about his wife all day.

He had not heard a thing from Elfriede, however, for there was still no
mail service. Doubt was gnawing at him—not because he doubted her
faithfulness, but because he had no idea whether things would ever work
out, and he did not know what would happen if they did not. His confidence had vanished; he had lost all courage. He could not see his way
clear any longer. Arie began to pity himself.

There was much work to be accomplished at the offices of the Van
Ommeren Shipping Company. Mr. Kroeze was happy that his right-hand
man had returned. He showed concern for this young man who told him
that he was married. The business at hand had to continue, however.
Business transactions with Germany began to get off the ground again,
and VanOmmeren established an office in Duisburg to facilitate all these

proceedings. There would be no objection if this young man would occasionally send a letter with the ships that would be sailing to Germany. The Dutch postal service was functioning poorly, and matters were even worse in Germany.

~

Amazing! How could it be that Elfriede was back in Braunschweig after a few months and received news about Arie exactly two days later? One of Arie's cousins served with the British Air Force and was stationed in Hannover. He happened to be home on furlough when Arie arrived in Rotterdam. Very willingly, he said to Arie, "This will work out fine. I will see to it that a letter is delivered in Braunschweig. As soon as I return to Hannover, I will stop by her parents and will see whether she is residing with them."

Arie immediately wrote a long letter in which he related his experiences but also expressed his concern and love for her. Arie's cousin took the letter with him, but it would still take several weeks before he departed. When he rang the doorbell at the Dillingerstrasse homestead, he met Elfriede, who had just returned a few days earlier. How happy she was! She knew that Arie was alive, and that he was doing well. She also realized that he had no knowledge of what had happened to her.

She considered it a blessing that Arie's cousin had not come any earlier. How worried her parents would have been, for they considered her to have been in the Netherlands already! They would have communicated this information to this cousin, and he would have returned to the Netherlands with that news. How worried Arie would then have been! However, all of this confusion was prevented by the Lord's wondrous, providential dealings.

~

"Can anyone help me learn the Dutch language?" That is how the small ad read in the *Braunschweiger Daily*—an ad that did not remain unnoticed. Thus Elfriede spent her evening hours learning Dutch from Mrs. Bertram, who was born in The Hague and had met Mr. Bertram there as an SS officer in hiding. They married after the war and made Braunschweig their residence. Although Mrs. Bertram was a nurse, she was quite capable of teaching Elfriede the basics of the Dutch language, and Elfriede did her best. Although she did not know what the future would bring, she was certain that all would turn out well, for the Lord would care for her. With this childlike confidence, she prepared herself for her departure to Holland. Perhaps it would happen shortly. Arie would certainly do his best in the Netherlands to secure all the necessary papers, and she would do her utmost in Germany to facilitate matters.

~

After four weeks, Elfriede traveled to Münster, for a fellow there had promised that he would have some news from Arie for her. Once more her journey proved to be quite an undertaking. One would normally travel this distance in one-and-a-half hours, but now it took an entire day. She had to wait, switch trains, ride along for a bit on a freight train, then switch trains again. Inch by inch, she was traveling in the direction of Münster. Finally she arrived again at the home with the Dutch flag. However, the gentleman who lived there told her that his trip to the Netherlands had been cancelled; consequently, he had no news for her.

Elfriede swallowed hard and tried to push aside her grief and disappointment. After thanking this gentleman, she began her return trip. Huddled in her coat, she once more spent a night at the train station. Although doubt was gnawing at her as to whether things would ever work out, she quietly brought her case again before the Lord as she had done so many times. She had no idea how to go on from here, but there was a deep impression in her heart that Jehovah's truth would stand forever. He would do what He has promised to do, and He has a wise purpose for all that He does—even though it made no sense to the slender woman huddled on the platform.

A train pulled into the station. It was a freight train with sliding doors that provided protection, and it was traveling in the direction of Braunschweig. Elfriede was happy when she found a spot, and she settled in one of the corners. The slow rhythm of the wheels caused her gradually to fall asleep. She was dreaming about the Netherlands, and she also heard people speaking Dutch. Suddenly she sat up straight, for she was not dreaming. She really did hear Dutch being spoken by men. Perhaps they could take along a letter for Arie. Her hope made her bold. She traversed the train car, and noticed two men.

They listened to Elfriede's question and responded, "There are so many women like that. We understand your concern." They would be willing to take her letter, and if she wanted to, they would take her along to the Netherlands as well. The men told her that they regularly crossed the border—not via official border crossings, but secretly. That is how they smuggled their merchandise to the other side of the border. They were prepared to take Elfriede with them, and then she would be in the Netherlands as well.

Elfriede felt so torn! Here was an opportunity for her to go to Arie. If she were to accept this offer, she could be with him tomorrow. Her head was spinning! She knew that she could trust these men, for she could see that they had no ulterior motives. Yet, she could not do it!

Elfriede felt in her heart that in so doing she would be going in the way of her choosing, a way outside of God's will and intent. That would not be right; therefore, she could not acquiesce in this plan. She would rather wait until the Lord opened the way, for in not opening a way, He also manifested His wisdom. Elfriede would rather wait upon God.

"Well, that's up to you. Give us a letter, and we will bring a letter back," replied the gentleman who introduced himself as Henk Van Mook. He lived in Schüttorf near Bentheim, a town near to the Dutch border. He was a former policeman who knew the area like the back of his hand. The only risk was that he had to be on guard for his own brother, who was also a policeman.

Slowly but surely the mail began to move again in Germany, and letters could once more be mailed within Germany. Elfriede therefore regularly mailed a letter to Schüttorf. Henk Van Mook would then take it with him on his cross-border ventures and deliver it in Rotterdam. Arie mailed his letters to the border town of Losser where Henk would pick them up and take them along to Germany. Henk neither became rich from his smuggling escapades, nor was this his motive. He knew that Elfriede had very little money, so he refused to accept any remuneration. "Nothing doing," he would say to her, "for he who gives all that he has, deserves to live."

```
              Brg., d. 1. 11. 4

Geachte Heer van Mook!

Vandag heb ik de post van U gekregen en ik dank
U hartelijkst. Mag ik U nu nog eenmaal een briefje
meegeven? Hoe zal ik U wel all dat, wat U gedaan
hebt voor mij, goed maken. Als ik toch ook voor U
een betjen doen kun. - Gaat U wel voor het Kerst-
feest nog eenmaal naar Ho.? Ik hoop er zoo op.

Ik hoop, dat het goed met U gaat en ben met de
hartelijkste groeten

                        Elfriede Elshout.

Er zijn zeker nog veel fouten in dien brief, maar
kijkt U astublieft niet daar op.
```

Elfriede's note addressed to Henk Van Mook

Translation: Dear Mr. Van Mook—Today I received your mail and thank you sincerely for this. May I once more ask you to take a letter with you? How can I ever make up to you what you have done for me? If only I could do something for you. Are you traveling again to the Netherlands prior to Christmas? I am so hopeful that you will. I hope you are doing well, and receive my sincere greetings—Elfriede Elshout (PS: There must be many mistakes in this letter. Please ignore them.)

Henk was the lifeline between Arie and Elfriede. Occasionally, he would spend the night with the Melzians in Braunschweig, and then again he would spend the night in Rotterdam—and for lack of space, in the same bed as Arie.

In every conceivable way, Elfriede attempted to secure an exit visa. She would travel to all the locations where the necessary Dutch paperwork was available. She traveled to Münster, Kleef, Hannover, and wherever else she had to go. Nothing could hold her back.

At this point only freight trains were in service. Time

Volumes of letters were written. It was the only way that Elfriede could maintain contact with Arie. Here are the folders containing all these letters— folders that have been preserved until today.

and again, Elfriede would find a spot on them. The round tank cars in particular would offer some protection. Via a steel ladder, you could climb to the top, but that was not advisable during the winter. The biting wind would lash her face and penetrate even the heaviest clothing. The steel would be frozen, so that one could not touch it. Under such conditions, Elfriede would travel from Braunschweig to Hamburg, and the next day she would return disappointed.

A day later Elfriede was in bed with a high fever. It did not take the doctor long to determine the cause: pneumonia. It was quite serious, and the doctor knew that a critical moment was imminent. Elfriede felt this as well. She feared that this crisis would be the end; she would never recover. Her thoughts drifted toward Arie. Would God's way then be different than she had thought? Elfriede prayed quietly. She did not know what all of this meant for her. She was certain of one thing, however: God's hand was in this event. It was therefore well, even if they would never see each other again. Even then all would be well. At the same time, there was a cry within her: "Has God forgotten to be kind? Shall I His promise faithless find?" (Psalter 209:6—Psalm 77). That was impossible! The Lord is true to His Word, for He cannot lie. The Lord would make it well. She believed with her whole heart that she would see Arie. With that thought, she fell asleep—a restless sleep.

Arie became discouraged. Time and again he would be turned down. "What do you mean?" officials would say. "You claim to be married to a

German woman. How can you prove that? You are telling us that her papers were taken away from her. Come on, that is obviously not true. How do we know that Elfriede Melzian really exists? Nowhere do we find any evidence of this person."

At night, Arie would write letters to all government agencies that might possibly be able to help him. Sometimes he would write twice or even three times if necessary. He often detected mistrust in the people with whom he was dealing. Obviously, there had been many women during the war who had profited from the fact that their husband was a Dutchman, or who wanted to profit from this fact even after the war. Arie knew that such was not the case with them. They had no ulterior motives. The Lord had brought them together and had forged a bond of love between them—a bond that was affirmed even now in difficult circumstances.

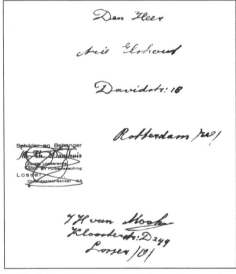

Henk Van Mook arranged the exchange of letters between Germany and the Netherlands.

Arie would therefore continue. Of course, he would persevere! Had not the Lord comforted him from His Word a few months ago when he felt so sorry for himself and had hard thoughts of the Lord? How bitter he had been! But then it was as if the Lord removed a veil in regard to his life. He could not express in words what he had then seen. His entire life was polluted with sin. The Lord would be righteous if he would pass him by. In his little attic room, which was also his prayer closet, he fell on his knees and confessed his guilt. This was the same room where four years earlier he had experienced such spiritual joy when beholding the atoning sacrifice of Christ who opened the way of salvation for him. Now, however, he expected nothing but well-deserved punishment. All he could do was to cry out for mercy—mercy from a righteous God who was both just and merciful. "Lord, I know that Thy justice must be satisfied," he prayed, "but is there yet a possibility for my wife and me that Thou couldest bless us?"

The answer was given to his question, "What must I do to be saved?" The answer was given, "Believe on the Lord Jesus Christ, and thou shalt be saved, and thy house" (Acts 16:31). These words dripped as heavenly ointment upon his wounded soul. By renewal, his soul was drawn to the Lamb of God, and he was privileged to lay the hand of faith upon the head of the sacrificial Lamb.

Suddenly, Arie realized that it said "thou...and thy house." All would turn out well after all! He would be reunited with Elfriede. How good God was for wretched people! Arie was resolved that he would doubt no longer, that he would stop pitying himself, and that he would persevere. The Lord was His shield and the lifter up of his head (Psa. 3:3).

By now, Arie and Elfriede had neither seen nor conversed with each other for two years. They could communicate only by way of letters—first via Henk VanMook and later directly by mail. That is how they had stayed in touch and encouraged each other.

During the following summer, Elfriede received a letter from Van Ommeren, in which he asked her to come to Düsseldorf (Germany) to pick up a package. It would be a long trip to Düsseldorf, especially because of the poor connections. But she obviously went.

Upon her arrival, Elfriede was received warmly. A few Dutchmen were present, and one of them handed her a package from Holland. "Do you have a moment?", he asked her. Elfriede responded affirmatively. She had no idea when the train would depart. The man explained to her that it was usually around this time that they had a telephone connection with the Netherlands, and then he said, "Your husband knows that you are here; perhaps there will be an opportunity for you to speak together."

Once Elfriede and Arie were connected by phone, she did not quite know what to say. Arie was on the other end of the line, and he was equally tongue-tied. It was so unexpected that they could hear each other's voices after two years. They hardly knew what to say to each other. They did spend these few minutes well, however. What new courage this opportunity gave them. Would everything work out well after all?

IHR MANN TELEFONIERT DAS IHRE EINREISE NAECHSTEN MONAT IN ORDNUNG KOMMT BENEHMEN SIE SICH MIT NIEDERLAENDISCHEM KONSUL BRIEF FOLGT = THEODOR KOEPENBRINK + VGL 56 +

Text of the telegram: "Your husband has called to say that your entry into the country will be arranged next month. Please contact the Dutch Consulate. Letter will follow."

Upon receipt of this encouraging telegram, it would take another half year before Elfriede received permission to travel to the Netherlands.

Elfriede was again traveling by train. She was tense. The day had finally arrived: October 7, 1947. Arie had received permission for his wife to come to the Netherlands. It had taken two years and four months. He had vacillated between hope and discouragement, but his quiet confidence in the Lord had not been put to shame. Arie had mailed the necessary paperwork, and now he had it in black and white that Elfriede, his wife, could be reunited to her husband and live in the Netherlands. She did not yet have an official passport. All she had was a temporary travel document—only valid for a one-way trip across the border.

Yesterday, all seemed to have gone wrong. When Elfriede arrived in Hannover to pick up her visa, the government official looked in the bins and could not find it. Elfriede showed him her paperwork. The visa had to be there, or else it would have to come soon, for tomorrow the train to Oldenzaal would depart. The official, who cocked his glasses and showed by his posture that he would not budge, said, "It is simply not here. You'll have to come back tomorrow." Elfriede too would not budge, however, and the official finally fetched the visa from another building.

In Osnabrück, Elfriede had to switch trains to catch the train to Oldenzaal. That would be no problem, for according to the schedule, there would be a layover of two hours. There was another train ready for departure at one of the other platforms. At first Elfriede did not take notice of this fact. Suddenly, however, she saw that the sign on the train said "Oldenzaal." How was that possible? Immediately, she grabbed her luggage and ran to the other platform. Huffing and puffing, her mother followed her, dragging some suitcases behind her as well. Elfriede waved to the stationmaster who was ready to blow the whistle for departure. He looked at her with annoyance and snapped at her that one needs a special permit to travel on this train.

"But I have that permit," Elfriede cried out. The man looked at her in disdain and blew his whistle. The steam began to hiss, and slowly but surely the train began to move. Elfriede was beside herself.

She now shoved her papers under the nose of the stationmaster. "Here, I have this special permit," she said.

The man obviously did not expect that response and looked rather embarrassed. He knew of a solution. "Hurry," he said, "at the other platform there will be an exchange of locomotives. Go there!"

Once more, Elfriede and her mother, dragging the luggage behind them, hurried to this other platform. Being assisted by a railway official, they walked directly across the tracks to catch the train that was about to depart. Exactly on time, they were able to hoist the luggage and themselves inside the train. They were out of breath as they collapsed on the benches. Things almost went wrong again, but happily they did not! There was a song in Elfriede's heart:

Wondrous beginning, glorious ending
When the wondrous and wise hands of God
Govern our coming in and going out!

The train stopped at Bentheim, and here Elfriede bade her mother farewell, for she was not permitted to cross the border. They did not know if they would ever see each other again, but they were both grateful that the Lord had opened the door.

Mother Melzian looked at her daughter as long as she could. There, only a few hundred yards away, stood her son-in-law Arie. How she would have loved to have seen him and spoken with him—especially to tell him that Father Melzian was completely at peace with the way in which the lives of his children were being led! But she was not able to speak to Arie. Only a few hundred yards separated them—yet it was so unspeakably far away. She sighed as she watched her daughter cross the border.

CHAPTER 8

He Hears the Needy when They Cry

The rhythmic motion of the train caused people to doze. The distance from Rotterdam to Oldenzaal was considerable. Even though the restoration of the railroad system was in full swing, traveling still was very time-consuming. The head of some travelers would hang somewhat sideways, and then it would suddenly jerk forward and rest on the person's chest. Arie, however, was not able to snooze; he was too tense. The day had finally arrived: October 7, 1947—the day he could retrieve his wife at the border. They had been separated for two years and four months. Although they had regularly corresponded with each other during that period, they had spoken with each other only on a few occasions.

Arie was pacing back and forth on the platform of the train station. It would still take several hours before the Scandinavia Express would arrive from Osnabrück. He was tense, and even the reading of God's Word in the train had not given him any rest. Would Elfriede truly be on that train? He hardly dared to believe it. What an undeserved favor that would be! He was convinced that all his distrust had made him unworthy of such favor.

After having repeatedly paced back and forth on the platform, he noticed a small blue sign with the letters *WC* (designating a restroom), and he entered it. The walls of this small room were tiled and covered with graffiti. As his eyes scanned these walls, it was as if a cold hand

BUREAU RECHTSHERSTEL
VAN HET MILITAIR COMMISSARIAAT ROTTERDAM

TELEFOON No. 35070
AFD.: Secretariaat
REF.: dVr.-Vo
No.: 3941   ROTTERDAM, 21 Augustus 194 5
BIJLAGEN: MATHENESSERLAAN 208

Den Heer A. Elshout
Davidsstraat 18
R o t t e r d a m.

    In antwoord op Uw schrijven van
25 Juli jl. delen wij U mede, dat U
zich inzake huwelijken met Duitsers dient
te wenden tot het M.C,R.H. te Den Haag,
tot welk bureau U een verzoekschrift in
duplo dient te richten.

                    Bureau Rechtsherstel
            v.h. Militair Commissariaat R'dam

A letter from the Office of Legal Restitution—
Countless letters had to be sent back and forth until
the marriage of Arie and Elfriede was recognized
by the Dutch government.

suddenly grabbed his neck. He took a second look and rubbed his eyes. How could this be? But what had been written was unmistakable:

Ask, and it shall be given you; Seek, and ye shall find; Knock, and it shall be opened unto you—Rev. G.H. Kersten, Rotterdam

He pinched himself, but he was not dreaming. Who could have written this message? It was very unlikely that Rev. Kersten himself would have put the text there. He was, however, certain of one thing: He knew Rev. Kersten personally, and the passage from Scripture before him provided him with fitting instruction for his circumstances. Arie perceived this handwriting on the wall to be a token from an omnipotent and omniscient God. Peace began to fill his soul at last. All that had transpired thus far had been good indeed, and all that would yet follow would be good as well. The Lord knew of their circumstances, and He would certainly care for them. After the bitterness of the past, He gave him the sweetness of the present.

There was a serious housing shortage in Rotterdam. Many young couples were therefore compelled to postpone their marriage—sometimes even for years. Having a home of your own was not even an option, and one could consider himself fortunate if he could board with someone. As soon as his marriage to Elfriede had been legally sanctioned, Arie immediately applied to secure an apartment. The waiting list was long, and they certainly would have to wait several years. Although he made numerous inquiries, he always came up short. Only one option remained: the attic room of his parental home at *18b Davidstraat*. His father and mother approved of this arrangement, even though there were still seven children at home. Although the attic room provided much needed privacy for Arie and Elfriede, in every other way they were simply integrated into the family.

United at last, Arie and Elfriede are standing in front of their first home—an attic room in Arie's parental home at 18b Davidstraat.

∿

Beneath a slanted ceiling and next to the chimney, a bed was located on one side of an attic room that was also furnished with a small table, two chairs, and a small heater. This furniture was all they possessed, and there would have been no room for anything else. It was not much, but it sufficed. The acquisition of this furniture had truly been a miracle.

Arie & Elfriede Elshout as a young married couple

Arie remembered vividly how the discussion went at Van Ommerens. The new salary-grid did not result in the pay raise that so many had anticipated. People were grumbling. When his opinion was solicited, he responded that all would turn out well. Is it not written in Psalm 42, "The LORD will command his lovingkindness in the daytime?" (vs. 8)?

The secretary responded, "Will that enable you to buy chairs when your wife arrives?" Arie responded in the affirmative.

There was hardly anything left in his savings account, however, and his salary was low. There was no money for chairs. This realization brought Arie to his knees. He experienced his dependency upon the Lord, not only in spiritual matters, but also in his daily affairs.

One Saturday morning, as he hung up his coat in the company wardrobe, located in the basement, he saw three chairs and a small dresser made of mahogany, along with a mirror. Arie was astonished and wondered what this furniture was doing there. It turned out that Mr. Bernard

Van Ommeren had refurnished his office and had placed the old furn-iture in the basement. He did not have to think twice. He overcame all hesitation and asked the financial comptroller of the company whether he could purchase this old furniture. He was aware of Arie's circum-stances, and Arie was therefore permitted to take everything free of charge. There was a song in his heart when on that very day he pedaled through Rotterdam with a special transport bicycle that carried three chairs and a dresser. Who could have ever imagined such a wonder? How cozy would the furnishing of his little attic room now be! Three chairs and a dresser!

He reflected on what the secretary had said, "Can you buy chairs with this?" The Lord had even provided a dresser as well.

Elfriede's reception in Rotterdam was rather awkward. Even though Mom and Dad Elshout embraced her warmly, it was quite an adjustment for her. Nevertheless, a mutual bond of love developed quickly. This bond did not exist, however, between Elfriede and many people in the neigh-borhood. After all, Elfriede was a German. The Germans were hated because of what they had inflicted on the citizens of Rotterdam. There was a collective aversion toward them. It was not Elfriede herself whom they did not like, but she took this treatment very personally. After a while, however, the attitude of the neighbors toward Elfriede began to improve, and they finally became friendly to her.

She felt this awkwardness most of all in church. Already on the first Sunday, Arie said to her, "Let's visit the consistory room. You will then be able to meet the consistory, and they will know that you have arrived."

The consistory members shook her hand, engaged in some small talk, and appreciated her broken Dutch—except for the minister. He looked right past her and refused to shake her hand. With tears in her eyes, Elfriede left the consistory room. Happily, there was Elder Van Kranen-burg, who supported Arie and Elfriede through thick and thin.

Elfriede's perception of the Dutch church also needed some adjust-ment. In Germany, the members of the Baptist church lived very sober lives. There was no alcohol consumption; no one smoked; no one wore earrings; short hair and dancing were considered sinful; and visiting the movie theater was denounced. Life was lived very modestly. Arie told Elfriede that many church people in the Netherlands wore black cloth-ing. Elfriede thus concluded that in Rotterdam people lived even more modestly and plainly than in Braunschweig. However, when she attended church for the first time, she thought she was attending a fashion show. Disappointed, she said to Arie, "I thought that people here lived so plainly!"

He responded, "No, I did not say that. I only said that here people often wear black clothing—which is not necessarily the same." Elfriede was not too impressed with this situation.

To become a member of the congregation, Elfriede was obligated to receive catechetical instruction and confess her faith once more. This instruction would also help her greatly in becoming conversant with the Dutch language.

Although Elfriede made public confession faith in 1948, distrust of her continued. Some people were offended when Elfriede partook of the Lord's Supper. The minister addressed her publicly and said, "You are a stranger among us. Let us hope that you are not a stranger before the countenance of God." After all, how could a German woman who grew up in Baptistic circles be converted? The implication was that this could not possibly be true.

Rev. H. Ligtenberg

Prior to the next Lord's Supper, Rev. Ligtenberg and an elder came for a visit. They were, after all, responsible for the sanctity of the table. This visit turned out differently than they anticipated, however. In all simplicity, but also with liberty, Elfriede told them about the way the Lord had led her—how He came into her life; how He caused a person who had considered herself to be converted to become unconverted; how she learned to loathe herself; but also how she began to trust more and more in the God of salvation; how in prison the doors of her spiritual prison were opened, and she found the way of salvation in Christ; how she was daily dependent upon grace; and how she, as a needy sinner, was privileged to take refuge time and again to this glorious Surety and Mediator who had become her life.

The minister and the elder listened to this testimony with tears in their eyes. They recognized and acknowledged the work of the Lord. Who would dare to challenge this testimony? On the contrary! Not only could Elfriede take her place at the Lord's Supper, but there was also a place for her in the hearts of God's children. Rev. Ligtenberg openly testified of this fact at the Lord's Table, quoting the words of a well-known Dutch hymn: "Though they may come from distant lands, their hearts will here readily melt together."

Arie, as well as Elfriede, perceived it to be a manifestation of the Lord's care that his wife was embraced by the congregation.

Arie's father literally had to make all sorts of twists and turns. Just outside of the attic room, there was a bit of space—very suitable for a stove. He had said to Arie and Elfriede, "It is time that you begin to live a bit more on your own. If I install a gas line, you will be able to cook for yourself and run your own household." Upon his father's orders, Arie handed him pliers and screwdrivers. Although his father was sighing and groaning, he succeeded in installing the gas line. Somehow they were also able to secure a stove. Arie and Elfriede were delighted with this arrangement. They were just able to make everything fit. Soon, following the birth of a little one, they would find a corner for the baby as well, for contrary to the expectation of many, they were indeed expecting a baby. Three physicians in Germany had affirmed that Elfriede would probably never be able to bear children. Transcending these physicians, however, was an omnipotent God who was able to accomplish the impossible. Arie and Elfriede made this desire a matter of prayer, for the Lord, as the Omnipotent One, was able to accomplish the impossible. Elfriede poured out her heart to the Lord and pleaded with Him to grant her a child. Like Hannah, she promised that this child would be set apart for the Lord's service. She did not

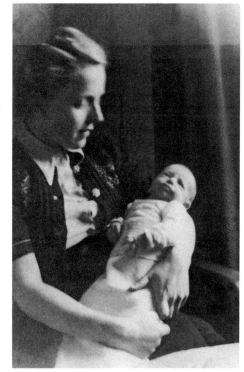

Little Bart, the child for whom they had prayed

mention this to anyone—not even to Arie. She believed firmly, however, that the Lord would be true to His Word and promises. It was a great wonder to them when on Sunday, February 20, 1949, their bassinet could now be put to use, for a son, Bartel, had been born. He was named after Opa Elshout. He was a child of prayer—a child destined for the service of God's kingdom.

It was an impressive moment when Arie and Elfriede stood before the baptismal font, and Rev. Ligtenberg, in the name of a Triune God, sprinkled water upon the forehead of little Bart. "Thy way is in the sanctuary, and is past finding out!" To whom did the minister address these words? To the congregation? The young parents perceived it to be God Himself speaking to them. The Lord confirmed this perception when the minister expressed the wish that God would also bestow upon the children the grace He had glorified in the parents. With teary eyes, Arie and Elfriede sang their favorite psalm (Psalm 118:7—Psalter 427:2):

> *Jehovah is my strength and tower,*
> *He is my happiness and song;*
> *He saved me in the trying hour,*
> *Hence shall my mouth His praise prolong.*

Every day, Arie took the twenty minute walk from Davidstraat to Parkhaven—the location of Van Ommeren, the place of his employment. He enjoyed his work there, and he would love to get ahead in the company. He spent his evenings studying, and he had already acquired three accounting certificates. The pathway to a management position in the company appeared to be open before him.

Yet, his thoughts would wander to the period prior to his departure to Germany. Spiritually, that period had been both a difficult and sweet time for him. It was not only a time when he was seeking the Lord, but also a time when he experienced His tender love.

On a given Saturday afternoon, Arie was reading his Bible. When he arrived at Matthew 9:37-38, he could not proceed, for there he read, "Pray ye therefore the Lord of the harvest, that he will send forth labourers into his harvest. The harvest truly is plenteous, but the labourers are few." Since this was a command, he closed his eyes, and he prayed earnestly that laborers would be sent forth into God's harvest.

As he did so, a thought arose within his heart that startled him. Should he also ask the Lord whether He would use him in His vineyard? He dared not do so, for that would be presumptuous. He asked the Lord to forgive him for having entertained such a thought, for he was too unworthy and too unfit. However, he could no longer suppress this thought, and on various occasions he felt compelled to pray this petition. Finally, he prayed, "Lord, I miss everything I need to do this work. Therefore, grant me

When little Bart was born, his great-grandfather, Jan Elshout, was 80 years of age.
From left to right: Bart (4 months), Arie (26), Bart (50), and Jan (80)

everything I need to enable me to shepherd Thy people and to serve Thee according to Thy will." Once he had uttered this prayer, peace came into his heart. He knew, however, that the Lord Himself must give the answer.

The Lord answered him by way of 2 Chronicles 1—a chapter in which Solomon asked the Lord to grant him wisdom and knowledge to lead His people. The Lord then responded, saying, "Because this was in thine heart, and [thou] hast asked wisdom and knowledge for thyself, that thou mayest judge my people, over whom I have made thee king: wisdom and knowledge is granted unto thee" (vv. 11-12).

To Arie, these words were an answer to his prayer, and he believed wholeheartedly that the Lord would use and equip him to be His servant to serve His people according to His counsel and will. He experienced a deep sense of amazement and joy in his heart. This was confirmed that same evening by means of Psalm 91 (Psalter 249:4):

Because on Me he set his love,
I will his constant Savior prove,
And since to him My Name is known,
I will exalt him as My own.

Arie obviously could not be silent about what the Lord had done unto his soul. However, he did not speak to anyone regarding his inclination toward the office of the ministry, and how God had spoken to him regarding this call. Others, however, spoke to him about it, and his mother said bluntly that she believed that one day he would become a minister. Others asked more discreetly whether he felt any inclination toward the office of the ministry, and whether he had had any spiritual exercises in that direction. It seemed as if it were written upon his forehead. Arie either avoided such conversations, or he remained aloof.

Instead, all of this implicit encouragement caused him much anguish and strife. There was a voice within saying, "There you have it. You so very much want this to come about, and you are therefore imagining these things." All of this greatly intensified, and it became increasingly impossible for him.

Arie went back to work after his lunch break. The words, "Not by might, or by power, but by my spirit, saith the LORD of hosts," continued to ruminate in his mind. He did not know the exact meaning of these words, nevertheless, he deemed them to be an answer from God. Did they pertain to the office of the ministry, however?

Although engaged in his work, the young man sent a sigh heavenward. The Lord then condescended so greatly in giving him again at this time an answer, saying, "Be not faithless, but believing" (John 20:27b).

Arie could not refrain himself from asking, "But Lord, what then must I preach?"

The Lord thereupon removed all resistance by speaking with power, saying, "He shall deliver the needy when he crieth; the poor also, and him that hath no helper" (Psa. 72:12).

This answer settled deeply into his heart and gave his life new direction. Things turned out quite differently, however, for he first had to go to Germany. He needed to learn to wait for God's time and to follow the Lord rather than running ahead of Him. He had to learn to fully trust the Lord and to take Him at His Word.

CHAPTER 9

This is the Lord's Doing!

Using a pencil and an eraser, Arie was drawing a sketch which he often would erase. The tip of his tongue was just visible between his lips. Although he was accustomed to dealing with numbers, calculations such as these were almost too much for him. How wondrous were the ways of the Lord! At first, Arie and Elfriede thought they would never have children. Within a year after the birth of Bart, they were expecting another baby. However, in addition to being overjoyed, this also confronted with the problem of a lack of space. Although there was just enough space in this attic room for Bart's little bed, there was not enough room to add a bassinet. Securing their own home was not an option, for the housing shortage had not decreased. They had an idea, however. If they were to install a hook and a pulley in the nook of the ceiling, they would be able to lower and elevate a little bed. That should work, and Arie proceeded to draw and calculate.

Once again, however, the Lord had other plans. When Arie arrived at his job the next day, he was asked to meet with Mr. Van der Sluis, the department manager. Arie entered his office without any idea of what the issue could be. When he left a few minutes later, he was smiling. What a remarkable providence! A basement suite was available for them at 69 Clementstraat. Van der Sluis was the owner of this home, and he readily made this suite available to Arie and Elfriede. The days following included some suspense, for an occupancy permit needed to be secured from various bureaucratic entities. Mr. Van der Sluis was willing to plead their case, however.

Arie and Elfriede's family moved at the end of 1949. It seemed that they now had an ocean of room: a living room, a bedroom, a kitchen, a hallway, and a hallway closet. A short set of steps enabled them to enter the backyard, which they could share with their neighbors—a childless couple.

This move also meant that they would be transferring their church membership to another congregation. The Elshout family joined the (Netherlands) Reformed Congregation of Rotterdam-South—the congregation where Rev. A. de Blois was the pastor.

A wonderful providence: a new basement suite at 69 Clementstraat

Rev. A. de Blois

Thus, on May 5, 1950, when little Meta was born, she did not have to be hoisted up. She was given her own spot.

Although there was great joy, there were also lingering concerns. The young couple really had to watch their pennies, and each penny was spent carefully. Having a low income meant that many expenditures would often prove to be challenging. Arie and Elfriede lived by the day, however, and the Lord provided their "daily bread." They even managed to save a bit to enable them to pay the bill of their gynecologist, Dr. Hoytema.

When they heard that friends were in dire straits, however, they brought this money to them. Although they had put this money aside, they realized that "he that hath two coats, let him impart to him that hath none" (Luke 3:11). Indeed, it is more blessed to give than to receive.

At the same time, Arie was concerned about the doctor's bill that was still pending. However, the bill did not arrive. He repeatedly requested that the bill be submitted, but no bill arrived. Once more he requested a copy of the bill, for he wanted to know where he stood. Subsequently, a bill was submitted, but the amount was far too low—an amount slightly higher than the charge of a family doctor. That could not possibly be correct. It was correct, however, for the specialist did not wish to receive more than that amount. Arie was thus able to pay the bill, and he did so joyfully. He perceived in the doctor's action the loving care of his heavenly Father.

The heart of man is "in the hand of the LORD, as the rivers of water: he turneth it whithersoever he will" (Prov. 21:1).

Elfriede was looking after the children, for it was Arie's turn to go to church. That afternoon Rev. de Blois preached about Lord's Day 21 of the Heidelberg Catechism. When question and answer 55 was read— "What do you understand by 'the communion of saints'?"—a deep joy pervaded Arie's heart. It pleased Christ, by His Spirit, to give the felt assurance that he was a partaker of Him and of all His benefits. He was filled with a deep sense of wonder when he considered not only what Christ had done *for* him, but also what He had been pleased to do *within*

The church building of the (Netherlands) Reformed Congregation of Rotterdam South—the congregation with which they affiliated after their move

Bart and Meta with Trolly—the little dog Uncle Werner Melzian brought with him
upon his return from having been a prisoner of war

him unto his salvation. In His great love, the Savior had delivered his body and soul from perdition, for Jesus had purchased him with His blood, and by His Spirit he was united to Christ. By faith, he was privileged to taste this blessed union.

At the same time, Arie realized that there was also a flip side: the Lord had a right to use his body and soul as He pleased. It was his duty of love to use all that he had received for the benefit and salvation of others, and to do so willfully and joyfully. However, Arie was not willing to do the latter—that is, he was no longer as willing as he once was. There was the prospect of the Van Ommeren Company's giving him a significant promotion. At last, he would have a good position and a much higher salary.

Furthermore, there were many troubling developments in the (Netherlands) Reformed Congregations. The unrest and tension surrounding Rev. R. Kok began to affect all the congregations. This tension negatively impacted the spiritual climate of these congregations. Arie was therefore no longer willing to give himself. As he listened to Rev. de Blois's preaching, however, everything he had asked of the Lord, everything he had promised Him, and his desire to serve in His kingdom—it all came back. Arie was moved in the deepest recesses of his soul.

The Lord had done everything to make him a partaker of Himself and His communion, and he was unwilling to surrender himself to be His servant. Arie bowed deeply, and he did not want people to see that tears were running down his cheeks. If he could have, he would have crawled under the benches for shame regarding his sins. Quietly, he asked for forgiveness, saying, "Lord, if Thou art still willing to have me, and if Thou wouldest still be pleased to use me, here I am. Be then pleased to open the doors and the ways that must be opened to make it possible for me to serve Thy people. In addition, be pleased to give me everything I need to that end, and I shall do what Thou art asking me to do."

Upon his return home, Arie could not hide from Elfriede what had happened. From that day forward, there was a yearning for all that would most certainly come to pass. He was certain that something indeed would come to pass.

Only a few weeks later, the young Elshout, who recently had become a member of the congregation of Rotterdam-South, was nominated for the office of deacon. He was elected, and he accepted his office. He did so quietly and thoughtfully, for the Lord would go before him. Yet, he also knew that serving as a deacon would not be the ultimate fulfillment of God's promise.

~

Arie attempted to show no emotion when his cousin (through marriage), a student at the Theological School in Rotterdam, asked him whether he had ever had a desire to preach the gospel. He tried to dodge the question but he did not succeed, for his cousin Tunis persisted. Finally, Arie admitted that there was indeed such a desire in his heart. A conversation ensued, during which Arie told him something of the way in which the Lord had led him. His cousin then responded, "If this is truly how matters are within your heart, why don't you ask the consistory for an attest?"

Arie's cousin, Tunis (Teun) Caberet, a student at the Theological School in Rotterdam—He "drew Arie out of his shell," so that Arie could no longer be silent about his call to the ministry.

The young Elshout did not quite know how to respond to this advice. He could not sleep that night. Although Tunis had urged him to seek an attest, this encouragement was not sufficient for him to appear before the Consistory. The Lord Himself would have to speak.

It became a restless night during which all of Arie's objections were taken away. Yet he remained doubtful, and he decided that he would seek the counsel of his minister, Rev. de Blois. He also advised Arie to approach the consistory for an attest to be examined by the Curatorium.

At the next consistory meeting, the young deacon spoke of the desire of his heart—a desire greatly assaulted at times. He spoke of the time when the Lord came into his life; how He conquered him with His love; how He humbled him; but also how He opened his eyes for that glorious salvation that is to be found in Christ Jesus. However, he also spoke of the way in which the Lord had given him a love for the office of the ministry, had inclined his heart, had called him, and had drawn him.

He subsequently had to wait outside of the consistory room. Upon his return, Rev. de Blois addressed him and told him that the consistory had freedom to give him an attest. Warmly and lovingly, the minister addressed him, and together they asked for a blessing upon this decision. They also prayed for the welfare of the churches in light of the high level of tension that now pervaded them. Arie felt strengthened, and he thanked the Lord for His help and His assistance.

When he met with the Curatorium on June 20, 1951, circumstances were quite different. Arie Elshout was the last to be examined of the seven men who had applied. One man after another had been turned down. The heart of the young man was pounding in his throat when he entered the room. He could feel the tension among the curators. While groaning inwardly, he gave his account. The curators required some additional explanation regarding his conversion, his calling to the ministry, and especially his marriage to a German woman, which had generated some rumors. After giving an honest answer to all these questions, Arie was asked to leave the room. It seemed to take hours before he was called back—and he did have to wait a long time.

Upon entering the meeting room, he could sense a tension so thick that it was palpable. The chairman stated that this body had not yet made a decision, for there were some additional questions that needed to be asked. Once more Arie gave an account of what moved him to request an attest. When finally one of the curators addressed Arie, saying, "It is a difficult decision for us. What do you think?"

Elshout did not have to think very long. He replied, "Brothers, I have placed myself in the way of the means to determine what the will and leading of the Lord is. I neither can nor am willing to have any part in arriving at a decision."

The secretary of the Curatorium, Rev. de Blois, responded, saying, "Brothers, this is indeed true, for *we* must arrive at a decision regarding this matter."

Again, Arie was asked to leave the meeting room. In the waiting area, he could hear that an intense discussion was taking place in the meeting room.

After a period of time, he was again permitted to enter. The chairman informed him that the Curatorium had no freedom to turn him down; therefore, they had decided to admit him. The student who had just been admitted left the meeting with mixed emotions. He did not know whether he should be joyful. Although he had indeed been admitted, in what manner and under what circumstances had this taken place? What would all of this mean? Upon his arrival at home, he placed his bicycle against a tree. Elfriede could not think otherwise but that her husband had been turned down. He looked perplexed and unsure of himself. He felt forsaken; the Lord was no longer mindful of him.

The next day he heard that one of the curators had called the Lord as a witness during a week night service, saying, "Thou knowest that one candidate was accepted today, and we may deem this candidate to be one too many."

"One too many..."—that obviously applied to him. This statement proved that everything had merely been imagination. There was great strife within the heart of the prospective student. There was neither any opening heavenward nor any perspective when looking either forwards or backwards. He felt like the Psalmist, "Refuge failed me; no man cared for my soul" (Ps. 142:4). He decided that he would inform Rev. de Blois that he would rather not proceed with this matter.

His minister, who was the clerk of the Curatorium, knew exactly what had transpired in the meeting, and he did not deny the palpable tension. The situation regarding Rev. Kok had caused division in the life of the church, and polarization was evident at all levels. Rev. de Blois then said to Arie, "The fact that you have nevertheless been admitted to the Theological School may truly be considered a wonder of God's omnipotence, and your acceptance is a sign that this is God's way regarding you." Arie could not argue with this conclusion, and he promised that he would present himself at the appropriate time.

His darkness did not lift, however, until his old friend, Elder Van Kranenburg, visited him. He claimed to have heard that his young friend had been accepted, and now he longed to hear how all of that had occurred. He did not tell Arie that Elfriede had contacted him, saying, "Please come and talk to Arie. He cannot get a handle on the situation, and he appears to be at his wits' end."

Van Kranenburg was a wise man who himself had been exercised in spiritual warfare, and he knew how to draw Arie out. Arie then began to tell how it all started, and gradually he spoke with increasing freedom and conviction. As he spoke, he was privileged once more to become assured of his calling. Light was arising for him in his darkness. Everything again became true for him. With opening, he could tell his story to his friend.

~

"Come here," said Mr. Kroeze as he beckoned Arie, who then followed him to the window. From this upper story window, you could look out over the parking lot on which the black Opels of the management team were parked. "Your car is among them," said Van Ommeren's manager, for when I retire in the near future, you will take my place on the executive management team."

A black Opel Record—"There is your car...if you stay."

Arie did take a look, knowing that he was giving up much indeed. However, at that moment he did not doubt. He would follow the Lord.

He had just tendered his resignation, and Mr. Kroeze was disappointed. Three times he asked Arie whether anything could be achieved by way of a significant raise. Arie, however, had made his decision—a decision that was resolute. At the same time, however, he felt a bond with the company and with Mr. Kroeze. They had always had a good working relationship. Arie had bonded with the company during the past twelve years.

Mr. Kroeze understood what all this meant, and said, "You are making a great sacrifice. I regret the fact that you are leaving us, but it is laudable that you are willing to make such a personal sacrifice for this purpose. Wherever in the world you are installed as a minister, I will be present."

It was quite an adjustment to attend the Theological School. Fortunately, the student could continue to reside in the home on Clementstraat. Yet there was only very limited space after the birth of Arie and Elfriede's third child, Frits. When traveling by streetcar to the Boezemsingel (the location of the Theological School), Arie could see the office building of his former employer from the bridges crossing the Maas River. One day, he felt an intense longing for his former occupation, and he yearned for the relaxed and open atmosphere of the Van Ommeren Corporation. At that moment, however, the words of the Savior were powerfully impressed upon him, "No man, having put his hand to the plough, and looking back, is fit for the kingdom of God" (Luke 9:62). Arie was ashamed. How slow he was to learn! This rebuke was more than sufficient.

The birth of Frits reduced the amount of living space at 69 Clementstraat.

Candidate L. Kieboom had just left the Theological School and had accepted the call to Waardenburg. Student W. Hage was in his last year. A.F. Honkoop still had two years ahead of him and had received permission to speak an edifying word. On Sunday, Student Honkoop would preach in various congregations, and he also desired to preach during the week. Consequently, he was reprimanded by his instructor, Dr. C. Steenblok, who felt that he was taking on too much. The Theological School was also attended by students T. Cabaret and L. Vogelaar.[10]

---

[10] The father of Rev. C. Vogelaar

Candidate L. Kieboom had accepted
a call to Waardenburg.

Student W. Hage

Student Elshout was the only student in his first year of study. Instructors Steenblok and Van Bochove looked after twenty-eight-year-old Arie. Soon he discovered that the tensions within the denomination did not bypass the school.

When not attending the Theological School, he found himself living as it were in a glass house. You had to be very careful as to what you either did or refrained from doing. Being a student, people would watch you like a hawk and often interpreted things negatively. For instance, going shopping together with your family was no longer acceptable. When Arie and his family were on their way to the wedding of Aunt Audrey, a man said to him, "How convenient when you are a student at the Theological School! Then you can go for a walk with your children during the middle of the day." Since Arie did not want to cause any talk or offense, he became even more careful.

Arie's first year was almost problem-free. Student Elshout thought very highly of Dr. Steenblok. He, in turn, was happy with this young man who was eager to learn. He recommended a variety of theological books to him, particularly the works of A. Comrie and W. à Brakel.

Enthusiastically, Arie delved into these works. Yet something did not make sense to him, for he read things that differed from what Dr. Steenblok was teaching him. Or, rather than reading different things, was he perhaps reading things differently? Therefore, he studied with even more diligence and presented his questions to his instructor. Dr. Steenblok taught him that he must preach the law to the unconverted, and that the gospel is to be preached to God's people. By preaching the gospel, he meant that people must be taught how God converts His people. He rejected the notion of a so-called offer of grace to all hearers of God's Word. Dr. Steenblok noticed that his student, of whom he had high expectations, began to doubt his instruction. He spoke about this feeling to a number of curators, and they became increasingly distrustful of Student Elshout. This feeling did not surface in the announcement of *De Saambinder* of June 26, 1952, however, where it was stated that "to everyone's satisfaction, Student Elshout had pursued his studies with great diligence, and he was therefore promoted to the next year of study."

During the second year of study, a theological student would be required to preach a number of trial sermons. Student Elshout was nervous when he was called upon to do so. His relationship with Dr. Steenblok had become strained, and he had given Arie very little guidance on how to construct a sermon. There was but a small

Student A.F. Honkoop

Mr. A. Van Bochove

audience when a trial sermon was preached: students, instructors, and curators. They were critical listeners, however. The students were less critical, for they were all in the same boat, and they would all get their turn. The instructors and curators were seasoned preachers who would not refrain from being openly critical for the benefit of the students.

Dr. Steenblok was particularly sharp in his criticism, and his assessment of the first trial sermon was not positive. Things did not turn out any better with the second one, for Dr. Steenblok did not like it when a student took too many notes into the pulpit.

The time had arrived for the preaching of the third trial sermon. Student Elshout looked up against this occasion immensely. First, the Particular Synod would convene, and thereafter he would have to preach

Dr. C. Steenblok

his trial sermon, for the curators and teachers would then be present anyway. Rev. de Blois warned Arie that on previous occasions all delegates had been invited to attend. That prospect rattled him.

This Synod would address the grievance that Rev. Verhagen had brought forward against the teachings of Dr. Steenblok. This circumstance generated an unusual level of interest for this particular meeting. Therefore, at the conclusion of an intense meeting, everyone was invited to hear the trial sermon of Student Elshout. The short amount of time that was left was not used by him to quickly scan his outline. Instead, he sought a place of solitude and fell upon his knees, beseeching the

Lord to assist and help him. How incapable and anxious he felt at this moment! If the Lord would not go before him, things would certainly not go well.

It went well, for the Lord went before him and granted him what he needed. Student Elshout himself was the one who was most broken about this deliverance. Again, the Lord had proven Himself to be faithful to His Word.

Student A.F. Honkoop, who was deeply moved, immediately went to Arie, saying, "This is the Lord's doing!" How true this was! Arie could not even entertain the thought of what could have happened if his trial sermon would not have been assessed favorably. It was, however, the Lord's will that he would become a minister, and therefore He granted him His help in an extraordinary manner.[11]

Shortly thereafter, in June 1953, a grievous schism occurred in the (Netherlands) Reformed Congregations. Dr. Steenblok was dismissed as an instructor. Rev. J.W. Kersten and Rev. L. Rijksen were appointed as instructors, and the Curatorium granted permission to Student A. Elshout to speak an edifying word. None of the students left the denomination as the result of the schism.

Rev. L. Rijksen

Student Elshout looked somewhat helpless. For the first time in his life, he would enter the pulpit and proclaim God's Word. He had been sent to Vlaardingen. It was a large and vacant congregation in which there was much unrest and polarization. The question was: Should they leave the denomination, or should they not? Also within the confines of the consistory, this question was a subject of conversation and discussion. Prior to the service, a discussion occurred that was not very edifying.

Student Elshout could no longer remain silent and said, "Brothers, I am about to preach God's Word for the first time. Please keep that in mind."

One of the elders supported him, saying, "Indeed, brothers, we need to stop. Would it not be better if we were to beseech the Lord to grant His help and assistance?"

The Lord did indeed help him. On this Sunday, the gospel was proclaimed in all its richness. Student Elshout was humbled when he considered that it had been affirmed that

> *He hears my voice, my cry and supplication,*
> *Inclines His ear,*
> *Gives strength and consolation*
> (Psalter 426:1—Psalm 116).

---

[11] Reflection upon this event yielded comfort to Rev. Elshout throughout his entire ministry.

A few months later, the Lord greatly encouraged him in Oudewater. A portrait of Rev. L. Boone hung in the consistory room. Many years earlier, this minister had baptized little Arie, his mother, and his sisters. Who could then have thought that this little fellow would once stand on

Rev. L. Boone

the pulpit of a congregation where Rev. Boone had preached so frequently? Elshout's thoughts were led back to 1941 when he refused to be present during house visitation. How wondrously all had turned out! "There is no God but Thee alone, nor works like Thine, O Lord Most High" (Psalter 233:5—Psalm 86).

It had not yet become a common practice for ministers and students to preach a third time in addition to conducting two Sunday services in a given congregation. After repeated requests, Student Elshout consented, however, and he agreed to serve the congregation of Stolwijk during the evening. An acquaintance, Wim Suijker, was prepared to be his driver.

Student Elshout arrived in the small consistory room of Stolwijk in plenty of time. Prior to the service, he asked the serving elder De Jong if he could make use of the restroom facilities. Of course he could; all he needed to do was to walk around the back, and he would find his way. Coming out of the light, Elshout stepped into the dark, and he could see absolutely nothing. He felt his way around as he sought to find the restroom facility. Instead of finding the restroom, however, he ended up in the middle of a ditch! The first thought that occurred to him was: "There you have it. This is what happens when you travel on Sunday."

At the same time, he uttered a prayer, saying, "Lord, if this is a manifestation of Thy displeasure, then let me know this by closing my mouth."

However, there was not much time for reflection. Elshout hoisted himself out of the water, and moments later he stood in the consistory, dripping wet.

Elder De Jong was perplexed, and said, "Oh, Reverend, what must we do now?"

The church building of the Stolwijk congregation (1954)

Student Elshout replied, "You had better remove your trousers, for I must soon enter the pulpit."

De Jong quickly responded by sending his wife to their home to retrieve another pair of trousers and shoes. In the meantime, the consistory room was transformed into a dressing room. The elder was far taller and more broadly built than the small student. Therefore, everything stayed in place only when Arie rolled up the end of the pant legs several times. The shoes were a bit more problematic. They were so big that Student Elshout had to curl his toes and take large steps to keep the shoes on his feet.

However, this incident did not prevent Student Elshout from proclaiming God's Word with great freedom. All circumstances fell away, and his eye was fixed upon the Author and Finisher of his faith. Powerfully and with liberty, he directed the congregation to look to Him. He urged the congregation to take refuge to the one and only Surety and Mediator, Jesus Christ, with their entire burden and guilt of sin.

No sooner had he said "Amen," however, when he was again confronted with the bizarre nature of the situation. Student Elshout had to hold on to his pants as he descended from the pulpit. In order not to lose his shoes, he turned around and descended backwards from the pulpit one step at a time. Upon arriving in the consistory room, however, the members of the consistory were unanimous in their opinion that it would be fine if the student would end up in the ditch more frequently if that would cause him to preach as he had done.

Eskampstraat, the new Elshout residence in Rotterdam-Overschie—
Their new apartment was on the top floor on the right.

Little Frits was growing well. He could already walk, and he was beginning to babble a bit. The home on Clementstraat, which at first appeared

Entrance to 14d Eskampstraat

to be as spacious as a palace, seemed to become smaller and smaller. That perception was obviously mistaken. Instead, the family was becoming larger, and everyone needed a place. When expansion of the family was again on the horizon, Student Elshout and his wife looked at each other with some concern. Where would there be room for this new child? One bedroom for six persons was simply not doable.

Just at the right moment, their prayer was answered. An apartment became available in Rotterdam-Overschie, located at 14d Eskampstraat. When Nellie arrived on December 30, 1953, a small room with a bassinet was ready for her.

CHAPTER 10

"I shall go there…"

As Candidate Elshout laid another call letter aside, he sighed deeply. He did not know what he ought to do. He had asked the Lord for light but had not received it. He had asked for clarity, and he still lacked the needed clarity. He had besought the Lord to give him an answer, but He remained silent. He had received call letters from thirty-five congregations. They all longed to receive him as their own pastor and teacher. They were undoubtedly praying that he would come. Upon receiving these call letters, he responded in writing to each congregation that had extended a call. He wrote, "Please accept my sincere thanks for the receipt of your call letter. Since your call is not the only one I have received, I have prayerfully laid it before the countenance of the Lord, beseeching Him that He would graciously teach me the way that He would have me go, and that He would grant me the grace to follow Him wherever He directs me to go."

Although he had written this thank-you letter rather quickly, the reality was different. There were attractive congregations—some were located in beautiful surroundings, some were centrally located, some were stable congregations, some had a good consistory, some had a beautiful parsonage, and some offered a good salary. The student years had not exactly been prosperous years, and Candidate Elshout felt the tempting attraction of all these matters—certainly now that there was another new baby in the bassinet. Little Arie had arrived on April 20, 1955. Yet, Candidate Elshout only desired to do the Lord's will. It was his prayer: "Make Thy ways known to me by Thy Word and Spirit."

He felt attracted to certain congregations—such as Scheveningen, for example. The times that he had preached there as a student were unforgettable. A bond was forged. He had alluded to this bond only to his instructor, Rev. J.W. Kersten.

The time for consideration expired, and the congregations were waiting for an answer. Yet, Candidate Elshout did not know where the Lord was leading him. Just imagine if the Lord would not make this known to him and there would be no answer! He was gripped with fear. He bowed his knees and begged the Lord to grant him light. In a childlike manner, he finally said, "Lord, I will lay all the call letters before Thee in alphabetical order. Should it be Thy will that I go to a certain congregation, cause me to be exercised with its call, and I shall go there, Amen."

Then he took some time to consider each call letter, laying each one before the Lord's countenance. He dwelt a bit longer on the letters of those congregations where he desired to go. That did not help, however, for the Lord neither spoke nor prompted him.

As the number of remaining letters dwindled, the tension increased. Arie thought, "There you have it. The Lord is not answering me. That can mean only one thing: the omniscient God does not concern Himself with me." Candidate Elshout was overcome by doubt. He began to question everything: the usefulness of prayer, the genuineness of his call to the ministry, his state of grace, and even the existence of God.

Yet, at precisely this moment, it would be confirmed, however, that "Thou calledst in trouble, and I delivered thee" (Ps. 81:7), albeit in an unexpected fashion. Candidate Elshout now had before him the call extended by the (Netherlands) Reformed Congregation of Utrecht. It was a congregation in turmoil, and her future prospects were far from favorable. The ecclesiastical conflicts of 1950 and 1953 had also profoundly impacted this congregation, causing confusion and polarization. Furthermore, the circumstances that led to the emeritus status of the previous pastor, Rev. J. van den Berg, had been very painful. No, Utrecht would not be a congregation for a freshman pastor. Only recently, Candidate Elshout had said to Student Molenaar as they were walking together, "You had better believe that Utrecht will have to wait a long time before they will again have a pastor."

Nevertheless, he could not lay the letter from Utrecht aside. In his mind, Candidate Elshout saw the congregation before him. He saw many young people seated in the balcony—young people who were in need of leadership and of hearing God's Word. The candidate attempted to push these thoughts aside, however. Were there not other congregations where there also were many young people? But no matter what he either did or thought, the call "Come over, and help us" became stronger and stronger. Inwardly, he was tossed back and forth.

On the one hand, he was praying, "Lord, let Utrecht not be the place where I must go." On the other hand, the need of this congregation was increasingly bound upon him, and a love for this portion of the church began to emerge. He was ashamed, for the King of the Church was obviously far more concerned about Utrecht than he was—he who himself had been the recipient of so much mercy. Not only was Arie made willing, but he was overcome with joy when he considered the *privilege* of preaching the gospel. Candidate Elshout was humbled by the wonders of God's favor and power. The Lord showed him the way. What a manifestation of His favor! He showed him His way irresistibly. What a demonstration of His power!

A few hours later, a delegation from the (Netherlands) Reformed Congregation of Scheveningen was sitting in the living room. They had come to inquire regarding the status of their call. They were not without hope, for Rev. Kersten had hinted to them that such expectation might be justified. However, upon their departure, it had become clear to them that Candidate Elshout was not destined to come to Scheveningen—in spite of the fact that he had not explicitly given this answer. A few days later, Candidate Elshout informed the congregation of Utrecht that he could not be disobedient to the heavenly vision (of the Macedonian man). Having been made willing by the Lord, he joyfully accepted the call extended to him by this congregation.

The (Netherlands) Reformed Congregation of Utrecht had just commemorated that thirty years ago, on May 25, 1925, Rev. H. Roelofsen had organized the congregation. At that time, a small group of families, primarily hailing from the adjacent city of Zeist, had been meeting in a building on Zandhofsestraat. Rev. M. Heikoop had served this congregation for many years. Judging by the growth of the congregation, it may be said that his was a blessed ministry. Soon the church building had become too small, and the congregation moved to a larger building on Boothstraat. The bond between Rev. Heikoop and "his" Utrecht was abruptly dissolved in 1944. Rev. Heikoop felt that the Lord had loosed him from the congregation of Utrecht, and he believed that he would have to go to Zeist. Consequently, he accepted the call of this congregation. However, God's way was different, for on November 6, 1944, he perished during a bombardment of Utrecht.

Two years later, Rev. J. van den Berg of Krabbendijke accepted the call extended to him by Utrecht. He was straightforward, well acquainted with church polity, and

During the ministry of Rev. M. Heikoop, the congregation of Utrecht grew rapidly.

Rev. J. van den Berg was a proponent
of youth ministry.

gifted in distinguishing the essentials of God's Word from human notions. He was a gifted speaker with an extensive knowledge of the truths of Scripture, and he knew how to engage the hearts of God's people. When slowly but surely the congregations began to implement a youth ministry, though opposed by a number of ministers, Rev. van den Berg was emphatically in favor of this move. Very quickly a youth group was organized, and the study of Scripture was pursued under the leadership of Elder Van Ginkel.

After some years, the health of Rev. van den Berg began to decline. Hardening of the arteries and high blood pressure not only sapped his physical strength, but also his spiritual strength. The consequences were tragic, for his walk of life became unacceptable. In July 1953, the consistory had to suspend him. Through the intervention of the moderator, Rev. A. Vergunst, this suspension was reversed after several months, and Rev. van den Berg was honorably granted his emeritus status. In the meantime, his health continued to decline, and he vacillated between grievous strife and hope. He drew comfort from the words of Romans 8:32, "He that spared not his own Son, but delivered him up for us all, how shall he not with him also freely give us all things?" A little over half a year after being granted emeritus status, Rev. van den Berg passed away on May 10, 1954.

In the meantime, other ecclesiastical storms had buffeted the (Netherlands) Reformed Congregations, and these storms had not bypassed the local congregation of Utrecht. Although the suspension of Rev. R. Kok did not affect Utrecht directly, it did lead to polarization—as it did in other congregations. Everyone had his own opinion regarding this matter, and few people kept their opinions to themselves. What happened in 1953 can never be divorced from what occurred in 1950. After Dr. Steenblok was dismissed as instructor at the Theological School, a number of ministers decided to break away from the denomination. Their congregations, or at least a portion thereof, decided to break away as well, and splits also occurred in other congregations. Breaches occurred in extended families, and even in some nuclear families. Tensions were on the rise, and mutual tolerance was obviously in decline. In Utrecht, a number of office-bearers decided to leave the denomination as well. As a result, another small (Netherlands) Reformed Congregation [12] came into existence. It was a bizarre situation, for in the (Netherlands) Congregation of Utrecht, one elder would read the exposition of the Heidelberg Catechism by Rev. G.H. Kersten during the evening services, and another elder would do the same in the break-away congregation located on Zandhofsestraat.

～

It was a solemn, impressive moment on September 8, 1955, when Candidate Elshout committed himself to the Lord and to the congregation of Utrecht by responding, "Yes, with all my heart." Rev. L. Rijksen, one of the instructors of the Theological School, installed the candidate with the words of Isaiah 62:6, "I have set watchmen upon thy walls, O Jerusalem, which shall never hold their peace day nor night: ye that make mention of

The sanctuary on Boothstraat was the second home of the congregation of Utrecht.

the LORD, keep not silence." Rev. Rijksen spoke of a weighty appointment, a responsible ministry, and a blessed motive for engaging in this task. God Himself appoints the watchmen upon the walls of Jerusalem, and according to the text, God's servants must labor day and night. For them there is no eight-hour workday, and they must be fully committed. Rev. Rijksen posited that when, so to speak, the sun is shining, this

[12]After the split of 1953 occurred, the break-away congregations (de "Uitgetredenen") organized themselves as "The Reformed Congregations of the Netherlands." The addition of "the Netherlands" served the purpose of distinguishing their congregations from "The Reformed Congregations" from which they had separated themselves. Thereafter, these original Reformed Congregations then sought to distinguish themselves by being called "The Reformed Congregations of the Netherlands and North America."

Bartel and Neeltje Elshout did not live to see the day that their oldest son Arie
was ordained as a minister of the gospel.

commitment would be easy to achieve, but during dark and troubling seasons, this commitment would not be that simple. Ministers need divine direction to be engaged in God's service. All their thoughts, words, and deeds must reflect the Name of Christ and be to the glory of God.

The installation service was held in the Reformed[13] "Oosterkerk," located on the Maliebaan. During the evening service, when Rev. Elshout proclaimed God's Word for the first time as pastor of his congregation, every seat in this sanctuary was filled. Father and Mother Melzian were seated on the first bench. There also was, however, the painful awareness of two empty places, for Father and Mother Elshout were absent. A little over a year ago, they both had passed away. They were merely 54 and 53 years old respectively, and they had died suddenly and successively. Mother Elshout passed way less than six weeks after her husband. These empty places were felt very keenly.

Opa Jan Elshout was present, however. Mr. Kroeze was seated several benches behind them. He had kept his word, and he, along with several colleagues, was present at this installation service. When the organ began to play the initial psalm, Rev. Elshout strove to maintain his composure. The selected psalm, Psalm 25:1 (Psalter 415:1), expressed precisely what lived in his heart,

---

[13]The North American equivalent would be the Christian Reformed Church.

The parents of Mrs. Elshout, Fritz and Meta Melzian (left), and
Opa Jan Elshout (above), witnessed the ordination of their son-in-law and grandson.

Unto Thee, O Lord Jehovah,
Do I lift my waiting soul.
O my God, in Thee I trusted;
Let no shame now o'er me roll.
On my enemy be shame,
Oft without a cause transgressing;
But all those who trust Thy Name
Honor with abundant blessing.

The Lord had truly heard that prayer. Never had He put that child-like confidence to shame. Oh, it had indeed been tested! How often he had been tossed to and fro! How often he had come short in this quiet waiting upon and trusting in the Lord! How ready the Lord was indeed to forgive, and how mindful He is of our human frailty!

The text for his inaugural sermon was 1 Corinthians 3:9, "For we are labourers together with God: ye are God's husbandry, ye are God's building." The young minister directed the congregation in the first place to the exalted Chief Laborer, God Himself. Secondly, mention is made of insignificant fellow-laborers, the ministers, and finally the text speaks of a chosen and privileged field of labor, the congregation. God has no need to be served by men. He can fully accomplish His own good pleasure. It pleases Him, however, to magnify and display His splendid attributes in His works of creation, providence, and grace. His fellow-laborers are but His humble instruments. They therefore so very much need the support and intercession of the congregation, and they must be strongly bonded to the congregation.

The newly installed pastor stated that he had come to Utrecht with the desire that both in his preaching and all his official labors, "he would not grieve those whom God does not want to be grieved, and not comfort those whom God does not want to be comforted." He could not have articulated his task more clearly than that.

Several addresses then followed. A small portion of them were spoken in the German language, which added an extra dimension to this service. It was almost conciliatory in tone. Fortunately, this was now possible, for the relationship with the neighboring land of Germany began to improve slowly but surely. Arie Elshout, who viewed himself as the chief of sinners, was emotionally touched when the congregation lovingly sang the solemn words of Psalm 20:1 (Psalter 43:1):

> *Jehovah hear thee in thy grief,*
> *Our father's God defend thee still,*
> *Send from His holy place relief;*
> *And strengthen thee from Zion's hill.*

CHAPTER 11
Love and Tact

Mrs. Elshout said little as she listened to her husband. A few days earlier, Elfriede had been born—a matter that humbled and amazed them. Once more the Lord had been pleased to grant new life, and He had displayed His omnipotence regarding that which formerly had been deemed impossible by doctors. The little girl lay in her bassinet, and Mrs. Elshout could hardly stop looking at her. Within her heart, she was preoccupied with her children—especially regarding their spiritual well-being. When doing her daily work, but also as she was resting in bed after the delivery, she would spontaneously beseech the Lord to have mercy upon them. She was convinced that they needed to be converted, and she was also convinced that the Lord was able to convert them. It was therefore her daily prayer that the Lord would indeed do so.

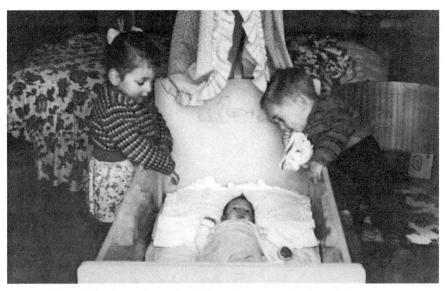

When Elfriede was born, the Elshout family consisted of eight persons.
Nellie and Arie are admiring their baby sister.

Her husband, however, was now sitting at the edge of her bed. Along with all that made him happy and grateful, he was also confronted with a problem. The money that had been set aside to pay for the delivery was depleted. He had to use it to support a family of seven, and now eight, persons. By now, he fully realized that raising children demanded a great deal. No money was spent on unnecessary items when they moved to 12 Maliestraat. The had been as frugal as possible. The curtains from their previous home were being used carefully, and washing them would help them to last longer. The young pastor used a motorbike for his pastoral work, resulting in significant colds and throat infections. Owning a car was not even an option.

The situation had become rather dire. The nurse, who had done an excellent job in assisting Elfriede after the delivery, also had to be paid. By now it was Saturday, and on Monday she would come for the last time. The needed funds still were not available. Mrs. Elshout listened and smiled. "Arie, look once above my bed. Didn't you put that text on the wall because you so firmly believed the truth that 'the Lord is my shepherd; I shall not want?' Was it true then, and have things now changed? The Lord is unchangeable, is He not?" She spoke to him of her hope and trust in this God who so often had helped them in the hour of need. He would not forsake them.

Her inner peace again gave her husband some courage. However, it also gave him some "homework." In his study, he pleaded for help upon bended knee, hoping upon the Lord's unfailing Word.

The sermons for Sunday had been prepared, the children were in bed, baby Elfriede had been fed, and now it was also time for the pastor to retire for the night. Arriving at the foot of the stairs, he stood still, and

12 Maliestraat—The parsonage of Utrecht (the left door is #12, a three-story home)

with amazement he stared at the doormat, for an envelope had been deposited on it. He picked up the white envelope, turned it over—there was no return address—and hastily ripped it open. A small, short, and unsigned note emerged, upon which was written, "Pray for the donor, for he is yet unconverted." Added to this note was a bank note of one hundred guilders. He raced up the stairs and showed it to his wife. How amazed they were! "I will, if thou plead, fill thine every need, all thy wants relieving" (Psalter 431:4—Psalm 81).

When the nurse departed on Monday, she received the wages she had earned. There was even some money left over, but that was quickly used for things such as food, clothing, medications, and the heating bill.

A few weeks after the Lord had so wonderfully provided for them, a similar situation occurred. Coal had to be purchased for the heating of the home. The order had been placed, but all funds had been depleted. That which happened two weeks earlier happened in the same way once more: on Saturday evening an envelope containing an unsigned note and a bank note of one hundred guilders was placed on the doormat. Since the handwriting was the same, it obviously came from the same person. For the minister and his wife, this matter was incomprehensible. Twice they had been helped, and all they could do for the unknown donor was to do what he had asked them in his note: pray for his unconverted and immortal soul.

The owner of a manufacturing firm in Utrecht was shifting restlessly on his chair. His wife asked him what was troubling him. "Wife, I don't know, but I keep on thinking about the minister. It must not be easy to make ends meet with such a large family. We know what it means to provide for a large family. Fortunately, we have no reason to complain. But I keep on thinking about the family residing on Maliestraat. The sixth child has just been born. Their financial needs must be considerable. I think that I am going to bring them some money. I have already done the math. Although our needs are also many, I am able to part with two hundred guilders. What do you think of this plan?"

The woman looked at her husband, and she saw that he was serious about this gift. He was certainly right. She responded, "You must do what lives in your heart."

It was on that Saturday evening that the small business owner left with his envelope containing two hundred guilders. He thought by himself, "This amount of money is quite a bit. What if they did not need that much? Do I have to give more than is necessary? I also have to work hard. I do not for a moment begrudge the minister this money, yet...."

He decided not to give two hundred guilders, but instead only one hundred guilders. That was also a substantial amount. He removed one bill of one hundred guilders, and moments later the letter was deposited into the mailbox. There was enough to pay the nurse and to fill the hearts of the ministerial couple with gratitude.

Upon his return home, the wife asked the business owner whether everything had gone as planned. He nodded affirmatively, telling her that he had given somewhat less, however.

The woman responded by shaking her head. "Hadn't you decided to give two hundred guilders? You should have done that. That which you felt in your heart was right, but instead, you have allowed your mind to overrule your heart."

Her husband did not say a word. He felt uneasy, and he was brooding. He couldn't help but think of Ananias and Sapphira. Oh no, he had not deceitfully tinkered with the amount. Everything was above board. And yet....

A week later, he again made a business trip, and he did not return until another week later. Upon his wife's question as to whether sales had been good, he shook his head. On the contrary, it had been a bad week. He said, "Let me quickly go and bring the other one hundred guilders to the parsonage, or else I will lose my entire business!"

The wife of this businessman met a member of the congregation in one of the streets of Utrecht. She engaged in a conversation with a woman who did not have it easy at home. Her husband was an outspoken atheist who wanted nothing to do with God and His service, one who mocked with all that pious nonsense. If his wife wanted to attend church, that was her business, but he did not want to be bothered.

The woman then told her that the minister had visited them. He naturally also engaged in a conversation with her husband—a conversation that was very intense. How could the minister be so certain that there is a God, and that this God involves Himself with human beings? Her husband had said that he believed all of that to be nonsense.

The minister then responded by telling a story—a story, according to the woman, almost too good to be true. She then proceeded to tell about the deliverances the minister's family had experienced. This deliverance happened twice, and twice it occurred at precisely the right time. The minister was convinced that the Lord had provided for them, and he asked this man whether he had an alternative explanation. Well, he did not, and he believed it to have been merely a stroke of luck, for he had never found such an envelope on his doormat. Yet this story had made an impression on her husband.

The wife of the businessman remained silent. Her heart was filled with joy, for now she knew that she and her husband had been the means to help in the hour of need. Politely, she said good-bye to the woman and continued her journey.

~

The Elshout's time in Utrecht had been a good time. Obviously, there were times of both joy and sorrow. Yet, Rev. Elshout knew from the outset that this was where he was meant to be. The preaching of the Word was not without fruit. However, the young minister also received instruction—sometimes unexpected lessons.

The pastor believed it would be good if during a preparatory sermon for the Lord's Supper, he would cross his "t's" and dot his "i's." There would be no harm in preaching a "sharp" sermon in which he would clearly distinguish between genuine and counterfeit spiritual life. The preparation of this sermon did not go well, however. This realization caused him to struggle and sigh—until with clarity these words were impressed upon his heart, "Comfort the feebleminded" (1 Thess. 5:14). It was as if the Lord impressed upon him that at this given moment he had to comfort the "little ones in grace." Being relieved, the minister chose a different text and made an entirely different sermon. First and foremost, his task was to comfort the feebleminded. He would never forget this lesson for the remainder of his life.

Following the first administration of the Lord's Supper, one of the office-bearers gently rebuked the minister by saying that he had invited too long—and perhaps he did. When no one else came to the table, the minister realized how many people remained in their seat. With all the love that was in him, he exhorted the congregation not to deny Christ if there was evidence of His work in the heart. Instead, they should come to His feet as poor and needy sinners. And then a woman came, bathed in tears. She hardly dared to take hold of the bread. At that moment, it flashed across the mind of the minister, "He binds their wounds and gently heals the brokenhearted ones" (Psalter 403:1—Psalm 145).

After the evening service, a deacon took Rev. Elshout aside and asked him to visit a certain woman who wanted to tell him something. When he visited her during the week, he recognized her as the last person who had come forward to the Lord's Table. She told him of the strife she experienced during the week of preparation. Oh, she was not a stranger of the life of grace. She was greatly tossed to and fro, however, and she had vacillated between hope and fear. During the preparatory sermon, a parenthetical reference to Isaiah 66:2b had given her some hope: "To this man will I look, even to him that is poor and of a contrite spirit, and trembleth at my word." But the power that accompanied these words had now vanished.

During the Lord's Supper service, she also had much strife. However, by renewal the same text from Isaiah was quoted. Would it yet be possible? Would she be permitted to go? Then she heard the admonishing voice of the minister, saying that one should not deny Christ. She experienced this directive as an admonition from the Lord Himself, and she neither dared nor was willing to be disobedient to the Lord's loving command: "This do in remembrance of Me." At the Lord's Table, the Lord granted her a peace that passes all understanding. By eating the Lord's flesh and by drinking His blood, she was assured of being a partaker of Christ. The minister was amazed, and it proved to him that he had not invited too long. The Lord was using him as His servant and instrument in the congregation of Utrecht.

Even the university students in Utrecht knew where to find the parsonage. Among the many who would come there to spend evenings engaged in discussion were Jos Blom, Arie de Reuver, Gerard van Leijenhorst, Stefan Paas, and Piet Haringsma. Rev. Elshout fully participated and always steered the discussion toward the essential issues. They searched together for answers to the many questions with which these students were wrestling. Thereafter, they would gather around the pump organ for singing. In turn, that made an impression upon the older children of the Elshout family, who during such evenings were permitted to stay up a bit longer.

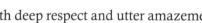

With deep respect and utter amazement, Frits looked at his father. Never before had he seen him do this. Accompanied by the Geijtenbeek and Van de Baan families, the Elshout family had traveled to the nature reserve "Huis ter Heide." This Saturday was a day off for the minister, and he had also reserved it for his family. The boys were playing some soccer, while the adults were engaged in conversation near the edge of the forest. Jan, Gerard, and Cor Geijtenbeek, the Van de Baan boys, as well as Bart and Frits were a good match for each other. It really became interesting for them, however, when the minister also joined in. They were flabbergasted, for he skillfully ran circles around these boys. They were unwilling to accept that, and on the field you could hear them yell, "Watch out for the minister! Watch out for the minister!" Frits had never seen his father play soccer, and only now had he discovered what talents his father had in that regard; that is, until something went wrong. The ball took an unexpected turn and forcefully landed on the face of the minister. Now it was his turn to be subdued, for his broken glasses were lying on the ground before him. All who were sitting in the front benches in church could see the next day that the frame of the minister's glasses now consisted of two fragments.

There were times of prosperity when the young minister could proceed in the power and strength of the Lord. There were also times of uncertainty, weakness, and strife. Satan, people, and the power of evil would do their utmost to thwart the Word. At such times, the running of the race was not as easy. When the Lord hid His countenance, the young minister became rather anxious. The regression of one's prayer life is often preliminary to troubling times being ahead spiritually.

One morning, Rev. Elshout went to his study, located on the third story of his home. First, he bowed his knees to ask for a blessing upon the labors of that day. However, it seemed to him that the door heavenward remained utterly closed. Shortly thereafter, the minster arose and sat down behind his desk.

A moment later there was a knock on the door. There was the voice of a child, the voice of Arie, saying, "Daddy, Daddy, please open the door."

"Why?"

"I have to ask you something."

"I don't have time right now. Go to Mom."

It remained quiet for a moment, and the minister proceeded with his work.

However, a little later, Arie knocked again. "I have to ask you something."

"I want you to go downstairs to Mom. The door will remain closed."

It now remained quiet for several minutes. Again, the minister proceeded to work on his sermon. Once more the subdued voice of Arie could be heard, "Daddy, please open the door. I have to ask you something."

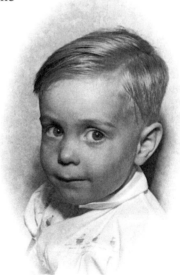

Three-year-old Arie knocked and asked, "Daddy, may I have a little piece of licorice?"

It was an annoyed Dad Elshout who opened the door. The two eyes of a child looked hopefully at him. "Daddy, may I have a little piece of licorice?"

Dad Elshout gave his child a piece of candy. At that very moment, these words were impressed powerfully upon his heart, "If ye then, being evil, know how to give good gifts unto your children: how much more shall your heavenly Father give the Holy Spirit to them that ask him?" (Luke 11:13).

How great the difference was between him and little Arie! That little boy persevered, even though the door remained shut, and he had been told to go away. He, the orthodox minister, had quickly arisen from his knees after he prayed because it would be to no effect anyway. The child persevered, even though he had only been asking for a piece of candy. And what about him? He did not persevere regarding something that was infinitely more important—something as indispensable as the Holy Spirit. Little Arie persevered, even though he could hear that his father was angry. He, the minister, did not persevere in prayer when there was not a single reason to think that the Lord would be unwilling to hear him. He was deeply ashamed, and once more he bowed his knees, beseeching the Lord to forgive him and be gracious to him for Jesus's sake. The lesson he had learned proved to be a blessing for him, and later he would be able to use it to comfort others.

People are slow learners, and the Lord must frequently intervene to instruct His children, teaching them to look away from everything outside of Christ by taking away all foundations other than this one and only Foundation. It pleases Him to grant such instruction also to His servants. How rich it is to receive such instruction! However, the way in which these lessons are given is not always a pleasant one.

Rev. Elshout felt comfortable in the performance of his ministerial labors. Conducting family visitation was not all that challenging for him, and in his preaching he felt himself sustained by his Sender.

Outside the sphere of his official labors, however, he was struggling. In the pulpit, he could speak with liberty, but as soon as he descended from the pulpit, he felt himself to be in bondage. Although he prayed to be delivered from this bondage, it had persisted and had already lasted for months. He did everything in his power to be at peace with himself and with the Lord. This struggle resulted in increased stress in his life. One morning he therefore decided that he would not arise from his knees until the Lord had resolved the matter for him. In his study, he engaged in prayer, and he was determined that he would not let go of the Lord until He blessed him. As he was praying, all kinds of thoughts were tumbling through his mind and something stirred within that he had never experienced with such force and intensity: enmity toward God. Why should he be groaning and be so oppressed? Why did he not get an answer? Instead of humility, there was rebellion in his heart. Thinking that there was no use in continuing his prayer, he decided to arise from his knees.

At that moment, however, his attention was directed to the words of the interceding High Priest, "And for their sakes I sanctify myself, that they also might be sanctified through the truth" (John 17:19). Through His mediatorial work, Jesus not only laid the foundation for the reconciliation of rebellious and wretched sinners such as Rev. Arie Elshout felt himself to be at that moment, but also for their sanctification. His high-priestly ministry was, is, and remains the means whereby sinners have been and shall be set free from bondage. In his heart, the minister grieved over his rebellion. However, at the same time his heart was filled with amazement and joy about the efficacy of the high-priestly ministry of the Lord Jesus on earth as well as in heaven. As a poor sinner, he surrendered himself into the hands of His Advocate, beseeching Him to be merciful to him. This surrender brought inner peace and yielded a blessed deliverance from his anxiety. Once more he was privileged to understand the wondrous ways of the Lord who "shall deliver the needy when he crieth; the poor also, and him that hath no helper" (Psa. 72:12).

The tension was palpable when Rev. Elshout opened the General Synod on June 6, 1956, on behalf of the calling church of Utrecht. As many men were singing the prayer of Psalm 123, he wholeheartedly joined them:

> *To Thee, O Lord, I lift my eyes,*
> *O Thou enthroned above the skies;*
> *As servants watch their master's hand,*
> *Or maidens by their mistress stand,*
> *So to the Lord our eyes we raise,*
> *Until His mercy He displays."*
> (Psalter 351:1—Psalm 123).

There was a good reason why he expounded Philippians 2:1-5, an exhortation to engage in like-mindedness and lowliness of mind. The tensions caused by 1953 were still evident in the congregations, and the conflict between the *(Netherlands) Reformed Congregations* and the *Reformed Congregations in the Netherlands* had not subsided. The contrary was the case. Although the young pastor wholeheartedly endorsed the doctrine of the (Netherlands) Reformed Congregations, he experienced the pain caused by the split nearly on a daily basis. So much damage had been done! Extended families had been torn asunder, and there was discord in many a nuclear family. This discord dishonored the Lord.

Yet he spoke with clarity in his opening message. When reflecting upon the events that had transpired during the past season, he noted the loss of nine ministers. Four had died, two now resided on the other side of the ocean, one had to be deposed, and two "had faithlessly deserted us." He proceeded, "There is almost no expectation that the wall of separation that now exists can be dismantled. A constructive dialogue appears to be beyond reach."

The Synod also had a surprise for Rev. Elshout when the work of distributing God's Word in Spain was discussed. It was the mind of Synod that this work was worthy of the support of the congregations. Synod decided that Rev. A. Elshout would be added to the Committee for Foreign Missions. The committee was authorized to allocate 5,000 guilders for the printing and distribution of Bibles in Spain.

Carefully and expectantly, the Elshout children observed the man sitting in the living room. He was a strange gentleman, one who seemed somewhat withdrawn. The children were rather reluctant to speak to him, for he would not always respond to their questions. At times it appeared that his thoughts were entirely elsewhere, and he would have a dark frown most of the time. Indeed, Mr. Saarberg somewhat resembled a hermit—but then a very sad hermit, for his eyes always reflected anxiety and pain. He lived alone in an apartment and was completely oblivious to others.

Mr. Johan Saarberg was able to overcome his grief and would contribute much to the congregation of Utrecht.

Little Meta was spontaneous and hardly understood that this man had already endured many afflictions, and that more afflictions were yet to come. She showed him her toys, babbled ceaselessly, calmly climbed onto his lap, and asked him whether he would play a game with her. Although Mr. Saarberg had already visited many times, it took a long time before, in some measure, he began to be part of the family. A gradual change began to take place, and he showed more interest and became friendlier. It was as if he were emerging from a cocoon. He loved visiting the parsonage, and he became a friend of the family. You could discuss anything with him. Sometimes he would talk about ministers from England and Scotland, for he was very knowledgeable regarding that subject. His children—he had two daughters— would often visit the Maliestraat parsonage. After a while, the Elshout children did not know any better than that Mr. Saarberg, the man who by grace was able to overcome his deep sorrow, simply belonged to them. He even accompanied the children to Germany to visit Opa and Oma Melzian. Obviously, not all children could come along at one time, and some of them were able to stay with "Ome Kees" and "Tante Gerrie Oskam." The latter were also friends of the family. These children would be next in line to go to Germany.

∽

Uncle "Kees" and Aunt "Gerrie" standing in front of their home in the village of De Meern—Later, Mr. Oskam would serve the congregation of Utrecht as elder for many years.

There was much work in Classis Utrecht, and the young pastor was appointed as the moderator of eleven congregations. He tried to serve them as faithfully as possible. In 1956, Rev. Dorresteijn decided to leave the denomination with a segment of his congregation; thereafter, Rev. Elshout was the only minister in the Classis. The residual tensions of 1953 were still manifesting themselves. Tensions were rising in Tricht. Zeist and Woerden were on the verge of splitting. Further alienation could be prevented in these churches partly due to the initiative, tact, love, and circumspection of Rev. Elshout.

How pleased Rev. Elshout was with Elder Kieviet—a wise man with much spiritual and ecclesiastical experience! Both men would discuss many concerns and problems when they met each other on Monday mornings.

Elder H. Kieviet was a spiritual father and a wise counselor for the young minister.

Rev. Elshout also regularly preached during the week. Since he did not own a car, Mr. Saarberg was his driver. On April 7, 1959, they drove to Haarlem, where Rev. Elshout was scheduled to preach. Following the congregational prayer and the singing, he began to expound the text for that evening: "Lo, I am with you alway, even unto the end of the world. Amen" (Matthew 28:20b). Shortly after he began, however, he observed a man entering the rear of the church. His uniform identified him as someone of high rank in the Merchant Marine. He sat down in one of the benches and listened intently. During the middle song, however, he arose abruptly and disappeared. Following the service, Rev. Elshout asked the office-bearers whether they were acquainted with this man. They shook their heads and stated that they had never seen him before. Then there was a knock on the door. To their amazement and joy, the Merchant Marine officer entered. He was a man of few words, and he asked the minister why it was on this particular evening that he found himself under the preaching he had abandoned as a young man. He told them that he had missed his bus connection to IJmuiden on this particular evening. He had therefore been walking rather aimlessly in the vicinity of the train station when he encountered an open church door. Since the lights were on, he decided to take a look inside.

Then he heard words dating back to his youth when as a boy he had been under the preaching of Rev. Geerts. The thrust of the message was the same. Memories began to multiply within him. He remembered how his God-fearing mother had urged him to seek the Lord, and how he had brushed her words aside. Worse than that, he was determined to remove himself from the supervision of his mother and from the ministry of Rev. Geerts. Deliberately, he misbehaved in such a way that he had to be placed in a special boarding school. He had his way, for now he no longer had to deal with his mother's admonitions, and he no longer had to listen to the sermons he hated so much. He became a machine operator in the Merchant Marine. During the war, he was actively involved in opposing the Germans. It was then that things took a turn for the worse, for he was captured and sentenced to be shot the next day.

It became a difficult, oppressive, and sleepless night for him. He had to die, and he could not die. He was compelled to reflect on his life. He would have to meet the God whom he had refused to serve. He did not dare to pray, and he was overcome by anxiety.

At that moment, the words of his mother came to mind: "My son, in whatever predicaments you may find yourself to be, call upon the God of your mother."

He then proceeded to call upon the God of his mother. Something amazing happened, for the young man who had been sentenced to death heard, as it were, a voice. Oh, no, he did not believe in visions, and yet he heard clearly and distinctly, "I have called thee by thy name; thou art mine" (Isa. 43:1b). The mariner could hardly refrain from weeping when he again uttered these words in the consistory room of the Haarlem church. In his cell, having been sentenced to death, he could confidently believe that he would not have to die. And indeed, he was not executed.

It was silent in the consistory room, for everyone was deeply impressed. What an astonishing story! The mariner then continued to tell them that after the war he completed his training as a mechanic, married, had children, and became a member of the Reformed Church.[14] He then said, "When I heard you preach tonight, I became troubled within. To whom did God say, 'I am with you always?' I do not recognize myself in what you described as being the marks of those addressed here as 'you'. That would mean that I do not belong to them, and yet no one can take away from me that I am a child of God, for He Himself said to me, 'I have called thee by thy name, thou art mine.'"

Rev. Elshout looked at this man speechlessly. What should he say to him? The minister was convinced that this mariner was somehow making a

---

[14]This is the Reformed church that came into existence at the initiative of Dr. Abraham Kuyper.

wrong application, but where, and in what way? In spite of all that this man had told him, the minister profoundly missed one thing: a humbling of himself before God. Even when the man prayed when death was staring him in the face, he merely asked to be delivered. He did not utter a word about his unworthiness before God. No mention was made of being drawn to Christ as the Mighty One upon whom God had laid help and whose blood cleanses from all sins. He did not say a word about humbly taking refuge to a crucified Christ so that by faith in His blood he might obtain the forgiveness of sins.

The minister was confused. He was by no means listening critically to see whether everything conformed to his own experiential blueprint. He was not so much concerned about words as he was about the essence of the matter. It did not bother him when someone could not express himself well. It did not matter to him if the furniture was not properly arranged, as long as all the pieces were there.

The minister did not doubt for a moment whether the Lord had truly spoken to this man. What then was lacking? Rev. Elshout did not quite know what he should say and picked up his Bible. Quietly, he beseeched the Lord to give him guidance and light, so that in love he could instruct this mariner. After turning some pages, he found the text: "I have called thee by thy name, thou art mine" (Isa. 43:1b). To whom does the Lord address the words of this text? He was addressing the entire congregation of Israel as His covenant people. God had redeemed Israel corporately, and by means of the preaching of His Word He called them by name. At Mount Sinai, He entered into a covenant with them! They were and are His people, and He had a just claim upon them in soul and body for His covenant's sake, and they were obliged to devote themselves to Him with body and soul.

Although the minister had already baptized many children, it had never occurred to him—and much less had he understood it—that the mentioning of the name of the child was significant. However, this evening something began to dawn on him. Clearly and by renewal, he perceived the significant distinction between the external and the internal call of the gospel. When does the external call of the gospel initially come to someone who has been born within the confines of God's covenant? He explained to the mariner that this call occurs at baptism, irrespective of whether the person is conscious of this call. At the baptismal font, God declares, among other things, that He desires to have dealings with the child that has been called by his or her name. Furthermore, though the child has been born and conceived in sin, He declares that for His Name's sake, for His Son's sake, and for His covenant's sake, He is willing to be his or her God if the child, by grace, responds to Him in the way of repentance and faith. Simultaneously, the Lord thereby declares that He has a claim upon the soul and body of that baptized child. This child is holy—not internally, but externally by virtue of his having been set apart unto a true covenantal union with Him. These baptized children belong to Him; they are His. This truth is also recorded elsewhere in the Bible, "He came unto his own, and his own received him not" (John 1:11). It is for good reason that they are called the "children of the Kingdom" (Mat. 8:12). That is far more significant than many recognize or are willing to acknowledge. Being called by our name is of profound significance for God as well as for us.

The mariner listened intently, and then he warmly bade the minister and the consistory farewell. He again disappeared into the darkness of the evening. Rev. Elshout prayed that the Lord would bless this instruction and that He would continue to deal with this man, who at his baptism had also been set apart by Him.

When Rev. G. Wisse, a seminary professor of the Free Reformed Churches, passed away, the General Synod was faced with a problem. In addition to all his other functions, he was also the driving force behind the Spanish Evangelical Mission. This organization published a Spanish version of the Bible, the Heidelberg Catechism, Bunyan's *Pilgrim's Progress*, and Calvin's *Institutes*. It was stated "that we can fully endorse these publications." It was decided that Rev. A. Elshout would fill the vacancy of the Board of Trustees, and it would be his task to see to it that this profitable ministry would continue.

Mr. Saarberg's car proved to be a blessing for the congregation and for her minister. He did not have the funds to purchase a car, but because his friend was willing to drive or occasionally was willing to lend his car, Rev. Elshout was

Rev. A. Elshout as the young pastor of the congregation of Utrecht

able to do much work in the congregation. It was not a satisfactory solution, but it was better than his having to travel on a moped in all sorts of weather—particularly because he had some health issues. As he was walking down Biltstraat, a black Opel came driving from the opposite direction. Immediately his thoughts drifted toward Van Ommeren where similar vehicles were also in use. A prayer arose within his heart: "Lord, Thou knowest all things—also that I so much need a vehicle for my work as well as for my health. Be pleased to grant me a vehicle, and open ways to that end, to the honor and glory of Thy Name."

At the next consistory meeting, without the minister having even hinted at this need, one of the office-bearers proposed that efforts be made to look for a good pre-owned car for the minister. The congregation would then purchase the car and make it available to the minister for his use. Quietly, Rev. Elshout thanked the Lord for His faithful care. A committee made work of finding a suitable vehicle, and they found an excellent car for a reasonable price: a black Opel Record. Since this car had to be insured by law, the consistory deemed it better to register this car in the name of the minister.

~

His work in Utrecht did not remain unfruitful. Unity was restored in a congregation that had been so divided. The preaching of the Word and the pastorate had proven to be the means whereby it pleased the Lord to bring forth spiritual life. This restoration of the congregation was accompanied by assaults of Satan—assaults apparent in the life of the congregation and in the personal life of the minister. However, time and again the Lord demonstrated that He knew of the needs of His servant. He kept him from being all too discouraged, doing so especially by enabling him to observe some divine fruits on his labors. The Lord blessed the labors of the minister among young and old, unconverted and converted persons, as well as among the little ones in grace and those who were more advanced in the knowledge of God and His ways. This realization humbled for him, but also repeatedly gave him new strength to continue.

One Saturday evening, the doorbell rang. A thirty-year-old, single young man told the minister that he had much inward strife and needed pastoral counsel in his spiritual distress. A few years earlier, this young man had made profession of faith but had not yet partaken of the Lord's Supper. With hesitancy and trepidation, he told his story. He had discovered that he was without God, and he expressed his sorrow and perplexity regarding this. He yearned for grace and that God would speak to him through His Word. He expressed his hope in the saving work of Christ but also shared how greatly all of this was assaulted.

The pastor then directed him to the preparatory sermon of the previous Sunday, and asked him, "Did the sermon include you among those for whom the Lord has instituted His supper?" When the young man affirmed this to be so, the minister replied, "Then I will not exclude you. Based upon what God has said in His Word, you also belong to those who are invited."

When the young man departed, he was somewhat relieved, though not convinced. The next morning the Lord's Supper was administered. It was customary that after the initial invitation, the consistory would first be seated at the Table of the Covenant. However, before the members of the consistory were seated at the table, this young man came forward and respectfully sat down. At night the minister

Mr. Sander Snoep became a deacon in the congregation of Utrecht, and in 1968, he was installed as a minister of the gospel in the (Netherlands) Reformed Congregation of Vlissingen.

again spoke to him. With joy the young man told him that the sermon of that morning so matched his circumstances, and so conformed to what lived in his heart, that all doubts had vanished. The Lord then gave him liberty to partake.

When the minister asked him why he was the first one to come to the table, he replied, "Pastor, when you preached about Abraham, you really stressed the fact that he always arose early to carry out what the Lord directed him to do. You exhorted us to follow his example, for the failure to do so puts us at risk of not doing it at all. This morning I thought of this example, and to prevent myself from once again remaining in my seat, I immediately came forward when you opened the Table of the Lord." A few years later, this young man, Alexander Snoep,[15] became a deacon, and at the age of thirty-eight, he was installed in Vlissingen as a minister of the (Netherlands) Reformed Congregations.

---

[15]Rev. A. Snoep (1930–1988) was also a brother-in-law of Rev. C. Harinck.

CHAPTER 12

Trusting in His Sender

O nce more Rev. Elshout received a call from Scheveningen. He knew
that this call would be forthcoming, for in 1955 the Lord had
already bound this congregation upon his heart. Among the thirty-five
calls he had received, the call from Scheveningen had stood out. He so
desired to accept that call, but the Lord did not give him the freedom to
do so. During the funeral of Rev. J.W. Kersten (1960), who had been
removed from the congregation of Scheveningen so suddenly, the love
for this congregation resurfaced with great intensity. However, upon
having received a call in March of 1961, he could not accept it.

Senior Citizen's Home "Elim" in the town of Beekbergen (c. 1961)

The establishment of a senior citizen's home in Beekbergen had
entered a critical phase. Rev. Elshout, along with Elder Schreuder of the
Amersfoort congregation, had fully and wholeheartedly committed himself to this task. His present departure from Utrecht could potentially
paralyze this endeavor, and he could not permit that to happen, for he
knew that the Lord Himself had called him to this task. He remembered
the moment in his study all too well when, after prayerfully searching the
Scriptures, the words of the Lord Jesus were bound upon his heart,

"[Son], behold thy mother" (John 19:27). He knew himself to be called to serve the needy among the elderly—especially those among them who feared the Lord.

On June 9, 1958, Hans (John) was born as the seventh child of the family.

When Chris was born, the Elshout family was complete and had now expanded to ten persons. Seated from left to right: Mrs. Elshout, Chris, Nellie, Elfriede, Arie, Rev. Elshout, and Hans (John); standing from left to right: Bart, Meta, and Frits

However much Rev. Elshout desired to accept this call, and however strongly he felt inclined to do so, he was not permitted to do so. He brought this matter before the Lord. Upon asking with a childlike faith that this matter might be delayed for a half year, he declined the call. Yet, from that moment on, he began to be loosed from Utrecht and from the senior citizen's home "Elim." Mr. and Mrs. Wilbrink were appointed as managing directors, and the doors of this home could be opened. Although Utrecht, his first congregation, had a special place in his heart, he sensed that he was being directed toward another field of labor.

When Rev. Elshout heard that Scheveningen had nominated him to be on a duo with Rev. A. Hofman,[16] he fully expected to receive the call. This turned out differently, however, for Rev. Hofman was nominated by the male membership of Scheveningen. An uneasy feeling took hold of Rev. Elshout. How could this be? Was it not the Lord who wanted him in Scheveningen? Just imagine if Rev. Hofman were to accept the call! "Commit thy way unto the LORD" (Psa. 37:5) was easier said than done. Prayerfully, the minister struggled with his unbelief. When Rev. Hofman declined the call from Scheveningen, it became clear to Rev. Elshout that his flesh needed to be crucified. In love, the Lord taught him a lesson, so that He would be glorified in His leading him to Scheveningen. He received a call from Scheveningen only a few weeks later.

Leaving friends behind is always difficult—
Mr. and Mrs. Ariese and their daughter Ans.

In the meantime, the family had expanded to include eight children. On June 9, 1958, Hans was born, and Chris on December 10, 1959. Bart was then nearly eleven years old. He and Meta understood very well that something special was in the offing, for when Dad and Mom conversed about Scheveningen, they sensed that there was a real possibility that they would move. However, they knew equally well that Dad would go only if the Lord would direct him to do so. They did not look up against a move, for it would be some-

---

[16] The oldest brother of the late Rev. H. Hofman, Sr., and the uncle of Rev. H. Hofman, Jr.

what exciting. There would be a different home, new surroundings, and different friends. They sensed that this move would be an adventure. No one looked sad when Dad told them before the Sunday morning service that he would announce his acceptance of the call.

Later they would recognize that moving would also mean having to say good-bye. They would have to leave behind good acquaintances such as Mr. Saarberg, as well as the Oskam and Ariese familes, all of whom were close friends of the family. That would not be pleasant. They were now looking forward, however, to their new residence in Scheveningen.

The historical roots of the (Netherlands) Reformed Congregation of Scheveningen went as far back as 1870. Albertus Hinderikus Geerts, who, along with some other members, at an earlier date had already severed himself from the Reformed Congregation under the Cross, had then organized an Old Reformed Congregation. He was ordained as a minister during the same year. The congregation initially worshiped at the Korte Houtstraat location, but later relocated to Keizerstraat in Scheveningen.

After the decease of Rev. Geerts in 1916, Rev. J. van Wier became the pastor of the congregation in 1920. A year later, the congregation purchased the Reformed Peniel Church, located on the Nieuwe Laantjes.

Rev. A.H. Geerts

In 1920, the congregation of Scheveningen received Rev. J. van Wier as their second minister.

The church was renamed as the Ebenezer Church. When Rev. van Wier departed to Rijssen in 1928, the congregation had already affiliated herself with the federation of the Old Reformed Churches.

The largest part of the congregation, however, decided in 1933 to affiliate with the (Netherlands) Reformed Congregation of The Hague. A minority continued as the Old Reformed Congregation. A lawsuit that went as far as the court in The Hague resulted in the latter group's retaining ownership of the church building. However, it was then decided that it would be sold to the (Netherlands) Reformed Congregation for 18,000 guilders.

During that period, the congregation of Scheveningen had a bent toward legalism. The consistory had strenuously opposed the use of bikes on Sunday. Only those who had received permission from the consistory were permitted to come to church by bike. In June 1950, the consistory decided that girls who entered the sanctuary without a head-covering would be denied admission. In addition, the church sanctuary could not be used for political gatherings. They would not even permit Rev. Du Marchie van Voorthuijsen[17] to give a lecture addressing the issues of the day. Two years later, however, this minister was permitted to speak on behalf of the SGP[18]—an exception they were prepared to make only for Rev. Du Marchie van Voorthuijsen. In 1951, one of the deacons proposed that those women who came to meet their husbands at church with their baby strollers would have to be rebuked. It is unknown whether this ever took place.

Rev. J.W. Kersten

The Sunday evening service was conducted almost weekly by the moderator, Rev. P. Honkoop.[19] The consistory insisted that he had to travel the distance between The Hague and Scheveningen on foot. This decision greatly displeased Rev. Honkoop,

[17]A well-known minister of the Old Reformed Congregations.
[18]This is the abbreviation for "Staatkundig Gereformeerde Partij"—the still existing Reformed Political Party in the Netherlands.
[19]Rev. P. Honkoop (1891–1963) was the pastor of the neighboring congregation of the The Hague (1933–1947) and assisted the vacant congregation of Scheveningen as moderator (or counselor).

and an elder from Scheveningen therefore accompanied him weekly on this journey. This somewhat eccentric pastor would embarrass the elder by engaging in extensive window shopping along the way. The elder would obviously urge him to continue and would admonish him that he should not be window shopping on Sunday.

The pastor responded, "Yes, you are right, but then you should not cause a man to be tempted by forcing him to walk...." In 1947, Rev. Honkoop departed for Rijssen, and six years would transpire before The Hague would again have its own minister, Rev. K. De Gier. He also became the moderator of Scheveningen.

Many things changed when Rev. J.W. Kersten came to Scheveningen in 1956. Congregational life flourished, and the bond of mutual love in the congregation became stronger. The proclamation of God's Word by pastors Honkoop, De Gier, and Kersten was blessed. The Lord had His children also in Scheveningen, and the preaching of His Word was the means to lead them into the truth, stripping them of all false foundations. They were thus led to rest upon the only Foundation, Jesus Christ, apart from whom there is no life. With a style that was uniquely his own, Rev. Kersten preached and labored in Scheveningen for four years. He died most unexpectedly on April 8, 1960, when a massive heart attack ended his life. "And he was not; for God took him" (Gen. 5:24).

Once more the congregation was vacant, but that would last only for a year and a half. When in September of 1961, Rev. Elshout of Utrecht was called once more, he responded positively to this call.

It is Christ who sends His servants into the harvest. The harvest season is of limited duration, and must therefore be used intensely—labor that is accompanied with strife and tears. Such were the words Rev. K. de Gier of The Hague spoke in expounding John 4:35b-37 during Rev. Elshout's installation service (December 6, 1961). He pointed out that God's servants also receive their reward. What could be a greater reward than to be privileged to gather fruit for an eternity to come? Granted, some servants may only sow, but others may then reap what was sown by the previous servant. Rev. De Gier declared, however, that all God's servants must remain focused upon the great Sower, who is also the great Reaper.

It was quiet when Rev. Elshout began his inaugural sermon that evening. The church was filled with attendees from Scheveningen and The Hague. Moreover, many members of the Utrecht congregation traveled to Scheveningen despite the inclement weather to attend the installation and inaugural services of their beloved former pastor. Rev. Elshout began by speaking a few words in commemoration of Rev. J.W. Kersten. The

Lord's ways are past finding out, for He releases one servant from his charge and causes another servant to enter into his ministry.

He then proceeded to preach about the text the Lord had used to incline his heart to accept the call from Scheveningen: "So, as much as in me is, I am ready to preach the gospel to you that are at Rome also" (Rom. 1:15). He spoke of Paul's longing regarding the congregation of Rome, addressing:

        1) The focus of this longing;

        2) The source of this longing;

        3) The fulfillment of this longing.

Paul was desirous to proclaim the gospel of Jesus Christ to the congregation of Rome—even though he had never visited this congregation. Nevertheless, he loved this congregation because of her reputation.

Rev. Elshout then stated, "In like manner, I have come to Scheveningen to proclaim the gospel to you—not in a manner that allows you to remain neutral, but rather so that Christ may be formed in you. I have not come for your possessions, but instead for you yourself. My desire to proclaim God's Word in Scheveningen proceeds from the fact that I am indebted to engage in the work to which the Lord has inwardly called me."

The family was received warmly by the congregation of Scheveningen. The Harteveld family was among the first to extend this welcome.

There was so much for the children to see: people wearing local costumes, the harbor, and the fishing vessels. Daily they could hear the rushing sound of the ocean. Never before had they walked along the beach, and now they could walk for hours along the water's edge, looking for shells and the teeth of sharks—or they would try to throw pieces of wood into the ocean as far as they could and then wait to see if the breaking

The Elshout children enjoyed everything related to Scheveningen: the costumes as well as the ocean.

edwaves would again cast them upon the beach. They would lick the salt from their lips and would be rebuked for the fact that their shoes had turned white.

The Elshout family gathered around the organ in the living room of their home in Scheveningen at 179 Frankenslag. From left to right: Hans (John), Nellie, Meta (playing the organ), Elfriede, Chris, Arie, and Mrs. Elshout

It was a wonderful time for the family. Bart was attending a local high school, while Meta, Frits, Nellie, and Arie were attending the local Christian elementary school, the Ebenezer School. The headmaster, Mr. Kalle, believed that Meta could also be enrolled in a local Christian high school for the following school year.

179 Frankenslag—The parsonage of Scheveningen (a three-story home)

The Scheveningen membership gave the minister's family a place in their hearts. With frankness and openness, they engaged the Elshout family. Many among them became family friends. Also among the elders there were those who visited the family as friends. It was only on a rare occasion that there would be no company on a Sunday evening. At times the family would gather with fellow believers, and at other times with young people.

～

It was a common sight on the streets of Scheveningen to see bakery vending carts (containing pre-packaged King Cornbread), milk vendors with their crates stacked high on their carts, as well as produce vendors

The exterior of the Ebenezer Church
of the Scheveningen congregation

with their horse-drawn wagons. There was, however, something that drew Rev. Elshout's attention. One could read "Help yourself" on all these vehicles, including those of coal dealers and even on the show windows of grocery stores. There evidently was a business cooperative by that name that rendered assistance in a variety of ways. This name provided the minister with an opportunity to connect with his congregation in his first sermon. As he wrestled to find a suitable text, beseeching the Lord for light, he noticed that the vehicle of an oil company was parked in front of the door on which the words "SELF-HELP" were written in giant letters.

Immediately, the minister was directed to the words of Psalm 89:19: "I have laid help upon one that is mighty." He had found a text, and the line of reasoning was self-evident: "HELP YOURSELF" evidently played a significant role in the lives of the people of Scheveningen. Rev. Elshout pointed out, however, that in reference to eternal things, one would deceive himself by relying on self. He was privileged to point to a better source for help: The Mighty One upon whom the Lord had laid help, Jesus Christ.

As the minister engaged in his pastoral labors, he observed that the people in Scheveningen also expected more from Moses than from

The interior of the Ebenezer Church of the Scheveningen congregation

Christ. The natural heart would rather seek for salvation in rules and regulations, and even in legalism, than relinquish all self-righteousness and by grace rest in the work of Another. The great Other, Jesus Christ, was the focal point of his preaching, and by God's grace one could observe a course correction in the lives of many of the members. Especially among young people, but also among older members, one could observe that Christ became preeminent in their hearts—a matter that is essential for enjoying the only comfort in life and death.

Rev. Elshout had his pastoral concerns. An enormous tent had been erected on the "Malieveld" fairgrounds, and evangelistic services were conducted in this tent during the evening. In and of itself, that was not a matter of concern for the minister. He was concerned about the content of the message that was being preached there. People were being cast upon themselves, and they were urged to believe. The need for the latter was certainly true. However, does not God's Word teach that faith is a gift of God, and that such faith must be accompanied by a confession of sin and a humbling of one's self before God? There was no mention of confession and humiliation in these tent services. Instead, a "help yourself" religion was promoted there.

Furthermore, an American faith healer was one of the speakers, giving it all a very charismatic and emotional flavor. Many young people of the congregation of Scheveningen also attended these meetings, and they returned home amazed and impressed. In the pulpit, Rev. Elshout asked the Lord to demonstrate that He is the God who works wonders.

The Lord affirmed this truth when the wife of Aart Verboom gave birth to a set of twins. Subsequent to the delivery, this young mother was in critical condition. Some of her intestines had become obstructed, and there was no hope that she would recover. The head nurse informed Rev. Elshout with great concern that this young woman would probably die. When the minister responded that nothing is too hard for the Lord, she looked rather troubled. This was obviously true, but....

This matter brought many in the congregation to their knees, including the minister. He besought the Lord that, for His Name's sake, He would undertake for this young mother and her family, so that people would know that they did not have to go to the "Malieveld" fairgrounds to witness or experience miracles. People need to observe that when they cry to the Lord for help, He will perform great wonders—that when utterly destitute sinners take refuge to Him, He will not put them to shame but instead will manifest His mercy, grace, and help.

To everyone's amazement, the woman was restored to health. Even the head nurse had to acknowledge that if ever there were a case of someone's being healed as an answer to prayer, it was certainly true in this situation. The members of the congregation perceived that what their pastor said in the pulpit was true: that which is impossible with man, is possible with God.

∼

The Lord's ways are not always ways of prosperity, however. The population of Scheveningen, consisting of fishermen, knew that their men were exposed to many dangers. Once they had left the harbor, their ship suddenly became no more than a nutshell being tossed around by both the sea and the wind. On various occasions, a fishing vessel and its crew would perish while out at sea. On shore, a woman would then wait in vain for her husband or son, or a boy for his father. When a gathering of people would suddenly become silent, the common expression in Scheveningen would be: "The minister is passing by."

That expression had an oppressive dimension in this fishing village. When the minister would be seen walking down the street, the question would arise, "Is he passing by?" There would be joy if he did, for if the minister would stop, it could be that he would come with evil tidings. If grown or young men would perish at sea, the minister would be called upon to convey that message to the home—a difficult and heart-wrenching task.

It was a sad day when Rev. Elshout went on his errand—an errand that pertained to young Mr. Korving. The trawling net of his ship became ensnared and caused the ship to vanish below the surface. Seven men drowned. It was a blessing that, by way of exception, his brother and father had not accompanied him on this journey, for otherwise three members of the family would have perished. The other victims did not belong to the congregation. Since Mr. Korving was a member, however, Mrs. Korving had to be informed. Rev. Elshout was acquainted with this young family. After a lengthy engagement, they were married, and it was only very recently that a baby had been born. Prayerfully, the minister went on his way, beseeching the Lord yo give him the right words to say. The predicament of this young family deeply moved him.

Mrs. Korving greeted him warmly, for she had no idea of the purpose of his visit. The minister then informed her, and there was not much to be said. However, his presence was a blessing for this woman. With only a few words, he directed her to the only Comforter. Upon his departure, he felt on the one hand a sense of sadness and felt deeply sorry for this woman. On the other hand, it filled him with joy that he was able to minister to her under these circumstances. He knew that he would never be a prominent minister, and he considered himself to be a man of only moderate gifts. However, a situation such as this was his niche—to be there in times of affliction and grief and "to speak a word in season to him that is weary" (Isa. 50:4). That role suited him well; therefore, he was also privileged to minister to those in need in Scheveningen.

Rev. Elshout readily found his way through the narrow streets, and he knew where both joy and sorrow prevailed. This led him to a woman who was in great spiritual distress. She was overcome by great despondency, and her anxiety and sorrow caused her to weep loudly. Whatever the minister said to encourage her was to no avail. The woman responded by saying, "That may be true for others, but for me it is no longer possible. Salvation is beyond reach for a sinner such as I am."

The pastor persisted in pointing out to her how God's Word directs us to an able, willing, and faithful Savior, Jesus Christ—the Lamb of God that takes away the sins of the world. As he was speaking, Rev. Elshout perceived a change in the woman's expression and disposition. The Lord Himself began to speak, and the Almighty did so by using the simple words of an insignificant servant. He caused His light to shine forth efficaciously into the heart of this woman.

"Pastor," she exclaimed, "You are right. Now I see, acknowledge, and believe that I too can be saved. What a wonder of grace that someone like me can also be saved! However, if it is possible for me, it is possible for the entire world." With a sigh, she concluded, "Oh, that the Lord would also reveal this to my old father!"

After coming downstairs, the minister encountered her father, and he briefly told him what had just transpired. The old man listened to him with much emotion. He did not say much, but his thoughts were greatly multiplied. Full of emotion, he shook his head, saying, "Again one of my children may enter the Kingdom of heaven ahead of me."

Not long after this visit, the minister was called to visit this man who had become seriously ill. He knew that this illness would be terminal, and that filled him with great fear. The minister would therefore visit him frequently. It was heart-rending to see how anxious this man was. The sorrows of hell had such a hold of him that he tossed restlessly in his bed. It seemed that not a single word of comfort could get through to him.

When Rev. Elshout again visited him, it dawned on him that this man no longer believed the expression, "Where there is life, there is hope." For him it would no longer be possible; for him it would be too late. However, was it right to have such thoughts? Wasn't God the Almighty One? This realization drove the pastor to his knees, and he humbly confessed his unbelief. He begged the Lord that He would grant him to believe with certainty that with Him all things are possible. Without that faith, he could neither do his work, nor could he any longer have a message. He besought the Lord that, for His great Name's sake, He would

The consistory members Elder De Jong (left) and Deacon Bosland were also present on the pastor's birthday. What better thing could the people of Scheveningen give their pastor than something related to their culture?

also prove to this old man that He could grant full deliverance even when death draws nigh.

His pastoral visit transpired as all other visits did. Lovingly and pastorally, Rev. Elshout pointed to the brazen serpent as the way in which we can be healed from our fatal disease of sin. When he visited the old man again, he met an entirely different man. He was overflowing with what the Lord had done in his heart, for mercy was also bestowed upon this old sinner for Jesus's sake. He lived a few more weeks, and his mind remained sharp until the end. His sickbed became his pulpit, and even old people were encouraged by his deliverance.

Rev. Elshout readily made use of examples from daily life in his pulpit ministry and in the pastorate. In so doing, he also followed in the footsteps of his Master who frequently taught by parables. After such illustrations would first have impacted him personally, he would pass them on to others.

The consistory of the (Netherlands) Reformed Congregation of Scheveningen
shortly before Rev. Elshout departed for America (1967)

From the consistory room, one could see the enclosed square in front of the home of the caretaker and his family. As he was waiting for a bridal couple to arrive, Rev. Elshout looked outside and saw the youngest member of that family in his playpen. The little fellow took hold of the spindles of this playpen with both hands and struggled until he finally stood on his two feet. Triumphantly, he looked around. However, a few seconds later he let go of the spindles and fell backwards. He wailed loudly, but in the end he turned over on to his belly, moved toward the spindles, pulled himself up once more, and again stood on his feet.

For the pastor, this was a beautiful illustration that he could use in his pastorate to instruct his people. Among them there were those who by grace and in faith would take hold of the spindles of God's Word. That was a matter of great joy. However, as they rejoiced, they would suddenly let go of these "spindles." He who thus reasons with flesh and blood will again lose his footing. When one is assaulted, it is better to persevere in praying, "Lord, I believe; help thou mine unbelief" (Mark 9:24).

Rev. and Mrs. Elshout during their stay in Scheveningen

Rev. Elshout was both careful and prudent in his pastoral work and manifested these characteristics in his own personal way. After someone had partaken of the Lord's Supper for the first time, the consistory noted that it would be good to visit this partaker of the Lord's Supper. Rev. Elshout did not comply, however. This matter was discussed again at the next consistory meeting. After a moment of quiet reflection, Rev. Elshout addressed one of the members of his consistory. Elder Hus was a landscaper, and the pastor asked him, "Hus, you are a landscaper, are you not?"

"Yes, pastor," Hus replied—a man who had been employed for many years as an employee of the Scheveningen Park Maintenance Service.

The minister then proceeded by saying, "Hus, after you have planted flower bulbs, and you see the first green shoots pushing through the earth, do you then dig up that bulb to see if it actually has some roots?"

Hus replied, "Of course not! That would be foolish. One must leave that bulb alone, or else it will die."

Rev. Elshout responded, "Well, that's also my method."

Hus looked somewhat dumbfounded, but then his face lit up, and he said, "That's a good lesson."

∽

Rev. Elshout regularly conducted the services on the Lord's Day. Only once was he unable to do so when he had to undergo throat surgery in 1964. After a few weeks, he had recovered sufficiently and was able to resume his pastoral labors.

His workload was increasing, for in addition to the preaching and pastoral ministry in his own congregation, he had to do a substantial amount of work as moderator of vacant congregations. Soon he was also called upon to engage himself for denominational mission work, for youth ministry, and for the Teacher's College, "De Driestar."

Did all of this contribute to the fact that Rev. Elshout began to have blood pressure issues? His doctor prescribed medication, but to no avail. He tried to exercise as much as possible by walking rather than using his car. Exercise hardly had any effect. The minister also adjusted his eating habits as much as possible by following a healthy diet—something he was already accustomed to doing. This attempt also proved to be of no help. On the contrary, his blood pressure became increasingly elevated. The minister was concerned about this development. What would happen to his family if he were to pass away? This question occupied him day and night, and this concern also was not conducive to having normal blood pressure.

The Elshout family in 1967, shortly before their departure to the U.S.A.—
Back row left to right: Bart (18), Nellie (14), Frits (15), Rev. Elshout (44), Meta (17)
Front row left to right: Chris (7), Arie (12), Mrs. Elshout (44), Elfriede (10), Hans (8)

During a wedding service, Rev. Elshout read the customary wedding psalm, Psalm 128. The words, "And thou shalt see thy children's children," sank deeply into his heart and were applied with power to his soul. At once all fear and anxiety dissipated. He knew that his death was not imminent; instead, he would live to see the good of Jerusalem and his children's children.[20] The Lord subsequently affirmed this by means of Psalm 91:16, "With long life will I satisfy him, and shew him my salvation." The Lord cared for His servant who perceived himself to be but a reed shaken by the wind. Although he knew himself to be but a weak and frail man, yet he trusted in His Sender.

---

[20]It is noteworthy how literally the Lord fulfilled this promise, for subsequent to his sudden death (August 10, 1991), no additional grandchildren were born. He was truly privileged to see all twenty-six of his children's children.

CHAPTER 13
The Ends of the Earth

The *Rijndam's* ship horn bellowed in low tones across the harbor of Rotterdam. The ropes that linked the ship to the docking location of the Holland America Line were released. The *Rijndam* began sailing toward the *Nieuwe Waterweg*[21] to commence its journey to North America. It would be the last scheduled journey of this ship as a passenger vessel. Traveling by airplane was becoming increasingly popular. In New York, the *Rijndam* would be refurbished as a cruise ship.

The *Rijndam* of the Holland America Line—the ship that carried the Elshout family to America.
Departure from Rotterdam: June 9, 1967—Arrival in New York: June 20, 1967

As Rev. A. Elshout held on to the railing, his wife stood next to him, and he was surrounded by his children. The children were excited; an adventure was beckoning them. However, they also felt somewhat unsure of themselves, for what would their future be like? Where would they end up living, and would they feel at home there? Their father had told them that all would turn out well, for he was not embarking upon a pathway of his own choosing. The Lord was sending him across the ocean to

---

[21]The shipping channel linking the harbor of Rotterdam with the North Sea

proclaim His Word also there. God Himself had promised that He would go before them.

~

When the mail was delivered in November 1966, Rev. Elshout picked it up and flipped through the letters as he walked to his study. One of the letters had arrived from America. Curiously, he opened the envelope and read the letter. It was a call letter from the Netherlands Reformed Congregation of Artesia, a suburb of Los Angeles. This congregation was truly at the other end of the world—located in California, in the southwestern corner of the United States. It was about six thousand miles from the Netherlands.

A small congregation of Dutch immigrants, who sought to better themselves economically, had been organized there in 1955.[22] Rev. L. Kieboom had departed five years earlier, after having served the congregation just short of four years (1958-1962). Prior to that, Rev. G. Zyderveld had served Artesia for a two-year period (1955-1956).

Rev. Elshout folded the letter and reinserted it into the envelope. The letter had little effect upon him. At an earlier point in his life, when he was still a theological student, the thought had occurred to him that he would end up in America. That notion had faded, however, for what would he do in that distant land with a growing family? No, that obviously would not be an option. At the dinner table, he informed the family of the receipt of this call, saying, "We could end up moving to America." Although the children were curious, they did not take it very seriously.

During the days that followed, the family discussed the call from America, but they would always do so in a general, inquisitive, and non-committal manner. All of that changed, however, when the Lord began to speak. Early one morning, Rev. Elshout read a daily meditation of J.C. Philpot regarding the text, "Look unto me, and be ye saved, all the ends of the earth" (Isa. 45:22). As was his custom, the minister subsequently asked the Lord to help him and equip him for his work. He asked the Lord to help him that day, beseeching Him that He would make that which he had just read, "Look unto me, and be ye saved," to be the focal point of his ministry and preaching.

Then, suddenly, his prayer stagnated, for Rev. Elshout realized that there was a call letter from "the ends of the earth"—a call to proclaim the gospel there. The minister was startled, and he attempted to continue his prayer and to suppress that thought. However, something had happened that could not possibly be suppressed. The lot had been cast.

---

[22]This congregation met for the first time in the living room of Mr. and Mrs. Aart Van Veldhuizen, the grandparents of Clarice Elshout, Bart's present wife.

Was the Lord calling him to preach in Artesia? He feared that such was indeed the case. Upon opening his eyes, he immediately thought of his wife. How would she react to this change?

Mrs. Elshout looked at her husband and said, "I knew that you would bring me to the Netherlands, but it never occurred to me that you would take me to America. However, if the Lord calls, I will follow."

The minister breathed a sigh of relief. Perhaps the Lord had removed the first and possibly the greatest obstacle. But the matter was not yet settled. The more he reflected on this matter, the more obstacles loomed before him. To cross the ocean with a large family of eight children could scarcely turn out well, and the minister therefore attempted to brush aside this calling. The contrary happened, however, for this call weighed all the heavier upon his heart. He could not find anything in God's Word on which he could lay hold in order to decline the call. Instead, he did find encouragements that the Lord will not forsake His children, even in the most difficult of circumstances. He who is the Author and Finisher of faith would lead him, and His imperative is that His gospel be preached to all creatures.

Objections arose within him as high as mountains and as deep as the oceans. How would all of this work out financially? He and his wife had learned to be frugal. They did not need that much, and they did not demand that much of life. Nevertheless, eight children needed to be clothed, adequately fed, and educated. How could a small congregation such as Artesia, consisting only of thirty-five professing members and an equal number of baptized members, provide for this need? Considering that there were only twenty families, he could do the math. In the call letter, he was given the choice between one hundred dollars per week or the contents of the collection box at the exit of the church. That was not a difficult choice for him, for he would never preach "on the box." He would rather be frugal and make do with a fixed salary than be dependent upon the whims and moods of the people. In the meantime, he heard from American ministers that he could not possibly make ends meet on such a salary. If he were to accept this call, he would not only have his salary reduced by ten thousand guilders, but it would also bring him into poverty.

However, wasn't the Lord calling him? Wasn't God's arm omnipotent to care for him even in America, as He had done all these years in Germany and in the Netherlands? Rev. Elshout then did what such circumstances require: he bowed his knees and cast all his burdens upon the Lord. He besought the God whom he loved, and whom he desired to serve wholeheartedly, to grant him clarity. In his heart, he hoped that the

Lord would give him the freedom to decline this call. The Lord gave clarity, but it was different than he had hoped. As he prepared himself for a Thanksgiving service in 's-Gravenzande, Rev. Elshout studied the parable of the rich fool. As he was reading Luke 12, he stopped at verse fifteen: "for a man's life consisteth not in the abundance of the things which he possesseth." The parable teaches that it is foolish to be of such a mindset—a foolishness the minister detected within himself at that moment. In Luke, the parable of the rich fool is followed by Christ's exhortation not to be anxious. Arie Elshout read that he should take no thought for his life, that God feeds the ravens, and that one cannot add one cubit to his stature.

A deep peace flowed into the heart of the Lord's servant. He continued to read, "How much more will he clothe you, O ye of little faith?... neither be ye of a doubtful mind...your father knoweth that ye have need of these things...it is your father's good pleasure to give you the kingdom" (Luke 12:28-32). He had asked for a clear answer, and this was a clear answer—though different than he had hoped. The heart of Rev. Elshout was relieved of a heavy burden. The Lord, as a loving, omnipotent, and caring Father, took the entire list of needs and concerns from him, saying, so to speak, "I will care for you, and you must go so that My kingdom may come."

For Rev. Elshout, this answer was also a wonderful affirmation of an old promise. His thoughts drifted toward the time when he was a student at the Theological School in Rotterdam. In *De Saambinder*, he had read an account of Rev. C. Hegeman regarding his ministry in America. He read of the need there: fields ready for harvest and a lack of laborers. The words of Acts 16 came to mind for Student Elshout, "Come over, and help us." Inwardly, he had then responded, "I will come." He was acquainted with a certain Mr. Winters in Grand Rapids, and without telling him why, he had asked him to send him an English Bible and some devotional literature.

Only once had he spoken to Rev. De Blois about this promise, but he responded curtly, "Forget about it! We can use you here."

Rev. Elshout had never been able to forget it, however. Occasionally, he would receive a call from America, but the cloudy pillar did not remove itself. Now that the latter was indeed the case, he understood that by first serving the congregations in the Netherlands for eleven years, he was being prepared for this moment. His involvement in the Committee for Youth Work had equipped him to speak to young people in America regarding the great deeds of the Lord. His involvement in mission work had taught him to look beyond national boundaries and take other countries and cultures into account. His study of the English language had prepared him to preach in English.

With increasing clarity, Arie Elshout now perceived how the Lord had been going before him when he had no inkling of His directing hand. It filled him with peace and a quiet confidence. One night, during a wakeful moment, his thoughts had gravitated toward America, and the words of this song came to mind:

> *Whatever the future may bring,*
> *The hand of the Lord will lead me.*
> *Courageously, I will therefore lift up my eyes*
> *To this unknown land.*
> *Teach me to follow without questioning,*
> *Father, what Thou doest is good.*
> *Teach me to deal only with today*
> *Doing so with a quiet and calm heart.*

That Sunday, another stanza of this song was sung as the family gathered around the organ. The words were still unfamiliar to the minister. By renewal, he was amazed at how precisely the Lord's care would match his circumstances:

> *Do not let me decide my own destiny,*
> *Even if I could do so, I would not dare;*
> *Oh, how mistaken I would be,*
> *If Thou wouldst leave the choice to me.*
> *Deal with me as a child,*
> *Who cannot find the way by himself.*
> *Take my hand into Thy hands*
> *And lead me as a child!*

There was only one thing that would withhold Rev. Elshout from accepting this call. Just imagine if the Lord were testing him as He tested Abraham when he was called upon to sacrifice his son—testing Arie Elshout as to whether he was willing to sacrifice everything that was dear to him. That possibility was eliminated when he read 1 Thessalonians 5:24: "Faithful is he that calleth you, who will also do it." These words settled into his heart with overwhelming power. Having been made completely willing, he promised the Lord that he would accept the call from Artesia. The next day a telegram was sent to America.

The family now entered a busy period. Although the younger children did not fully understand what was happening, the older ones did all the more. What would the consequences be for Bart? A fierce war was raging in Vietnam, resulting in many American casualties. Within a half year upon his arrival in the United States, Bart would receive a summons to be examined for possible military service. The same would happen to Frits—though perhaps a bit later. Intense doubt gripped the boys. In addition, it had not been an easy year for Meta. During her high school final exam period, she had a traffic accident and was confined to her bed for six weeks with a concussion and an injured leg. It was a wonder that she was able to take her exams and would be able to be enrolled in the Domestic Academy near the Peace Palace in The Hague. Upon completing her first year, she would have to select a specific career track, and she would probably choose to be trained as a dietician.

The minister and his wife left the choice to their children. This choice was not a difficult one for Meta, for she was in a transitional year as far as her studies were concerned, and she would thus be able to make the transition to America. Rev. Elshout told Bart that the possibility of his having to serve in Vietnam had been on the list of burdens made known to the Lord, who had promised him that His care also pertained to this specific need. Even in Vietnam, Bart would be able to count on the Lord's protection and help. However, the choice as to whether he would accompany them or remain in the Netherlands was his.

During the night, Father and Mother Elshout heard someone opening their bedroom door. Bart entered and sat down upon the bed. He had

A picture of Rev. Elshout and his brothers and sisters taken shortly before his departure to America—Standing left to right: Bart, Arie[†], Jan[†], & Jacques (Sjaak) Seated left to right: Katrien[†], Sija, Adrie, Bep, & Nel[†]

[†]deceased

long been plagued with doubt, and he intended to remain in the Netherlands. He could believe, however, that his father was correct: the Lord would also care for him in America. He would go. After some conversation, Bart quietly returned to his bed.

Just after Father and Mother had again fallen asleep, the bedroom door opened again, and Frits stood before their bed to tell them the same thing. They were filled with gratitude, for the Lord had inclined the hearts of their children. This event was also a manifestation of His care. When someone asked Hans whether he was afraid to cross the ocean by boat, and later to travel by airplane, he looked somewhat surprised. He responded, "Afraid? No, the Lord is calling my father to go to Artesia, and He will therefore also protect us."

To keep the costs for the small congregation of Artesia at a minimum, the Elshouts had decided to apply for immigration, for the Dutch government would then assume responsibility for their move. This meant that they would have to journey by boat. It would save the congregation of Artesia a large sum of money, even though this mode of travel would be less convenient for the family than traveling by airplane. Education was free in the state of California. This was a relief, considering the educational needs of the older children. How all of this would fall in place was unknown to them. Would Rev. W.C. Lamain and Rev. M. Romeyn be correct that their family would be reduced to poverty, or did the Lord's care also extend to the ends of the earth, and all would turn out well? Rev. Elshout, like Agur, prayed neither for riches nor prosperity. Neither did he pray for poverty, but rather for "food convenient," for that which would be in their best interest.

He said to his children, "All will turn out well. Artesia is a small congregation, however, and we will have to adjust ourselves to the living standard of these people. If they must make ends meet with little, we must also endeavor to do so."

The *Rijndam* exited the *Nieuwe Waterweg* and entered the ocean. The ship's destiny would be New York—a journey that would last twelve days. This passage was an adventure for the children, but Mrs. Elshout looked up against it. How could she keep an eye on her eight children on such a humongous ship? What a blessing it was that the Van Zomerens accompanied them on this journey! This couple from the congregation of Scheveningen had anticipated visiting their family in Canada for quite some time. However, "Aunt Riek" and "Uncle Arie" had decided to make a detour of 1,400 miles to support the minister's family in their journey to Artesia.

There was no time for the children to be bored on the ship. There was also an English teacher on board who instructed them daily in their new

language. The ship itself resembled a city. There were stores, a barbershop, a chapel, an auditorium, and even a swimming pool. Often the children could be found on one of the decks on which the black and white contours of the game of shuffleboard were painted—a game which required that large disks be shuffled across the playing area.

Rev. Elshout quickly established contact with the other passengers and with the crew. He discovered that there were two other ministers on board, and they agreed to conduct a joint worship service on Sunday. Rev. Eberlein, the ship's resident chaplain, would preach in German, Rev. Elshout in Dutch, and the American minister, Rev. Reynold Hoover, in English.

There were plenty of games on board the ship. Much time was spent on the upper deck playing shuffleboard.

The weather was stormy, waves were rising high, and the ship that had appeared so humongous in the harbor was now no more than a tiny vessel.

There were practices with life vests in the event there would have to be an evacuation with lifeboats.

Most passengers were absent during mealtime. Being sea-sick, they were either in bed, or they were miserably hanging over the railing to empty their stomachs. The captain had to smile when he observed that the entire Elshout family was seated at the table. Not one member was absent. There was a moment of consternation, however, when one of the waiters dropped a bowl of peas due to a sudden movement of the ship.

After twelve days, the *Rijndam* approached New York. There was, however, very little visibility, for the ship was enveloped in heavy fog. The radar indicated that a few small vessels were in the vicinity of the ship, but radio contact could not be established. The captain then decided to stop the ship until the fog lifted. The wait was long, and the tension was palpable. The horn of the ship would be sounded regularly to keep other ships at a distance.

Finally, the journey could proceed, and on June 20, 1967, the *Rijndam* docked in the New York harbor. On shore, Rev. W.C. Lamain and his brother-in-law, Deacon Nieuwenhuis (Franklin Lakes, NJ, NRC), were waiting. They would bring the family to the airport. When Rev. Lamain saw the family disembarking from the ship, he shook his head and sighed. Ten people! What would become of them in distant Artesia? He sighed repeatedly.

In a friendly way, Rev. Elshout said, "Brother, do not sigh, for that does not help us. Instead, please carry one of our suitcases." Surprised, the older minister complied with this request.

After engaging several taxis, the journey proceeded to John F. Kennedy Airport, where an airplane destined for Los Angeles was waiting. The children were overwhelmed by all the new impressions. Everything was new for them: the cars were big, the roads were wide, the office buildings were tall, and the billboards were in your face. Everything exuded self-confidence. New York also appeared to be chaotic, however. Was this beautiful America, and was this Manhattan with its famous skyscrapers? The busyness, the disorderliness, and the grime of the city were not exactly what they had expected.

Rev. Elshout was of good courage, however, for hitherto the Lord had helped. Ebenezer! His thoughts wandered, for many years earlier his father, Bartel Elshout, and his brother-in-law, Jan Bije, had also been here looking for work. For Rev. Elshout, there was work awaiting him— work that pertained to eternal things. What a privileged man he deemed himself to be!

Mrs. Elshout did not say much. She wanted her children to absorb and enjoy everything. Her heart was not really in all that was happening, for her thoughts drifted to the other side of the ocean. Would she ever see her parents again? What would lie ahead of them? The Lord had promised to be with them. She clung to that promise and got hold of herself. Perhaps everything would turn out better than expected.

The Holland America Line Pier in New York (Manhattan)—
the point of arrival in the U.S.A. for the Elshout family on June 20, 1967

A small group of people were waiting at the airport of Los Angeles, California's largest city, to welcome the minister and his family. The Elshout children stood there somewhat bewildered, for the people spoke a mixture of English and Dutch. Even Bart, who for several years had studied English in high school, could not quite figure out what was being said. The family was then asked to step into cars—large American "boats." They then proceeded to drive to Artesia on a ten-lane freeway. The driver was a friendly man, but since he was continually chewing on his cigar, his English—which actually was Yankee-Dutch—was rather unintelligible.

At the home of Deacon VanRavenswaay, the coffee was ready, and there was a warm reception for the family. Welcome to Artesia! But the children were rather quiet, for everything was so American—so different from the Netherlands. The homes were different, for they were not built as solidly. Due to the sub-tropical climate, there were different trees and plants. Daily life was different and more extravagant. Everything was so different, even though the children were unable to identify what it was.

The entire family was then ushered to the garage, and there stood a shiny and brand-new Pontiac Catalina station wagon as a gift of the congregation for the minister. Quietly Rev. Elshout reflected on these words:

"Your heavenly Father knoweth that ye have need of all these things." He had already asked himself how this matter could be resolved. The distances in America were great, and a car would be indispensable. Not only had he received a car, however, but he had received a quality American car that could accommodate the entire family!

The parsonage on 21309 Bloomfield Ave., Hawaiian Gardens, California, with a new Pontiac Catalina station wagon in front of the door

Two Sundays later, on July 2, 1967, Rev. M. Romeyn[23] was present to install the Dutch pastor. The inaugural service was slated for the afternoon, and Rev. Elshout had selected Isaiah 45:22 as the text for his inaugural sermon. How could it have been otherwise? In this text, the Lord spoke by the mouth of His prophet, saying, "Look unto me, and be ye saved, all the ends of the earth, for I am God, and there is none else." Artesia's new minister expounded this text in both English and Dutch—sentence after sentence in Dutch, followed by the pastor's own translation.

The pastor did not yet realize that the language issue was a matter of offense and discord in the congregation. The conflict was intense, and relationships were rather strained. Added to the mix was the fact that the majority of the congregational members hailed from a variety of congregations in the Netherlands that differed in spiritual disposition. Some

[23]Rev. M. Romeyn served as the pastor of the Netherlands Reformed Congregation of Chilliwack, British Columbia (Canada), and was the moderator (counselor) of the Artesia congregation.

sought to impose their Dutch customs upon the American members, and others, in turn, were opposed to the "dutchification" of congregational life.

The pastor decided to preach three times on Sunday—twice in English and once in Dutch. "We are here in an English-speaking country," he reasoned, "and for the sake of the young people, we must speak the language of the land. Do you not transact your business in the language of the land?" Thus he did not support the Dutch members who tenaciously wanted to cling to their Dutch customs. Unintentionally, he was drawn into a conflict in a congregation that was being torn asunder by friction and internal turmoil.

Rev. M. Romeyn (4th from the left, middle row) traveled to Artesia from Chilliwack, British Columbia (1300 miles), to install Rev. Elshout in his new charge.

The pastor quickly adjusted his preconceived notion that this was a congregation that struggled financially. Half the members of the congregation were wealthy—exceptionally wealthy. However, many of them sought to use their prosperity to manipulate their minister. They failed to achieve their goal and the pastor began to experience resistance and opposition from these people. From others, such as the Kuperus, Schoneveld, Van Beek, Van Ravenswaay, and Veenendaal families, the family received much help and love.

California's public education system enabled the entire family, with the exception of its youngest members, to attend summer school to learn English. The pastor already had considerable knowledge of the basics. Prior to the family's departure to America, one of the Americans with whom he corresponded wrote, "If you speak the language half as well as you write it, we will be satisfied." The pastor smiled and asked himself what he should make of this comment.

The children learned the English language quickly. After the family had been in the United States for three months, little Arie was reprimanded by his teacher: "Arie, you are making this mistake for the second time. I have told you how it should be. Why don't you get it?"

Arie replied, "Teacher, I am really doing my best, but I have been here only three months."

The teacher responded with amazement, saying, "Weren't you born here?" Then she realized that instead of speaking poor English, Arie's English actually was very good.

During the summer vacation, the entire family was enrolled in summer school to learn English. Everyone attended his own class daily in order to master the English language as much as possible. The pastor and his wife enrolled themselves at the local Cerritos College to improve their facility with the English language. The congregation observed this effort, and it was appreciated by some.

Mrs. VanderWeide understood what it meant for a mother to leave her family behind daily. She promptly said, "Twice a week I will assist you with your housework. That should make matters a bit easier for you."

Following the summer vacation, all the children were enrolled in a Christian school in the nearby—except Bart who attended Cerritos College. In spite of their very meager salary, the pastor and his wife had

The campus of Cerritos College—A picture taken in 2005 when Bart visited the Artesia area for the first time since having left in 1969

decided to send the children to the local Christian school. They had no idea how they would pay for their education. They were convinced, however, that the promise they made at the baptism of their children to teach them the Christian faith still needed to be honored.

Elfriede was ill at ease, for she perceived that the children in her class were laughing at her. There she stood with her pigtails and plaid skirt—something that was perfectly normal in the Netherlands but not at all fashionable in America. The other children found it strange that she packed a lunch for school, for during the lunch break they would eat cake and chips. She did her best to speak the language, but her classmates considered it primarily as "broken English."

There was very little contact with other congregations. Although Sunnyside was the nearest congregation geographically, it was actually located 1,200 miles to the north of Artesia. The work in the congregation demanded a great deal of time, yet there was more time available for the family than had been the case in the Netherlands, strengthening the bond of reciprocal love among the members of the family.

Serving the churches in North America necessitated either flying or embarking on a lengthy journey by car. Rev. Elshout did the latter in

To serve other congregations, great distances had to be traveled—usually by plane. During the summer, however, the trip would be made by car with the entire family (here in 1967).

August, for he decided that he and his family would visit the neighboring congregations. This trip would enable his children to become better acquainted with the vastness of the country and allow them to establish contact with young people from other congregations. The Pontiac Catalina was loaded to the brim.

The famous Mount Rushmore Presidential Memorial in South Dakota was one of the stops as the family traveled to other congregations.

After traveling two-and-a-half days, the family arrived in Sunnyside. After a few days in Sunnyside, where Rev. Elshout preached on several occasions, the family continued their northbound journey to Canada—a journey that was delayed by a flat tire. The car had to be emptied to exchange tires, and the flat tire had to be repaired at the next service station. The service manager expressed concern, stating that the factory-installed tires were not the best. It would be better to replace all four tires. Would this be expensive? Yes, indeed, but that would be a far safer option, particularly with such a fully loaded vehicle. Rev. Elshout decided to follow the mechanic's advice, and all four tires were replaced. Within a short period of time, however, three of the tires blew out, and only then did it became evident that this service manager had installed tires that were too small. Although this had been a profitable deal for him, he jeopardized the family's safety. What a blessing that God had protected them! In each of these incidents, the family escaped all harm and injury. The words of Psalm 121, read prior to every journey, proved to be true: "Thy Protector is the Lord" (Psalter 345:2—Psalm 121).

❧

The congregation of Artesia did not prosper. A sharp division became increasingly evident, for the minister, and especially his preaching, met with resistance. Although some fruit became evident among the young people, there were many others who resented his preaching. Rev. Elshout's preaching differed from that of some of the older ministers of the Netherlands Reformed Congregations—not in terms of content, but rather as to his style and emphasis. His preaching was direct and convicting, and confronted sinners with their responsibility toward the gospel.

The church building of the Artesia NRC

This small congregation also proved incapable of bonding together and of practicing mutual tolerance. There was more talk than prayer, and they kept a wary eye on each other. The minister's family bore the brunt of this tension. Mrs. Elshout was deeply affected by the suspicion and insinuations, and her health declined visibly. Her family doctor even urgently advised her to attend church as seldom as possible, arguing that this was too stressful.

Furthermore, there was yet another matter of concern: the home on Bloomfield Ave. was only a rental property. When the owner decided to sell this property, she first offered it to the consistory. Since, however, the home was too small for the minister's family, the consistory declined this

Pulpit view of the sanctuary of the Artesia NRC

offer. This meant that the brothers necessarily had to look for a different
and larger parsonage. Not everyone was happy with that proposal; one
of the members said bluntly, "If we had known that you had eight children, we would never have called you." It could not have been said more
plainly than that!

The consistory located another home in the vicinity of Bloomfield
Avenue. It was a new home, not too expensive, and very suitable as a
parsonage. However, the membership rejected the proposal to purchase
this home. Some members stated that if the minister were to depart, they
would be saddled with this home. The minister was exceedingly troubled
by this attitude, for he had been in this congregation merely one half of
a year, and the thought of departing had not even remotely occurred to
him. Given that the Lord called him to labor in this locality, why was
there already talk about his departure?

The membership meeting was a troubling event. Serious accusations
were hurled at the minister and the consistory, and the members ultimately decided that another rental property would be the only option.
Rev. Elshout was deeply grieved—not so much because of the house, but
because of the bitter accusations and the distrust expressed by the members. He addressed the members, stating that he could testify before God
and man that he never aspired after the money and material goods of the

congregation. On the contrary, he had applied for immigrant status so that the congregation would be spared the expense of his move. All moving expenses had therefore been paid by the Dutch government. He had made no demands regarding either his salary or the house. His coming to Artesia had not been motivated by a desire to emigrate. The call of the congregation was for him the call and commission of God Himself.

One of the members callously responded, "If God has sent you here, He will also provide a home for you."

The family was despondent. Did they have to come to America to be maligned and to see their mother waste away? The minister then encouraged his wife and children, saying, "This member of the congregation who made this loveless and cutting remark will certainly be proven right. The Lord shall take care of us, for He has promised that all that we need shall be added to us. Will He not do what He has promised?" Father Elshout was certain that Zion's God would help in the hour of need, "for the gold and silver are His. He will even use men to confirm His Word to us."

The next evening someone knocked on the back door during the supper hour. Deacon Hans Kuperus entered. He was as distraught as all other members of the consistory about what had occurred. He said, "Reverend, I will buy the home on Cortner Ave., and I will then permit

The new parsonage at 18617 Cortner Ave., Cerritos, CA—
Hans (John) and Chris quickly mastered the basic skills of baseball.

A cozy Dutch living room under an American roof at the Cortner Ave. parsonage—
Elfriede is playing the electronic organ.

the congregation to rent it for the amount I need to service my debt. We will thus comply with the wish of the congregation, and you and your family will have a good home."

The minister was speechless. He did not quite know what he should say. How could this be? Kuperus was by no means a wealthy man. By working hard as a small businessman, he was earning a living for his wife and five children.

Rev. Elshout therefore asked, "But, Kuperus, what motivates you to do this?"

He then stated how, at the dinner table, he had opened the Bible to the history of Elijah in Zarephath. Elijah requested that something first be prepared for him. The widow then first provided for Elijah, and there-after for her son and herself. "That impacted me greatly," he said, "so I said to my wife, 'We must buy that house!' My wife immediately agreed with me."

Rev. Elshout was so moved by this account that he responded to Deacon Kuperus, "Hans, you will not be able to earn heaven with this, but the Lord will bless you."

The gospel of free grace will not always be received joyfully. The truth that we cannot be saved by the works of the law is incompatible with

pharisaical piety. To be reconciled with God on the basis of the mediatorial work of Another is a way that is too easy for some. "Jesus alone"
is a truth that is ultimately too "light" for them. They would rather cling
to their external religion and be at peace, thinking that thereby they are
pleasing God. Such people do not want to be awakened. Instead, they view
preaching that focuses on resting and abiding in Christ alone as problematic, considering the one who thus preaches to be an unwelcome troubler
of the waters.

Rev. Elshout experienced this criticism also during a Thanksgiving
service in one of the Canadian churches. After the service, he noticed that
there was some commotion among the deacons. When the minister
asked them what was going on, one of them showed him a slip of paper
that had been found in one of the collection bags. A Bible text (Matthew
8:34) had been written upon it. The paper was not signed. The deacons
had already located this text: "when they saw him, they besought him
that he would depart out of their coasts." The faces of the consistory
members betrayed confusion.

However, the minister responded differently than they had anticipated:
"Brothers, why is this so upsetting to you? I consider it a great honor that
the same thing is happening to me that happened to my Lord and Master.
To endure His shame belongs to the doing of His will. It is also the fulfillment of what He had foretold would happen if we follow in His footsteps.
You should pity the one who wrote this note, for he loves his pigs more
than the preaching of the gospel of Jesus Christ and Him crucified."

Fortunately, there were also other reactions to his preaching. Fruit
became evident, for there were broken and humble hearts, asking the
question, "What must we do to be saved?" Wherever the Lord works, the
devil will not be idle. Yet he shall not be able to prevent the progress of
the Lord's work!

California is a region prone to earthquakes. Several plates of the earth's
crust are sliding across each other, and experts believe that Los Angeles
and San Francisco could potentially be struck by earthquakes so severe
that not one stone would remain upon the other. In the building industry,
such quakes were anticipated, for large buildings, and even skyscrapers,
were built upon adjustable foundations that were capable of absorbing
such quakes.

The first time the Elshout family experienced an earthquake was just
after the meal had been served. Mrs. Elshout thought that she was
becoming lightheaded, and she became nauseated. She was just about to
say to her husband that she would rather not eat, when she saw him
sitting with his eyes fixed on her. He did not understand what was hap-

pening, for one moment his wife went up, and then again she went down. Then it slowly dawned on them what was happening. The minister immediately summoned the family to leave the table, and he ushered his children and his wife out the door and into the backyard. They could see how the car on the driveway was swaying back and forth, and a deepening tear was beginning to manifest itself. Then the quake faded away. Later the radio reported that it had been an earthquake that measured 6.5 on the Richter scale. Their hearts trembled even more. The minister felt in his heart, however, that the Lord had delivered them out of this distress. At night, they still felt some aftershocks. The next day, Artesia assessed the damage inflicted on several buildings and roads. Although people resumed their daily routine as if nothing had happened, yet they did so, anticipating that someday there would be another quake.

Rev. Elshout's ministry in Artesia remained challenging. The internal tensions in the congregation had a detrimental effect upon his pastoral work and his preaching.

Frits, posing with the customary gown and graduation cake, upon graduating from Valley Christian High School.

When he received a call from the congregation of Corsica, however, he felt compelled to decline it. The Lord had not given him any direction regarding this call.

In the meantime, his wife was not doing well. Rev. Elshout sensed that if this situation were to continue, it would culminate in her having a nervous breakdown. Could he permit this to happen? Would the Lord permit this to happen? He laid his concerns before the Lord and besought Him to send deliverance. He wrestled before God in prayer not only for the congregation of Artesia, but also for his wife and children. Wouldn't the Lord be able to initiate a turnaround and grant mutual love and peace within the congregation?

The Lord answered his prayers, albeit differently than he had anticipated. His thoughts began to focus upon the congregation of Kalamazoo, recognizing that also there would be a field of labor for him. As he wrestled with this matter in prayer, the minister became convinced that the congregation of Kalamazoo would call him, and that he must and may go there.

The next morning, he said to his wife, "Try to persevere a bit longer, for we are leaving Artesia."

"Where are we going?" she asked.

"To Kalamazoo," he replied.

"When?"

"This summer."

"How do you know this?"

Rev. Elshout responded, "The Lord has shown me."

He did not discuss this conviction with anyone else, not even with his children. Two months later, a call letter came from Kalamazoo. The receipt of this letter would indeed have far-reaching consequences, and yet, it was truly an answer to prayer and an affirmation of what God Himself had spoken. He is a God who is true to His Word. The minister and his wife very much experienced it as such: "Gracious is the LORD, and righteous; yea, our God is merciful" (Psa. 116:5)!

> *Whene'er to God I cried,*
> *He hastened to my side*
> *In all my tribulations;*
> *From Zion's mountain fair*
> *He looked on my despair,*
> *And heard my supplications*
> (Psalter 414:2—Psalm 3)

Undoubtedly, there were those in the congregation who breathed a sigh of relief. The taskmaster would finally depart. It became evident, however, that there were also others who had wholeheartedly supported the minister and his family, and they were ashamed about all that had transpired. The bond of love with the consistory of Artesia now manifested itself. They had endured so much tribulation together during the past two years. It pained the minister that he had to leave these people behind with all their concerns. Although he had experienced a sense of relief, he grieved over the fact that people had been unwilling to submit to the Word of God and be led by the Spirit of Christ, refusing to be conquered by the love of Christ. Rev. Elshout realized all the more, "It is not of him that willeth, nor of him that runneth, but of God that sheweth mercy" (Rom. 9:16).

In spite of some opposition in the Artesia congregation, the Elshout family also experienced a great deal of loving friendship. This was particularly true for Mr. and Mrs. Richard Van Ravenswaay, fondly referred to by the children as Uncle Rich and Aunt Minnie.

CHAPTER 14

"Be it unto thee even as thou wilt."

Elder Thomas Moerdyk from Kalamazoo called, and said, "Reverend, do you remember that you preached for us a year-and-a-half ago? Both the consistory and the congregation could endorse your preaching. Already then it was my desire that you would become our minister. However, it was not yet the Lord's time. It is now my delight to express the joy of the congregation. We have been vacant for forty years, and we have extended many calls—but always in vain. At last, the time has now arrived that the Lord has answered our prayer, and He has been pleased to grant us our own pastor." Mr. Moerdyk could not refrain from weeping. There was, however, also something else he wished to discuss, but he could not communicate that by phone. A few days later he would travel to Artesia.

As they were driving from the Los Angeles airport to Artesia, he told his story. Prior to this visit, Mr. Moerdyk had corresponded with Rev. Elshout about the offer of grace, and they were evidently of one mind. Both men felt a great kinship with Boston, the Erskines, and other Scottish divines. They both felt a burden for the congregations in which the matter of the offer of grace was frequently addressed in an unbalanced and one-sided fashion. Such discussions had even resulted in church splits, and there still was confusion in the churches regarding this matter. Mr. Moerdyk felt a kinship with this minister. During the night, he had literally laid his letter before the countenance of the Lord, just as Hezekiah had done with his letters. He fervently besought the Lord that He would send Kalamazoo this minister with whom he felt such kinship. The Lord answered by saying, "Be it unto thee even as thou wilt."

Mr. Moerdyk was amazed that it rendered him speechless. That did not last long, however for the thought occurred to him that he did not even know whether these words were in the Bible. Perhaps it was all imagination. He questioned Rev. Lamain about these words, but even he had to do some searching. However, a few days later he responded by saying that these words are found in Matthew 15:28, where the Savior Himself uttered them to the Syro-phoenecian woman. Mr. Moerdyk was relieved. It was indeed the Word of God, and it was His promise.

At the next consistory meeting, he could not refrain from telling what had transpired. He proposed that a call be extended to Rev. Elshout. The consistory responded cautiously, however, asking whether they could legitimately call a minister who had not even been in his present congregation for a period of two years. A decision was made to leave this matter to the discretion of the male membership's meeting. Rev. Elshout's name was placed on a duo, and the membership voted to call him.

It was quiet in the car, for Rev. Elshout was reflecting on what had transpired. Finally, he said, "Well, Mr. Moerdyk, you have told me of being exercised in prayer during the night. When exactly did this occur?"

It did not take Mr. Moerdyk long to respond: it was in February. It was now Rev. Elshout's turn to be amazed and speechless. All of this had transpired during the same time that he had unburdened himself to the Lord, when he had become convinced that he was called and permitted to go to Kalamazoo. The Lord is a great and holy God indeed, for it had been affirmed afresh "that before they call, I will answer" (Isa. 65:24).

Once they arrived in Artesia, Mr. Moerdyk had another surprise in store for the family. He extracted a container from his suitcase that contained architectural drawings for a new parsonage. After Rev. Elshout had accepted the call the previous Friday, Mr. Moerdyk, at the direction of the consistory, had contacted a builder. The question was whether it would

Due to the united effort of many members of the congregation, a new parsonage was built in only nine weeks!

be possible to build a parsonage in such short order. There was more than sufficient room to do so on the grounds surrounding the church building. The builder told Mr. Moerdyk that he had a set of plans that were eminently suited for a parsonage, and some adjustments could be made if necessary. The party for whom these drawings had been prepared had cancelled their contract that week. Rev. Elshout, standing next to his wife, was again speechless.

The moving van in front of the Cortner Ave. parsonage, and Chris is standing in front of the truck. The move from Artesia to Kalamazoo was an adventure for the children.

Three months later, on August 5, 1969, Rev. Lamain installed his fellow minister in Kalamazoo. There was a larger audience than customary—more than three hundred people. Rev. Elshout was conscious of the fact that he was called to be a fisher of men also here in Kalamazoo. He felt led to preach about 2 Corinthians 5:20b, "Be ye reconciled to God."

In the rear section of the church sat sixteen-year-old Joel Beeke. He was deeply moved by the inaugural sermon, and he listened to the message with tear-filled eyes. His heart yearned so deeply to be reconciled with God, and yet from his side, it seemed so impossible. As a sinner, he had utterly forfeited this reconciliation, and he felt himself to be so far from the kingdom of God. Rev. Elshout said that God seeks those that are lost, and though he believed that to be true, he felt that God would pass by one as lost as he was. The Lord used this sermon to teach this young man that salvation was unattainable from his side. Subsequently, he was privileged to learn that whatever is impossible with man is possible with God.

In the elder's bench, Elder Peter Beeke was deeply impressed. How precious was this preaching in which salvation was so freely offered to lost sinners! It filled him to overflowing. The next day he stepped into his car to go hear Rev. Elshout preach in Grand Rapids, a one-hour drive from Kalamazoo. He was hopeful that that the minister would preach about the same text, and that was indeed the case. But Mr. Beeke squirmed in his seat, for the sermon seemed so different. Why was it that yesterday there had been food for his soul, and today he could not even find a crumb? Then an incident that Ralph Erskine had encountered came to mind, and he understood. A member of Erskine's congregation had been richly blessed under his preaching. When she followed him to a different location, however, the sermon did nothing to her. Erskine commented: "That makes sense, for earlier it was your desire to hear the voice of Christ, and now you wanted to hear Erskine, and therefore you came up empty." With shame, Mr. Beeke returned homeward, concluding that he had done likewise.

Kalamazoo was a congregation that was made up of immigrants, and most members had their roots in the Netherlands, in spite of the fact that many families had resided in the United States already for generations. Between 1800 and 1830, the first Dutch families had established residence in the state of Michigan.

The congregation had been vacant for forty-one years, and the arrival of their own pastor caused quite a stir. For so long they had yearned to

The Kalamazoo church buildin with the parsonage in the background

be blessed with a pastor, and their prayers had been answered at last. The congregation received Rev. Elshout with open arms, and his preaching was well received. Grace was proclaimed to poor, helpless sinners who could no longer find anything in themselves. Although God's good pleasure and His electing love were emphasized, the door remained open for the sinner. From God's side, salvation was always possible. God's good pleasure was a central component of Rev. Elshout's preaching. Election is indeed a given, for had there been no election, no man would ever have been saved. At the same time, however, he fully affirmed the teaching of Scripture regarding the responsibility of man. Man is fully responsible for his own salvation. As a fisher of men, Rev. Elshout cast the gospel net week after week, doing so with but one objective: to catch men in the net of the gospel. His prayerful aim was that sinners, by grace, would become subjects of Christ Jesus.

The minister's reception into the homes of the members was also friendly and generous. He and his wife made many visits. Strong friendships developed with the Beekes, the Johnsons, the Moerdyks, and many others. This friendly and tender-hearted minister was greatly appreciated.

However, his task was not always that easy. A young woman from the congregation had asked the minister to marry her, and he readily agreed. However, shortly thereafter it became evident that this wedding was compulsory, and the minister had not been informed of this fact. Once he knew it, he immediately dealt with it—not because the wool had been pulled over his eyes, but because God's honor was at stake. He engaged in a pointed, yet pastoral, conversation with this young couple, and it resulted in their confession of guilt. The matter was then resolved before the Lord and the congregation; therefore, no one could any longer point a finger at them. Rev. Elshout was indeed a tender-hearted man, but he was also upright and at times unyielding.

"Blessed are they that mourn, for they shall be comforted." With love and compassion, Rev. Elshout preached about this text—a text that must be read correctly. It does not say, "Blessed are they that weep." That would pertain to an entirely different matter, for there is much weeping about matters that are not addressed in this text. The text focuses upon those who mourn after a God that they miss and also about their sins.

Shortly thereafter, Rev. Elshout paid an acquaintance visit to an elderly man in the congregation. He soon noticed that the man was not very happy with his preaching, especially not about the sermon regarding this Beatitude from the gospel of Matthew. In former days, the man had often been moved to tears under the preaching of God's Word. However, that was no longer the case, for he had not shed a single tear under Rev. Elshout's preaching. The pastor carefully questioned the man, and he came to the conclusion that those tears were the foundation of this man's hope. The pastor gave careful but pointed instruction: his tears could not save him. To that end, he needed the Savior, Jesus Christ. Only a true faith in Him would culminate in salvation. Tears of contrition, and especially a mourning over sin—albeit with dry eyes—are components of genuine faith, but they cannot be the foundation upon which God promises salvation. This man did not deny it, but inwardly he could not believe it. It would take several years before he would understand this truth experientially. He was later hospitalized, and what he had heard in the sermons of Rev. Elshout—but had not accepted—then became reality for him. Being faced with death, he discovered that he could not move God with his tears. By grace, he was privileged to put his hope in the Person and the work of the Savior, Jesus Christ, and he truly experienced, "Blessed are they that mourn, for they shall be comforted."

Rev. Elshout's preaching in Kalamazoo bore fruit by the Holy Spirit who was pleased to use his preaching to transform hearts. He caused people to humble themselves and repent, teaching them that they had no standing before God. They had to learn to find life outside of themselves in Jesus Christ. When the consistory convened, it was customary to discuss the family visits. It was noted with joy that here and there stirrings of new life were detected. The evidences of new life could be observed. God's work will progress, and Satan can do nothing to prevent it.

The Lord's work in the congregation also became visible in Rev. Elshout's own family. Some of his children were impacted by the preaching. A godly sorrow about their own sins, and a yearning for grace were no longer simply familiar terms but became experiential realities.

Upon administering the Lord's Supper, Rev. Elshout was greatly affected by the fact that his daughter Meta was seated at the table and was privileged to receive the bread and the cup. This occurrence also caused a stir in the congregation. There were diverse reactions among young and old. Some viewed it as a blessing and fruit upon the preaching, whereas others dismissed it as presumption and will-worship. Shortly thereafter, Joel Beeke also could no longer refrain from partaking of the Lord's Supper.

～

One Saturday evening, Bart came to his father's study. He wanted to talk with him, for the following morning the Lord's Supper would be administered, and his heart was filled with questions. He could no longer remain silent about them. He told his father about the changes in his life—his yearning after God, his sorrow over sin, and his heartfelt love for the Lord and His service. However, he also had significant doubts. His life had been changed, but the question was whether this change was God's work, or whether it was of his own making. Was it presumption, or was it of a true and saving nature? It brought him into a bind, and while he was prayerfully wrestling at God's throne, a portion of Scripture came to mind that filled him with amazement: "I have loved thee with an everlasting love: therefore with lovingkindness have I drawn thee" (Jer 31:3). Bart could not arise from his knees, for he was overwhelmed

During their stay in Kalamazoo, Rev. and Mrs. Elshout were privileged to commemorate their 25th wedding anniversary.

and filled with amazement. He understood the words of Mephibosheth when he said, "such a dead dog as I am," and yet the Lord was mindful of him and had loved him *"with an everlasting love."*

However, after some time doubts again surfaced, for how could it be that the Lord loved him, let alone love him with an everlasting love? Once more he prayed, "Lord, I dare not believe that Thou hast loved me, dost love me, and wilt love me—that all that has transpired in my life is the result of having been drawn by Thee, for I have not experienced such great fear and anxiety of which I have read regarding the lives of Thy children." By renewal, the same words of Jeremiah 31:3 came to mind. However, this time the emphasis was evidently upon the latter portion of the text: "therefore with lovingkindness *have I drawn thee.*" Bart told his father that it was as if the Lord communicated to him that he should not render suspect that which had transpired within him. That which he had experienced was not contrary to God's Word; instead, it was in conformity with it.

In quiet amazement, Bart's father listened to his son's pouring out of his heart, and he was privileged to instruct him from the Word of God. That which Bart had read in the book of Petrus Immens was so true and so biblical: The one is led by way of a bitter Mara, and the other will be led to the heavenly Canaan by way of a sweet Elim. There was therefore no reason to suspect the Lord's dealings. Instead, there was reason for thanksgiving. Rev. Elshout extracted the following lesson from this experience: Never measure yourself and others by the unique aspects of the life of someone else. The next day, Bart, along with several other young people, partook of the Lord's Supper for the first time.

This attendance met with resistance from some older members, and there was also division within the consistory. Rev. Elshout said, "Brothers, let us not judge too rashly. Instead, you should speak with these young people, and listen to see if you can detect something of the Lord's work."

Some office-bearers did so, and they were amazed about God's work in them. Others would not yield in their assessment, and some even claimed that the preaching was to be blamed. As a result, the seed of division had been sown within the consistory, and the pastor sensed opposition to his preaching, even though it came primarily from one office-bearer. This opposition profoundly impacted him, and he subjected himself and his preaching to self-examination. He readily acknowledged that there was much in which he had been deficient and remiss. However, he neither could nor was willing to change his preaching in any way—unless one could demonstrate that it was either unbiblical, unreformed, or fostered erroneous sentiments. None of that had occurred.

Many young people felt a bond with their congregation. The Youth Group flourished, but they also wanted to be engaged practically. Being encouraged by their pastor, they organized Bible Truth Books. Good books were selected and made available at greatly discounted prices. Thousands of books that articulated sound and Reformed doctrine found their way into the hands of many—and also into many families. On a small scale, this organization also engaged in the distribution of existing gospel tracts. Bible Truth Books needed a great deal of money to operate, but time and again the Lord provided the necessary means. Not only did it teach the young people to be dependent, but it also taught them to trust in the power and grace of the great and faithful Helper.

With a loud thunder, the airplane roared down the runway. It carried Frits, who was on his way back to the Netherlands. Father and Mother Elshout had to brush back tears. For the first time, the unity of the Elshout family was broken—at least as far as everyone's dwelling together. The pastor and his wife now had to experience letting go of their children. Obviously, they were very supportive of Frits for whom a long-standing wish was being fulfilled. He so much wanted to become an organ builder, and the Flentrop Company in Zaandam was willing to accept him as an apprentice. This was an extraordinary opportunity. As the wings carried the airplane, so Frits was carried upon the wings of prayer—and especially the prayers of his father and mother.

Frits is ready to return to the Netherlands (1970) to begin his life-long career with Flentrop Organ Builders in Zaandam, the Netherlands. He concluded his career as president of the company.

The pastor and his wife again found themselves at the airport a few months later. Bart was departing. His educational objective was to become a teacher of the German language, and he wanted to further refine his skills at the University of Braunschweig, the city in which his grandparents resided.

Finally, Meta would also cross the ocean. She would pursue her education at a hospital in Rotterdam to become a lab technician—and then as a lab technician to be employed in the tropics. Her desire was to be engaged in medical mission work, and such training would therefore be

Meta ready to return to the Netherlands to be employed at a hospital
in Rotterdam (Havenziekenhuis)

Bidding Meta farewell at the Detroit Airport
From left to right: Nellie, Elfriede, Hans (John), Meta, Chris, Mrs. Elshout,
Rev. Elshout, and Arie

beneficial. Meta had already discussed this desire with her father on an earlier occasion. He was rather guarded in his response, however, for he knew what it meant to be involved in mission work. As a member of the Mission Committee, he was intimately acquainted with the fact that the proclamation of the gospel among the heathen is a difficult task, and it is often a plowing upon the rocks. At bottom, he did not want to subject his daughter to this task—unless it was the Lord's will that she be engaged in mission work. He also hoped that the Lord would make this matter very clear to her.

～

Hardly anyone noticed it—and yet, something was changing. The attentive church-goer would hear it. Rev. Elshout did not like to become emotional in the pulpit. He strenuously avoided the shedding of tears, for he believed that tears were inappropriate for the pulpit. The Word must have the preeminence, and it must not be inhibited by an excessive display of emotions. Yet he could not control himself as well as he otherwise did, and his emotions manifested themselves more readily. Although he was still able to preach, he was tormented by irrational fears. He could no longer view in proper proportion the stress that he had always been able to process effectively. Molehills became insurmountable mountains.

The pastor was ill, suffering from mental burn-out and all its residual symptoms. It grieved him that his wife, his children, and his congregation had to suffer because of this illness. He viewed himself as a hypocrite and as a dismal failure. He responded differently to things than was customary for him. Sometimes he was irritated, and sometimes he would be angry for no reason at all. His wife no longer recognized him. When visitors entered through the front door, the pastor disappeared through the back door. He could no longer handle even the company of visitors.

His spiritual warfare increased. In his mind, he could already hear his enemies, as well as those who opposed God's work in the congregation, rejoice. There you have it: he is no partaker of God's salvation. He began to understand Elijah, who preferred death over life, and who asked the Lord to take him away. Gradually, these tensions began to overwhelm him.

Then it dawned on Mrs. Elshout what was happening. Her husband was ill and needed to see a doctor.

"Go see a doctor? Of course not, for I am simply over-tired. Some rest will do me good," he responded. Others advised him to leave for a few weeks—perhaps to Florida. Although such advice was well-meant, the ministerial couple did not have the money to "just" travel to Florida. Furthermore, they needed to care for their family. The pastor could not find any rest, and he continued to pace back and forth like a polar bear—doing so over and over again. He was restless and anxious, and no longer able to sleep.

Being at her wits' end, Mrs. Elshout called Rev. C. Harinck, asking him whether he and his wife could come for the weekend, and whether the pastor of Franklin Lakes could talk with her husband. They were lovingly received by the family. His condition did not improve, however.

As a caged animal, Rev. Elshout paced through the house. Sometimes—and occasionally at impossible times—he wanted to speak to his colleague: "Cor, have I preached correctly? Have I not been sharp enough in my preaching? Cor, even though you are now affirming it, yesterday you said it differently. Did you not say that my preaching was deficient? Just tell me honestly!"

Rev. Elshout preferred to go for a walk—at least he called it a walk, for Rev. Harinck was unable to keep up with him. For hours on end, these two would walk and speak together. They would primarily speak about two matters: Rev. Elshout's calling to be a minister and his preaching. On Monday, the ministerial couple departed for Virginia. Perhaps it would do them some good to go away for a few days—to enjoy nature and go for some walks.

Pastor Elshout struggled greatly, and it seemed to him as if death were imminent. There was nothing within but turmoil. He was gripped with a sense of anxiety, fear, uselessness, and worthlessness. Satan was assaulting him, causing him to pray day and night—even though

Rev. C. Harinck, pastor of the Netherlands Reformed Congregation of Franklin Lakes, New Jersey (1971-1974)—For hours he would walk with his brother, Rev. Elshout.

he did not dare to call it prayer. He did not even know how to articulate his needs and concerns. He found no comfort and instruction in the Word of God, and he felt inner rebellion. His childlike faith that he had been able to exercise in such a rich measure was now frequently eluding him. All his spiritual experiences since his eighteenth year were of no benefit to him. Experiences of which he believed that nothing could erase them from his memory were assaulted intensely. He thought within himself, "Everything has been my imagination; otherwise I would never be in this predicament. My faith was nothing but a temporary faith, and all my experiences were only those of a presumptive Christian."

The reflection upon seasons of spiritual prosperity in his life only made his anxiety greater. He became convinced that the words of Hebrews 6:4-6 were also applicable to him: "For it is impossible for those who were once enlightened, and have tasted of the heavenly gift, and were made partakers of the Holy Ghost, and have tasted the good word of God, and the powers of the world to come, if they shall fall away, to renew them again unto repentance." Thoughts were rummaging through his mind, and he reasoned with himself: "But you have not become an apostate, have you? You still pray and are reading your Bible. That may very well be, but my heart has apostatized. I am no longer willing, and there are moments that I am sick of it all. I have sinned the unpardonable sin. It is written in God's Word, 'Whosoever speaketh against the Holy Ghost, it shall not be forgiven him, neither in this world, neither in the world to come'" (Mat. 12:32).

Rev. Elshout was experiencing a deep spiritual crisis. He did not realize, however, that this crisis was not caused by specific sins, but was due to mental and physical burn-out. He descended ever more deeply into his depression. He was despondent, had no energy, and had no interest in doing anything. Indeed, he could not do anything. It seemed as if his will to do anything had been paralyzed.

During the night, he was tormented with dreams. Time and again it seemed as if he were sitting in an automobile that roared down the road at great speed. There were no exits. There were only signs saying, "Dead-end-street," or "Highway will end in a few miles." Anxiously, he stepped on the brake, but the brakes were not working, and the car roared on. He wanted to jump out of the car, but he did not dare to do so. Anxiety was choking him, and there were deep ravines on all sides. He did everything in his power to escape, but he remained behind the wheel as one who was paralyzed. At that moment he awoke. He stepped out of his bed, walked to the sink, and turned on the light. He saw a pair of wild, anxious, and despairing eyes. He thought, "Is that me? Has it come this far with me?"

He staggered as he walked toward the edge of his bed, and then he took his Bible and began to read Psalm 42. Here David speaks of "deep calling unto deep;" David was thus also familiar with this struggle. For a moment, this realization gave some relief. However, immediately the powers of hell took hold of him again, suggesting, "But you are not David. Don't think for a moment that you are a partaker of that salvation." A mental straight-jacket again caused him to be tormented and be in severe bondage.

On another occasion, he read Job 7:13-15: "When I say, My bed shall comfort me, my couch shall ease my complaint; then thou scarest me with dreams, and terrifiest me through visions: so that my soul chooseth strangling, and death rather than my life." Was Job also acquainted with such circumstances as his? That would mean that even people with a tender life of faith, who live godly lives, can come into similar circumstances. But then the thought occurred, "But you are not Job, are you? Do you wish to compare yourself with this righteous man?" He found himself in bondage again. Life had become a burden to him.

Rev. Elshout was overcome with the restlessness that followed each night. He wanted to drive, walk, and thus run away from himself. During the weekends, they would return to Rev. Harinck, and during the week, they would travel through Virginia. After three weeks, they had to return to Kalamazoo. Mrs. Elshout was driving. Holding the steering wheel with one hand, she needed her other hand to keep her husband inside the car, for time and again he wanted to get out to walk home. However, given the distance, that was obviously not an option. Prayerfully, Mrs. Elshout drove onward, making repeated efforts to divert her husband's attention. Finally, they arrived in Grand Rapids at the home of Rev. Lamain.

Using both tact and his persuasive powers, Rev. Lamain convinced his brother in the ministry that he had to see a doctor. Rev. Elshout agreed, and then they made the trip to Pine Rest Hospital in Grand Rapids.

CHAPTER 15

The Long Road to Recovery

R ev. Elshout inspected his nightstand once more to see if anything had been left behind. He then checked the windowsill, the bathroom, and underneath his bed. All his belongings were in his suitcase. He was going home, and his wife was coming to pick him up.

He had been a patient at Pine Rest, a Christian psychiatric hospital located in Grand Rapids, Michigan, for six weeks. During the first days after his arrival, he had done nothing but sleep; his medication resulted in his spirit getting some rest. Consultations with resident physicians had as their objective the correction of his thinking pattern, thereby teaching him to view things again in their correct proportions. His stay at Pine Rest had been to his benefit, although he did recognize that he was far from being well again. Yet he was grateful for the loving care he had received. What a blessing it is that there are people who care deeply about their fellow men and are willing to help! What a blessing it is that medical knowledge can be of such benefit—also for those who are mentally afflicted! Moreover, what a wonder it is when an omnipotent God is pleased to use men and their knowledge by blessing the treatments they are administering!

Christian psychiatric hospital, Pine Rest, in Grand Rapids, Michigan (2008 Picture)

How often he had blamed himself for being anxious and fearful during his illness! He had greatly abhorred himself, blaming himself for the fact that his wife, children, and congregation were so severely impacted by all that had occurred. It was all his fault, and his fault alone! However, the Lord did not abandon him, for He instructed and comforted him by means of Isaiah 53. So often he thought that the Lord did not hear his cries for grace and mercy, thinking that God in wrath had abandoned him. Nevertheless, God had not forsaken him.

When he had one of his bouts of anxiety, he was privileged to read Matthew 26, the account of the suffering of the Lord Jesus in the Garden of Gethsemane. He read and re-read these words, "And he…began to be sorrowful and very heavy" (Mat. 26:37). He who knew no sin was sorrowful and greatly oppressed—so oppressed that His sweat even changed into blood. It flashed through his mind that the book of Hebrews records that Christ "was heard in that he feared" (Heb. 5:7). God's Son, the Sinless One, feared when His impending suffering weighed Him down and when Satan assaulted Him.

There was nothing sinful in that He feared. Instead, His fear proceeded from having a weakened human nature that responded as such due to the extraordinarily heavy burden that weighed Him down. Thus His being fearful and anxious in such difficult circumstances was not something that was worthy of a rebuke or reprimand. Instead, He was being tempted in all things, except for sin. What a lesson, and what an encouragement for all who are anxious and despondent! This lesson shed some light on his own life, giving him some renewed hope. God's grace and goodness were great, and the Lord was leading him—albeit slowly—out of the prison of self-accusation and self-condemnation.

Rev. Elshout thought about his wife and children with warm affection. Every day his wife had sat with him. As soon as the children came home from school, and she had taken care of her daily family affairs, she stepped into the car and drove to Grand Rapids. Every day she would be with him, listen to him, and walk with him. If mutual love between husband and wife was ever evident, it was now. The presence of his beloved Elfriede confirmed for him that she would be faithful unto death. Not only her compassion, but also her common sense and steadfastness were helpful to him.

The children were also very much engaged. Although three of them were residing in Europe, they continually stayed abreast of the situation. The other children adjusted themselves to the new circumstances. By now Nellie was training to be a nurse, Arie and Elfriede attended high school, and John and Chris attended elementary school. Although they sensed the challenges of the situation, they made a united effort to relieve their mother's burden. If at all possible, one or more of the children accompanied her to Grand Rapids. Since the older children already had their driver's license, she did not always have to drive.

Ahead of time, Mother Elshout determined whether it would be beneficial if the children came along. At first, Rev. Elshout preferred that they would not come along. He felt such a sense of shame, even in connection with his children. Gradually this feeling changed, however, and he and the children would be happy to see each other and engage in some casual conversation. Dad was not forgotten in their individual prayers. They were hopeful that the day would come when Dad would join them again, talk and converse with them at the table, help them with their homework, and also play some soccer with them.

Medication, rest, and instruction from both God and men were the means that enabled him to recover from his spiritual and mental exhaustion. Gradually, his depression began to lift, albeit along a trajectory of ups and downs.

As his mental state gradually recovered and was restored, his spiritual life also began to revive. The efficacious impact of the gospel increased and was of longer duration. The subjective experiences of believing, hoping, loving, sincerely grieving over sin, an inner yearning after God, His favor, and His people, accompanied by an active believing in the efficacy of Christ's blood, in the richness of His grace, God's faithfulness in fulfilling His promises, and the desire, strength, and courage to live— all of this, and much more, gradually returned.

Although Rev. Elshout's illness was of a much longer duration, it was only for a two-month period that he was unable to preach. On March 24, 1972, he officiated at a wedding, and on May 28 he again preached once in his own congregation of Kalamazoo—a congregation that expressed a great deal of loving interest and concern. A week later, he preached twice, and thereafter he no longer needed to absent himself. His progress was, however, rather sluggish. His medications had an inhibiting effect on him, and he knew very well that he was not yet free from depression. His despondency, though less intense than it had originally been, would not yield. Often he would feel so useless, so hypocritical, and so much more.

He was greatly assaulted when called upon to administer the Lord's Supper. He considered the option of not partaking of the broken bread and the shed forth wine. Immediately, the enemies within assaulted him. Who could answer his many "why" questions—questions that tormented his weary and fatigued soul? Although he was surrounded with much love and compassion, he often felt lonely and forsaken. Doing his work was very difficult for him. It was a cross for him. Even the least demanding task that he had formerly performed with delight was now a burden to him.

He was very open in his conversations with his family physician, Dr. Richard Lemmer. Rev. Elshout did not hide the inner strife of his soul from him. The doctor listened intently, asked specific questions, and finally said, "I believe that someday you will be a writer. You know what spiritual anxiety is." Rev. Elshout looked at him with disbelief.

Rev. Elshout was greatly encouraged when his former congregation of Utrecht extended a call to him in 1973. He was amazed and speechless. Although its members knew about his condition and his health, the congregation that he had been privileged to serve for six years again desired him as their shepherd and minister. This call was fresh water for his thirsty and yearning soul. Although he had to decline the call, he warmly thanked the congregation of Utrecht for their expressed confidence in him. This experience gave him new courage, and he sensed that God used it to strengthen and sustain him. He also realized, however, that there was a desire in his heart to return to the Netherlands, to his family, to his brothers in the ministry, and to the congregations. Yet he was certain of one thing: the time to return had not yet arrived.

At this time there were also other concerns. Mrs. Elshout had health issues and she needed to undergo surgery. The Elshout couple now understood what was meant by the poet when he exclaimed, "Thou, Lord, hast proved and tested us as silver tried by fire" (Psalter 174:1—Psalm 66). The surgery was successful, but the bill for this procedure was problematic. There was no money to pay the bill. Considerable expense had been incurred as a result of Rev. Elshout's illness, albeit that the deaconry of the Kalamazoo congregation had responded to their need. This concern became a matter of prayer for the ministerial couple, and by renewal the Lord showed that He does not change. As wonderfully as He had helped them in the past, so He would help them today. A letter, accompanied by a check of one thousand dollars, arrived from a friend in the Far West. He expressed his warm greetings and stated that he was certain that the minister would be able to use this money. That was certainly true! Without realizing it, this donor had mailed the exact amount that was needed, for the remaining bills could now be paid.

Slowly but surely, with ups and downs, Rev. Elshout began to regain some of his strength. He again dared to see light at the end of the tunnel, and he again experienced the nearness of God and His invigorating grace. His emotional life began to function again. His anxiety and his

Rev. Elshout rejoiced in the marriage of his son Bart and Joan Sweetman.

lack of self-assurance were gradually diminishing. Contributing factors were events that brought great joy to him, such as the marriage of Bart and Joan Sweetman. They were married on December 27, 1973, in Franklin Lakes, New Jersey, near the city of New York. Being the father of the groom, Rev. Elshout was privileged to officiate at this wedding. According to American law, the minister also functions as a civil servant.

He returned home by plane, and his family traveled by car. Mrs. Elshout was driving, and the children were trying to sleep. After a few hours, one of the boys would take over the wheel. The Interstate ran westward through Pennsylvania to Ohio. From there they would travel in a northwest direction to Michigan. It was cloudy, the temperature was considerably below freezing, and it began to rain lightly.

Within a very short time, the road turned into a skating rink, and Mrs. Elshout had to slow down considerably. As she approached an entrance ramp, another car was merging onto the highway. Due to traffic behind her, Mrs. Elshout could not yield and therefore had to apply the brakes. Immediately, the car began to slip and slide. She could no longer control the vehicle. Finally, after incurring considerable body damage, the car came to a stop against the guardrail. Rudderlessly, an enormous truck came gliding by as a dark shadow, and it appeared that they would be crushed by it. However, the truck barely missed them and slid by. Although everyone was very frightened, their gratitude was even greater. Once more God's care was evident, for no one had been injured. How amazed they were, for even at this perilous moment the family had been protected—as had happened so frequently!

Bart looked at Arie with surprise. His father had received a call from Slikkerveer in the Netherlands. As far as he knew, his father was not exercised with this call. He had no reason to be concerned that the family would return to the Netherlands. He did not even want to entertain such an idea. Not only were there strong bonds of love between all members of the family, but there was also a strong spiritual bond between Bart and his father. Arie said, "You had better not be so sure of yourself, for there is a possibility that Dad will accept this call. At first, the call did not affect him at all, but that has now changed." Arie's assessment was correct.

The congregation of Slikkerveer was not unknown to Rev. Elshout. As a student, he had once preached for this congregation. It had been an unforgettable service, for a woman became ill on her way to church and passed away just outside of the church building. Student Elshout sensed how dismayed everyone was, and he prayerfully ascended the pulpit. He put his sermon notes aside and spoke "a word in due season" for the circumstances of that moment. He sensed that his words were accompanied with divine unction.

But he also clearly remembered that he had preached there as a minister in 1964. The congregation was rife with tension, and it appeared that this tension would culminate in a split. Such a split did not materialize, however, and, humanly speaking, Rev. Elshout's sermon was instrumental in preventing this split. This congregation had obviously not forgotten him, and he appreciated that. More was needed, however, to accept a call. Although he sensed once more a deep longing to return to his native land, he realized that the Lord would have to direct him accordingly. If He would not go before Him, he neither wished nor dared to proceed.

Rev. Elshout sat behind his desk and read the decline letter once more. As was his custom, he had bowed his knees prior to writing the letter, asking the Lord to give him light and wisdom so that he would make the correct decision. Without anything in particular prompting him, his thoughts wandered to the history of Exodus 3 in which Moses was commissioned to visit the Israelites who as slaves lived in bondage in Egypt and were crying out to the Lord. Moses would be instrumental in helping them and in leading them out of Egypt. If they were to ask him who he was, or who had commissioned him to come, he would have to answer, "I AM hath sent me unto you" (Ex. 3:14). With amazement, Rev. Elshout asked himself what this meant for him. He sensed that the Lord was speaking to him. Trusting in the I AM THAT I AM, he consequently felt directed to accept the call.

He walked over to his wife and let her read the letter. She nodded, for if there were nothing else, and therefore not a clear calling, he would indeed have to decline that call. Rev. Elshout stated that there was something else, however, and he expressed his sentiments to his wife. But as he was speaking to her, doubts began to resurface. Was it not all imagination? One can so easily assume things to be true when in reality they are not. He was again gripped by uncertainty, and he requested the congregation of Slikkerveer to grant an extension. He needed more time to arrive at a settled conclusion. This extension period had expired, however, and he had now to make a decision regarding the call extended to him.

The telephone rang, and it turned out that Rev. Mijnders of Ridderkerk was calling him. Rev. Mijnders wanted to know the status of the call that had been extended by his neighboring congregation. He had been exercised with it, and he felt strongly inclined to make this phone call. The two ministers had a lengthy conversation. With a sense of relief, Rev. Elshout concluded the phone conversation, and he decided to accept the call.

Rev. J. Mijnders, the Moderator of the Slikkerveer congregation, had a strong desire to call brother Elshout.

When Elder John Beeke stopped in, he told him that he intended to accept the call extended by Slikkerveer. When Elder Beeke replied, "I already knew this," Rev. Elshout looked at him with surprise. That morning Elder Beeke had laid this call before the Lord in prayer, and he believed—had to believe—that the congregation of Kalamazoo would again become vacant.

Rev. Elshout tried unsuccessfully to make a telephone call to the clerk of Slikkerveer, Elder Den Hartigh, to inform him that he had accepted the call that had been extended to him. He made several attempts but did not get a connection. What he did not know was that Elder Den Hartigh was meeting with the consistory to prayerfully lay this call before the Lord. This call had a different effect on the consistory than previous calls. The consistory observed that the congregation was also being exercised with it. People were talking and praying about it. Elder Den Hartigh had therefore proposed that the consistory convene to petition the Lord regarding this call. There was support for this proposal, and the consistory convened in the consistory room of the church building on Oranjestraat. Earnestly and fervently, they called upon the Lord, and when they concluded their prayer, the members of the consistory knew he would come. That same evening they received the anticipated phone call from America. On the same day, Rev. C. Harinck of Franklin Lakes accepted the call extended to him by Dordrecht.

Bart and Meta had a difficult time accepting the fact that their parents would now depart from America. Bart had married in the meantime, and Meta was scheduled to be married to Tom Moerdyk that week. She still harbored a deep desire to be engaged for the cause of God's kingdom—especially in missionary ministry. Tom had the same desire. They had made known their desire to be engaged in missionary ministry, but the Mission Committee of the Netherlands Reformed Congregations did not yet have a mission field. It was therefore obvious that Tom and Meta would also remain in America.

Nineteen-year-old Arie had to make a decision: accompany the family or remain behind. He chose the first option. The other children also had not been yearning for the family's departure from America, for they enjoyed living in America and had assimilated into American culture. They all realized, however, that the Lord was leading their father in a different direction. They knew how their father and mother had always fully surrendered themselves to the Lord, and how the Lord had often so wonderfully manifested His care for them and their family. No one had any doubt as to whether their father's decision was indeed the correct one. Yet, as obvious as this was to them, it was not an easy way.

Rev. Elshout accepted the call of the Slikkerveer congregation during the week that Meta Elshout and Tom Moerdyk were united in marriage.

Mrs. Elshout had no issues with their return. Although she never discussed it with her husband, it had been her intense desire to return to the Netherlands. Although it would be very difficult for her to leave two of her children in America, in the Netherlands she would again be closer to Frits. Her second son intended to get married to Nellie Buitenhek in July in Scheveningen. The tickets had already been purchased for this event, but they could now be changed from round-trip tickets to one-way tickets.

Frits Elshout and Nellie Buitenhek were
united in marriage in July 1974.
His parents had returned to the Netherlands
just a month prior to that event.

It was not easy to bid farewell to the congregation of Kalamazoo. A bond of love had been forged due to the love and support shown by the congregation, also during troublous times. Rev. Elshout had found a place in the hearts of young and old. His family had become part of the congregation, and his children had established friendships. God's cloudy pillar was removing itself, however, and therefore they had to depart.

On June 28, 1974, Rev. Elshout preached his inaugural sermon in Slikkerveer. The choice of a text was not difficult: "I AM hath sent me unto you" (Ex. 3:14b).

CHAPTER 16

The LORD Made Room

A congregation gathered for worship in the cafeteria of the Electro Smit Company in Slikkerveer the day after Christmas in 1946. Rev. Van de Woestijne, pastor of the (Netherlands) Reformed Congregation of Ridderkerk, stood at the location where during the week laborers would be eating their lunch and enjoying a cup of coffee. He was preaching about the Bread of Life and an opened Fountain for thirsty souls. The turnout was good, for approximately fifty people, seated on folding chairs, were in attendance.

From that day forward, two services were conducted every Lord's Day in this cafeteria for the rental fee of 2.5 guilders per Sunday. To lay the groundwork for the future organization of a congregation, the mother church of Ridderkerk conducted a membership meeting in which J.A. Don and C. Van Noppen were elected as elders, and C. Den Boer and P. van der Linden as deacons.

The attendance continued to increase, and soon the cafeteria was too small. The increased attendance called for a newly constructed building, but the Department of Restoration[24] determined that only a semi-permanent building could be erected. On April 6, 1950, this provisional church building, with a seating capacity of three hundred, was dedicated.

Three years later, the formal organization of the congregation took place in a service conducted by Rev. M. van de Ketterij. From that moment on, there was an autonomous (Netherlands) Reformed Congregation in Slikkerveer.

In 1960, Rev. W.C.J. Bosschaart became the first pastor of the congregation. What a great disappointment it was when in 1963 this minister had to be suspended due to his sinful walk of life! Approximately one half year thereafter, he laid down his office and withdrew himself from the congregation.

The church sanctuary was indeed a provisional structure. Rather quickly, many defects began to emerge that were a direct consequence of cheap construction and the inferior quality of building materials. Already in 1961, architectural drawings had been prepared for a new church build-

---

[24]This department of the Dutch government was established immediately following World War II to facilitate and manage the reconstruction of the war-ravaged country of the Netherlands.

ing. The construction of this building had to wait, however, for priority had to be given to the issues pertaining to their delinquent pastor.

The arrival of Rev. G. Zwerus in 1967 was a matter of great joy for the congregation. It would, however, be a joy of short duration. It was but recently that their pastor had become a widower, and he was not in good health. He passed away only a year-and-a-half after his installation in

Rev. G. Zwerus

Slikkerveer. By this time, the number of members had grown to nearly six-hundred, and plans for the construction of a new building were once again being considered.

When the new Ebenezer Church was dedicated in 1971, it could accommodate six-hundred attendees. A few years later, a new organ was built in the sanctuary by organ builder Leeflang of Apeldoorn. Although to all appearances the congregation was prospering, the absence of a pastor was keenly felt. This need was truly bound upon the hearts of some members of the congregation, and it became a matter of prayer for them.

Thus there was great joy when an affirmative response to their call letter arrived from America. Slikkerveer would again have her own pastor, for the I AM Himself had sent him.

When the call had been extended, the parsonage was still occupied by the A.J. Zwerus[25] family. This family would have to find another home, and that was not easy. Although the date of Rev. Elshout's arrival was approaching, a new home for the Zwerus family had not yet been located. This situation generated some stress, for soon the new minister would arrive, and there would be no home for him and his family.

However, the consistory was very confident, and someone remarked, "Soon the house will be available, and then there will be other reasons preventing the minister from occupying it." And so it was, for when he arrived in Slikkerveer, the container with his household belongings had not yet arrived. The Elshout family temporarily moved into the home of a member of the congregation who had agreed to move in with her daughter.

---

[25]A son of Rev. G. Zwerus

Rev. Elshout's ministry in Slikkerveer was a rich blessing—for the congregation as well as for himself. Christmas of 1974 particularly became unforgettable for him. The initial period of his ministry in Slikkerveer had been rather difficult. This difficulty was precipitated neither by Slikkerveer nor by his wife and five children who were attempting to reintegrate themselves into Dutch society. The Lord was most certainly not to be blamed, for it was Arie Elshout who was again at odds with himself and felt once more that he was declining. There was nothing he could do to halt this decline, for his former depression and anxiety were again manifesting themselves. Had the move and the new environment been too strenuous? Had his decision, in consultation with his family doctor, to radically discontinue the ingestion of all medication not been a wise one? He did not know what to make of it, and once more he felt the oppressive bondage of his depression. Must he again go through such a deep valley? How grievous that would be for him and his family! He was very despondent.

With great interest, his family doctor listened to him, for he wanted to know what precipitated his renewed bout of depression. He proceeded

The new Ebenezer church building was dedicated in 1971.

to formulate his response carefully, saying, "Reverend, depression is precipitated by what still must transpire in redemptive history rather than by what has occurred already."

Rev. Elshout reflected on this remark and realized that he lived too much by what his feelings were telling him. Although he again felt so cold, empty, barren, and lifeless, he must instead live by what is written in God's testimony. He felt ashamed. What a slow learner he was! Why was he inclined time and again to look within where he would never be able to find spiritual security? Again, he was groveling within himself rather than casting the anchor of his hope outside of himself into the anchor ground provided by God in His Son and in His Word.

The advent and Christmas sermons were particularly efficacious for the minister himself. After having preached about the conclusion of Psalm 90, he was privileged to return homeward, having received a blessing for himself. That for which he had prayed so often now became true for him: "Make us glad according to the days wherein thou hast afflicted us, and the years wherein we have seen evil." He perceived that all oppressive and anxious feelings had to yield, and his bondage vanished. He was privileged to breathe in the pure and liberating atmosphere of the gospel. It gave him liberty—the liberty with which the Lord had made him free. The Lord had made room, and he was fully assured that by God's grace he had overcome his depression.

Living again in the Netherlands was a major adjustment for the four youngest members of the family. They had not been in the Netherlands since 1967, and they had truly become young Americans. Since the difference between America and the Netherlands is not one that merely pertains to language and distance, the children found it difficult to connect with their peers. There was such a profound difference regarding the way of life, for everything in the Netherlands was small and cramped. Having already for some years enjoyed driving a large vehicle with an eight-cylinder engine, made a small motorcycle, even with a souped-up engine, seem like a toy. It simply did not compare to a Pontiac or a Plymouth.

In turn, the Elshout children, due to their Yankee manners, caused some young people to raise their eyebrows. The Elshout children were rather forward in expressing their opinion about everything. It appeared that a measure of humility was not something that America had taught them. They experienced real culture shock. Their experience differed significantly from what they had encountered seven years earlier in Artesia. There, everyone had a measure of compassion with these brand-new Dutchmen who, after all, were unacquainted with America. However, there was no such compassion in 1974. After all, were they not Dutchmen who had returned to their own country? It was therefore expected that they would again behave themselves like Dutch people.

Upon her return to the Netherlands, Elfriede pursued training to become a home care nurse in Bergen op Zoom. However, this also meant that she had to reside in the dorms of the training institute, the *Besselhof*. Thus she experienced a double change. She would spend her weekends at home where some adjustments had to be made to provide everyone with a suitable place to sleep. The garage was remodeled to be the pastor's study, and this arrangement enabled the family to use all the bedrooms.

Nellie and Arie, who were twenty and nineteen years old respectively, found themselves to be in a predicament. Both really felt at home in America. Nellie had her diploma as a registered nurse, and she had a responsible job in a Kalamazoo hospital. Arie had already completed the first year of his training to become an accountant. They quickly realized, however, that their certificates and training would not be recognized in the Netherlands. For a long time, they vacillated but finally decided that they would accompany the family rather than remain behind and be alone in Kalamazoo. They first wanted to see what staying in the Netherlands would turn out to be. Returning to America could always be an option. Although the differences between life in America and the Netherlands were significant, both Nellie and Arie adjusted fairly well.

Quietly Hans went his way. You cannot tell a book by its cover, however. Dad Elshout knew that returning to the Netherlands had been very difficult for his son. He reflected on what had transpired earlier, and he smiled. June 9, 1967, the day they travelled from Braunschweig to Bremerhaven, and then to Rotterdam, was also Hans's birthday—a fact that went unnoticed by everyone. The next day his birthday was celebrated on the boat.

Although Hans had really enjoyed living in America, he changed his name to "John." "Hans" was an unknown name, causing him to be nicknamed "Hunts Ketchup." This obviously resulted in his name being made fun of, and thus it was changed into "John." John had one bosom friend, Jim VanGiessen,[26] and they were two peas in a pod. Other than that, John always went his own way—quietly and unpretentiously.

It was painful for Rev. Elshout to reflect on the time period when he had been admitted to Pine Rest. This time had been very difficult, particularly for John. He was around fifteen years of age and very much needed a father. Fortunately, he found a second home with the Johnsons, the assistant custodian and his wife. Rev. Elshout could never be grateful enough for their assistance during this period. Upon his return to the Netherlands, Hans quietly and independently went his way. Circumstances

---

[26]After Hans returned to the Netherlands, Jim tragically drowned in Lake Michigan. His remains have never been found.

had compelled him to grow up prematurely. There was no doubt in the pastor's mind: Hans would return to America.

The transition to the Netherlands also was very difficult for Chris, the youngest member of the family. He had lived half of his life in America and considered himself to be an American. He hardly had any knowledge of the Dutch language. In America, he had received very good grades, and that meant that he should be enrolled in an academically oriented high school. His deficient knowledge of the language proved to be detrimental, however.

He also had difficulty coming to grips with the cultural transition. An anti-American mindset prevailed in the Netherlands. The Watergate scandal was reaching a climax, and President Nixon was abhorred by many in Western Europe. In addition, teachers of the Reformed Christian High School could not refrain from expressing their aversion for America.

This sentiment did not make any sense to Chris. What was wrong with America? He had very good memories about this country and its population. He had no desire to leave a country he loved but had been compelled to leave. He was torn between the spaciousness of America and the oppressive confinement here in the Netherlands. Having enjoyed a delightful sense of freedom, he now lived on a street and in a home where you could hear the conversation of your neighbors. Playing baseball and basketball outside was no longer possible, and tinkering with cars was impossible. People would talk about it.

In fact, what was, and what was not permitted? In America, you could not ride your bike to church, for that would surely be deemed controversial. Riding your bike on Sunday would be viewed as engaging in sport, and that would be unthinkable. The Boonzaayer family, however, were not of that opinion. They had come to America quite recently, and on Sunday they all came to church on their bikes. Yet, in the Netherlands you were not permitted to come to church by car; therefore, you had to come by bike—or better yet, you should walk to church. Chris could not reconcile these things.

When things did not work out for Chris in school, his father and mother decided to send him to a technical high school in Rotterdam. The practical training provided there was his cup of tea. However, his "American" conduct frequently precipitated friction with school management.

Chris arrived home with drooping shoulders, for he had again been expelled from school. After hearing his story, his father responded resolutely and said, "Get in the car, Chris. We have to talk about this."

Chris did not have high hopes, for it was not easy to deal with the principal, Mr. Groenendijk. Chris had to wait in the hallway, while his dad entered Mr. Groenendijk's office. He remained there for quite a long time, and Chris concluded that Mr. Groenendijk obviously would not budge. Finally, when Chris had given up all hope, the door opened. He was completely puzzled, for his father and Mr. Groenendijk were laughing loudly as they exited. Tears were running down their cheeks. His father said, "Well, I wish you the best, and we will just forget the idea of expelling him."

Mr. Groenendijk waved and said, "Of course, and we will talk again in the future."

Chris could hardly contain his curiosity. In the car, he exploded. What happened? How was this possible? What exactly had his father said? His father responded by saying, "Actually, I did not say anything, for when I saw Mr. Groenendijk, I immediately recognized him as one of my former pals. We both were not exactly what you would call sweet little boys. Together, we were responsible for quite a few pranks, and that's what we talked about."

Chris looked at his dad proudly. His dad! As was true in America, you could also really count on him here. When he played a baseball game there, his father had come to watch him even though he was not really in favor of his playing. Thus Chris knew with certainty that his father remained *his* dad.

Many in the congregation of Slikkerveer exerted themselves to integrate this immigrant family into their midst. The Youth Group made a genuine effort to reach out to the children, and the ready accessibility of the parsonage resulted in healthy interaction with the families of the Slikkerveer congregation. Things went so well that before long Elfriede was dating Henk Huijser, and Arie was dating Marjan den Hartigh.

Slikkerveer yielded its own surprises: after three months, Arie was courting Marjan den Hartigh…

… and a few months later, Elfriede and Henk Huijser became a couple.

Nellie sought to find a suitable work environment. Although her American diploma was not recognized in the Netherlands, she succeeded in acquiring a Dutch diploma by completing a two-year nursing program.

The continuation of a college education proved to be no option for Arie since the educational systems of America and the Netherlands did not dovetail at all. A return to school would mean that he would have to enroll in high school again. Due to the mediation of a deacon of the local congregation, he was employed by a small accounting firm in Dordrecht. His evening hours were devoted to study required for securing his Dutch professional diplomas. Arie had to swallow hard, for instead of being a second-year college student, he was now the freshman employee at an accounting firm. During the evening hours, he was enrolled in a course to learn the basics of accounting.

After a year, another surprise awaited him. Arie was notified that he was required to serve in the Dutch army. Bart, the oldest of the children, had not yet served in the army in 1967, and he had remained in America. The so-called "brother clause" was therefore not applicable to Arie, and he had to transition from his office to the army barracks. After fourteen months, Arie could resume his work for the accounting firm in Dordrecht. However, his employment there did not last long. Although he really enjoyed his work as an accountant, he could not ignore the following advertisement: "The Mission Committee of the (Netherlands) Reformed

Elfriede and Henk were privileged to receive their fourth child, Nelleke. The other children are Arie, Peter, and Elfriede.

Congregations is looking for an administrator who has an affinity for mission work and is conversant with the English language." Wasn't this another piece of the puzzle for him? Although the ways of the Lord are truly past finding out, He has a purpose in all that transpires in our lives. Arie was hired, and six weeks subsequent to his marriage to Marjan den Hartigh, he was employed by the Mission Committee of the (Netherlands) Reformed Congregations.

~

During the summer of 1975, Dad and Mom Elshout again embraced their son Bart and his wife Joan—and not only them, but also little David, their first grandchild. When Rev. Elshout held the little fellow in his arms, he became emotional. Once more the Lord had been faithful to His Word. His mind wandered to the time when he, as a young man, was unsure whether the Lord would be pleased to bless him and his wife with children. He then couldn't help but think that he would not become old. In the presence of his wife, he had repeatedly brought these matters before the Lord in prayer. The Lord answered him with Psalm 128:5-6: "The LORD shall bless thee out of Zion: and thou shalt see the good of Jerusalem all the days of thy life. Yea, thou shalt see thy children's children."

That moment had now arrived, for he held the child of his child in his arms. He was oblivious to the thousands of passengers that surrounded him. He looked at little David, and a prayer ascended from his heart that the Lord would care for his children and grandchildren as He had cared for him—that He would glorify His grace from generation to generation. The Lord had said in His Word, "I will...be a God unto thee, and to thy seed after thee" (Gen. 17:7).

~

The words of his family doctor that the day would arrive that Rev. Elshout would be a writer proved to be true. Upon a request from the editor of *De Saambinder*, he wrote a series of articles about pastoral care for people who are afflicted and/or terminally ill. His own experiences proved to be of inestimable value in addressing this subject. He knew how people can feel, and how reticent people can be to being encouraged when they are discouraged. He perceived clearly that spiritual and mental problems can readily be intertwined and consequently cause a great deal of inner confusion. The tone of Rev. Elshout's articles was also fitting: not patronizing, not condescending, and certainly not pedantic. On the contrary, he knew how to come alongside those who were ill and show them pastoral compassion.

The reaction to his articles was overwhelming. Not only did they generate a steady stream of thank-you letters, but Rev. Elshout also received a large number of letters from people who were distressed, and who opened their hearts to him. Thus, in addition to his labors in the congregation, he was now also engaged in an invisible pastorate. He would refer people to professionals when necessary, however. He often groaned within the quietness and solitude of his study, for a staggering measure of suffering and concerns were confidentially communicated to him. Once more he recognized that sin and its consequences did not bypass the (Netherlands) Reformed Congregations. The devil knows how to ensnare even the Reformed community in all that is to be encountered in the world, and the consequences can be far-reaching. These pastoral labors yielded much information and provided much food for thought.

Rev. Elshout decided to use his series of articles as the basis for a book. Upon completing the book *A Helping Hand*, he besought the Lord to bless it, and to use it to help people in mental distress—to guide them toward counselors and to the mighty God Himself. In so doing, he reflected with amazement upon the words of Paul: "Blessed be God, even the Father of our Lord Jesus Christ, the Father of mercies, and the God of all comfort; who comforteth us in all our tribulation, that we may be able to comfort them which are in any trouble, by the comfort wherewith we ourselves are comforted of God" (2 Cor. 1:3-4).

Not long thereafter, two other books were published: *This Do in Remembrance of Me*, a book addressing the Lord's Supper, and *Once More a Helping Hand*.[27] Again, the reactions were positive. Many people could identify with the content of these books. To Rev. Elshout's surprise, they were strengthened by them. He considered himself to be but a small helping hand in the large hand of the great Helper in need—an insignificant comforter of the feebleminded in the service of the great Comforter, a feeble soldier under the command of the great Warrior. The mighty Captain Jesus assisted him.

There was a growing awareness within the (Netherlands) Reformed Congregations of the prevalence and reality of mental suffering. The General Synod decided to constitute a special committee to address this concern, first under the umbrella of the Committee for Families and the Elderly, and later of the Committee for Diaconal Matters. As chairman of this committee, Rev. Elshout wrote additional articles for *De Saambinder* about pastoral care for people who are suffering and/or dying. This was helpful in removing the stigma attached to this subject.

It became increasingly evident to Rev. Elshout that there was a need for the type of mental health care provided by Pine Rest in America.

---

[27]The English title of the third book, *Once More a Helping Hand* is *Overcoming Spiritual Depression.* These titles have been published by Reformation Heritage Books.

The initial publication:
A Helping Hand

The sequel: *Once More a Helping Hand*
(published in English as *Overcoming Spiritual Depression*)

Although such care was not available in the Netherlands, there was an urgent need for it.

Rev. Elshout gladly agreed to serve as chairman of the Commission for Youth Ministries of the (Netherlands) Reformed Congregations. His heart was knit to young people, and he was very supportive of youth ministries. He reflected on the fact that he had not always had such an evident affinity for youth ministry. Prior to the Lord's gracious dealings with him, he had not been associated with any youth society. The only society that mattered to him had been the local soccer club.

After the Lord had dealt with him in mercy, he became too "pious" for youth work. Although he had never visited a session of such youth societies, he neither liked what he heard about them, nor did they in any way appeal to him. He would rather visit with older, God-fearing people or study the Bible at home in the solitude of his room. He was convinced that such societies were made up of "know-it-alls"—or, at least, that they would foster such an attitude.

However, when young Arie Elshout became a seminary student at the Theological School of the (Netherlands) Reformed Congregations, he recognized that he could no longer avoid dealing with youth ministry. He was inclined to dispense with this matter once and for all. On a Sunday afternoon, he sat down to write down all arguments against youth ministry. He wrote down all the dangers as he saw them: a know-it-all attitude, erroneous influences, the fostering of a presumptive faith, and so forth. He then proceeded to write down all the arguments in favor of youth ministry. That was easier than he had anticipated. In contrast to all his objections, there were also many positive matters. Involvement in youth ministry can be very educational, and it also can offer support to young people in an increasingly challenging environment for church members. By meeting each other, young people can interact regarding their experiences, and encounters can also take place that, with the Lord's blessing, could culminate in a Christian marriage. When this began to dawn on Student Elshout, he became deeply ashamed, and he promised the Lord that he would be supportive of ecclesiastical youth ministry.

The history of Peter's being unwilling to go to the Gentiles repeated itself. The very next day two young men rang his door bell. One of them, Chris van der Poel,[28] was the spokesman. Both of them were members of the executive committee of the Youth Society, and on behalf of this committee they asked Seminary Student Elshout whether he would be willing to become the chairman of the Youth Society in the (Netherlands) Reformed Congregation of Rotterdam-South.

When serving his first congregation in Utrecht, it did not take long before he was asked to chair the National Federation of Boys' Clubs. Although it meant a great deal of additional work for him, it was not a burden. It was his delight to be as much among the young people as possible, and the young people were delighted when he was among them. During the summer months, he would visit various youth camps—a new initiative of the Committee for Youth Ministries that generated some controversy. In inclement weather, the young people would gather inside with Rev. Elshout. He would then talk about a variety of things he had experienced in his life. He had the gift of using examples from everyday life to illustrate spiritual truths. In favorable weather, he would play soccer with the young people who were amazed at the minister's skill, the force with which he would kick the ball, and the precision with which he scored—until photographs began to circulate, and he was accused at ecclesiastical gatherings of denigrating his office.

Upon his departure from the Netherlands in 1967, the Committee for Youth Ministries gave him an honorary membership—a gesture he valued. The young people were bound upon his heart, and he upon theirs.

---

[28] As Rev. Chris vander Poel (1932–2016), he would serve the (Netherlands) Reformed Congregations from 1965–2001. He was the pastor of the congregation of Yerseke (Zeeland, the Netherlands) for this entire period.

Having now returned from America, it did not take long for this committee to contact him again. First, he became the chairman of the 16+
division (1976–1981), and in 1978 he became chairman of the full Committee for Youth Ministries. He and his wife together would be in charge of
many summer camps and youth weekends—until he noticed that he was
advancing in age. The time had come for a younger chairman, who, in turn,
would have more affinity with the young people. In 1992, Rev. J. Driessen
assumed the chairmanship of the Committee for Youth Ministries.

In Slikkerveer, Rev. Elshout's preaching did not differ from what he had
preached in the other congregations he had served. It was plain, trans-
parent, and scriptural. His sermons gave evidence that he was well-read.
He had fully assimilated the forefathers.

Everyone has his favorite psalms. Psalter 290:4, 5 (Psalm 106:3) were
Rev. Elshout's favorite stanzas:

> *O Lord, remember me in grace,*
> *Let me salvation see;*
> *The grace Thou showest to Thy saints,*
> *That grace reveal to me.*

> *Let me behold Thy people's good*
> *And in their joy rejoice;*
> *With Thy triumphant heritage*
> *Let me lift up my voice.*

He would frequently quote it from the pulpit, and he would often ask
the congregation to sing these verses.

He rejoiced when he noticed that the members of his congregation
evaluated his sermons in light of the Word of God, the confessions, and
the old writers. He even encouraged this evaluation, and he would point
to the Christians in Berea who did likewise. Rev. Elshout knew that he
was not a polished orator. However, in all simplicity, he sought to recom-
mend the service of the Lord. He would speak without an avalanche of
words and with clarity, keeping in mind even the beginners in grace. In
addition, he also sought to minister to people with mental afflictions.

Upon the advice of his doctor, Rev. Elshout walked frequently, and he
did not consider it a waste of time. He paid close attention to what he
saw and heard, and many of the common things of daily life would yield
spiritual lessons. The congregation often knew when the minister had
been for a walk. On one occasion, he saw some goats grazing on a dike.
The one had a long leash, and the other one a short one. From his study
he could observe a bird's nest in a hedge. The one bird opened its mouth

more widely, and therefore received more food. He also observed how stubborn sheep could be. He would then subsequently instruct God's children by way of such examples.

Rev. Elshout strongly opposed the drinking of alcohol and smoking. He made no effort to hide his aversion for these vices. When expounding the Ten Commandments in his catechism sermons, he would address these matters with unmistakable clarity. One of his sermons became known as the "tobacco sermon."

When visiting a birthday party, Rev. Elshout observed how some of the guests declined to avail themselves of all the delicacies. He then said, "This reminds me of what happens on Sunday, for then there are also many people who decline to partake of that which is good."

In the backyard of the Slikkerveer parsonage at the occasion of the
35th wedding anniversary of Rev. And Mrs. Elshout (1980)

When a truck driver asked him for directions, Rev. Elshout obliged by riding along to show him the way. However, he simultaneously evangelized the driver by starting a conversation with him, saying, "Look, that is also my work on Sunday. Then I try to show people the way to Christ."

Sometimes a minister is also in a hurry, and when Rev. Elshout ignored the directions of a crossing guard, whose job it was to help school children cross the street safely, the boy said, "Sir, I do not stand here for nothing!"

Rev. Elshout stopped, returned, and allowed himself to be guided by the crossing guard. This was a good lesson for him, and he incorporated it into his sermon on Sunday.

Rev. Elshout was not interested in outward show. He would say, "Just act in a normal manner. All the things we have are but gracious gifts." He would also practice what he preached, sometimes in an unsettling way. Once, when returning from Izi, he came walking from the plane in Schiphol with bright yellow slippers on his feet. He had given his shoes away to a Nigerian who could put them to good use. This certainly would not have happened if Mrs. Elshout had accompanied him on this journey. She would by no means have begrudged any Nigerian a pair of shoes, but there are limits to what may be done.

As his spouse, she kept an eye on him. When on a Sunday morning, Rev. Elshout discovered that he had forgotten part of his false teeth, he wanted to continue walking to church. What difference would it make? He did not think it was necessary to go back home to retrieve them. Fortunately, his wife thought otherwise!

Rev. Elshout was very busy, and his calendar was filled. In order to be available to everyone, he decided to implement a visitation hour. He informed the members of his congregation that on every Saturday morning, anyone would be welcome between 9:00 and 10:00 AM. At 9:00 AM someone knocked at his door.

Upon saying, "Come on in," his own wife walked in and asked whether the minister would also have some time for her. Not long thereafter, however, he discontinued the practice of having such a visitation hour. It was not a suitable way to engage in pastoral work in the congregation.

CHAPTER 17

The Spirit's Work Encompasess
All Kindred and Nations

Tom and Meta Moerdyk had been waiting for quite some time. The
Mission Committee of the Netherlands Reformed Congregations in
North America had accepted them as mission workers, and they were to
be sent to the mission field. This event would be the fulfillment of their
heartfelt desire. Meta always had this goal in mind as she pursued professional training—first as a nurse, then as a mid-wife, and eventually
her training for employment in the tropics. Having secured a degree in
tropical agriculture, Tom was also able to make a major contribution.
Following his return from Vietnam, he pursued this degree at Michigan
State University in Lansing. Employment on the mission field was his

In 1966, Rev. A. Elshout and Rev. H. Rijksen, as members of the Dutch Mission Board,
paid their first formal visit to Nigeria. On this occasion, the Bethesda Hospital
in Ikachi was dedicated.

ultimate objective. Rev. Elshout rejoiced in this prospect, for he saw in his children a reflection of his love for mission work.

Long before this moment, Rev. Elshout already had an interest in the proclamation of God's Word to people who never had heard the gospel. He had been a minister only a few years when he was appointed to serve on the Synodical Committee for Foreign Missions in 1959. It was a time when much was at stake for denominational mission work. Gerrit Kuijt had been accepted by the denomination for training as a missionary minister, and a mission field had to be selected. Rev. H. Rijksen, the chairman of the Mission Committee, approached the selection process rather theoretically; therefore, he tended to forget practical consequences.

Rev. A. Vergunst, the secretary of the Mission Committee, changed his mind rather frequently. One week he was convinced that Africa should be selected, and a week later he would be equally certain that they were being led to South America. In the end, Papua, New Guinea, was selected.

In 1966, Rev. Elshout, accompanied by committee chairman Rev. H. Rijksen, traveled to Nigeria, where the Mission Committee co-labored with the Methodist Church in the Igede region. It was the first time in the existence of the Mission Committee that such a formal visit had been undertaken. As members of the committee, both men were called upon to ascertain the progress of this missionary endeavor, as well as to inquire about the well-being of the Mission workers. The local Bethesda Clinic would also be formally dedicated. This event transpired in typical Nigerian fashion—an elaborate ceremony, consisting of many speeches and, of course, a meal. When one of the mission workers took Rev. Elshout to the Anyim River, separating the Igede and Izi regions, he was hopeful that God's Word would also be proclaimed and bear fruit on the other side of the river, and that Igede would serve as a launching pad from which God's Word would be proclaimed beyond this region.

His departure to America also meant that Rev. Elshout resigned as a member of the Mission Committee. He was subsequently appointed to serve on the American

Upon his departure to America, Rev. Elshout vacated his position on the Mission Board. At the annual Mission Day, all the attendees sang a psalm (121) whereby they wished him God's blessing.

Mission Committee, however. As clerk of the latter committee, he maintained contact with the Dutch Mission Committee, and it was mutually agreed that Tom and Meta would be given on loan to the Dutch Mission Committee. They would be sent to Nigeria.

Meta viewed this as an affirmation of her calling to this wonderful work. While attending high school in California, a missionary, Rev. Smith, gave a presentation about Nigeria that kindled her love for this nation. He had labored there for twenty years without observing any fruit upon his preaching. Thereafter, however, he was privileged to gather in a significant harvest. Rev. Smith had even written a book entitled *The Nigerian Harvest* as an account of that which had transpired. Meta listened to this man intently, and for the first time a prayer ascended from her heart that the Lord would also use her in His service on the mission field.

Tom and Meta Moerdyk in Izi, Nigeria, with their children Eric, Paula, and Mark

When she subsequently discussed this desire with her father, he did not show much enthusiasm for this idea. On the contrary, Meta felt that he really put a damper on it. Only later, instructed by the Holy Spirit, would she understand that her dad was not (yet) ready to have his daughter engaged in this work. He knew how difficult and challenging mission work could be—how much patience, perseverance, dedication, and self-sacrifice were required. However, the seed had been sown in Meta's heart, and it germinated and began to grow. Being engaged to Tom Moerdyk only strengthened this desire, for she had no other desire but to follow the Lord and to serve in His kingdom. Tom and Meta became the first missionary couple of the American churches. They would need to wait two years before a visa would be granted and before they could actually depart for Nigeria. Working with the Dutch mission team that had already labored for some time in Nigeria, they began to engage in missionary work in Izi, located on the other side of the Anyim River.

~

Rev. Elshout read and reread the letter. The date was correct, and it also began with "Esteemed Brother Elshout." However, the letter as such seemed peculiar to him. Was he not the pastor of Slikkerveer? In this letter, the Mission Committee asked him whether he, contingent upon ecclesiastical approval, would be willing to labor in Nigeria.

Although Student C. Sonnevelt was preparing to become a missionary minister, he had by no means completed his training. The mission team in Nigeria needed pastoral care, and there was also much work to be done for the church in Izi. Mr. J. Commelin, the missionary who had pioneered the work there, had to return to the Netherlands due to family circumstances.

A period of eighteen months would have to be bridged, and the Mission Committee wrote in the letter that it was aware of Rev. Elshout's love for mission work. Furthermore, he also was conversant with the English language and would therefore be able to serve in Nigeria. Although the Mission Committee never before had made such an appeal to anyone, the situation was urgent.

Rev. Elshout was amazed, for a love for mission work had always lived in his heart. Although he was able to contribute in a meaningful way as a member of the Mission Committees in both the Netherlands and North America, he had not entertained the idea that he himself would be commissioned, for that seemed unrealistic to him. During his vacation, he had read the book of Marshall Broomhall about Hudson Taylor, and it rekindled within him a yearning to be engaged in mission work. Would the Lord have used the reading of this book to prepare him for this request from the Mission Committee? In his heart, Rev. Elshout was prepared to travel to Nigeria with his wife and his youngest son, Chris.

However, his consistory was not quite prepared to acquiesce in this undertaking. Was it truly necessary? Couldn't their pastor do much good work in Slikkerveer? What would happen to the congregation if their pastor were to be absent for more than a year? Rev. Elshout then proposed to his consistory that pulpit supply be provided by guest ministers for all the services that he would normally have conducted. Finally, after careful consideration, the consistory agreed that permission would be granted if the congregation would also support this proposal.

A letter was sent to all congregations and to all active ministers with the request that one Sunday would be designated for Slikkerveer in addition to the regular twelve "free" Sundays. Arrangements were made for exactly all forty Sundays. The membership also endorsed the temporary leave of absence of their pastor.

During the weeks of preparation, Rev. Elshout frequently visited the Mission Office. One morning he met his brother and former fellow student, Rev. A.F. Honkoop, who lived in the parsonage adjacent to the Mission Office. Naturally, the conversation gravitated towards Rev. Elshout's anticipated journey to Nigeria. The fact that he would reside there for several months was no small matter. Although Rev. Honkoop was very supportive, he said to his brother, "Quite an undertaking, Arie! You are quite courageous!"

Rev. Elshout responded immediately by saying, "Adrie, I do not know if I am all that courageous. But do you know what I dare not do? Be disobedient! This task has been bound upon my heart, and I have already had to learn the hard way what the consequences of disobedience are." Both brothers were in full agreement.

Between the medical clinic and the Anyim River stood a small home. It was small even by Nigerian standards, and it was in great need of repair. Its location was a bit out of the way and in close proximity to the river. The walls should have been plastered white, the garden and surrounding area were dried out, and everything was quickly covered with red dust. All one could find around the house were those trees and shrubs that could withstand the hot and dry climate—thus, it did not amount to much.

The baptismal font was a stainless steel bowl. That was no impediment, however, for the administration of Holy Baptism to little Mark Moerdyk, Tom & Meta's youngest child.

The Anyim River—the boundary between the Igede and Izi regions

Mr. Commelin, the missionary, had already crossed the Anyim River a few years earlier to establish initial contacts with the Izis. A large round hut functioned as the medical center, even though referring to it as such was a bit of a stretch. Mr. Commelin, a missionary in both word and deed, built a home there, and it had subsequently even been enlarged—large enough for Rev. Elshout, his wife, and Chris.

The mission team in Izi was growing. In addition to Mr. Commelin and his wife, as well as Tom and Meta Moerdyk, Dr. Scheer and his wife Ria, and Celia Renes, were members of the team. A few months earlier, Hielke Visser and his family had joined them as well. The first spiritual fruits of their ministry among the Izi population were becoming visible. Rev. Elshout was amazed when he heard the testimonies of a population that had been exposed to the ministry of the gospel for only such a short period of time. Of course, not everything was as it appeared to be, for there was also much opposition, apostasy, and the existence of a "bread" Christianity (i.e., following Christ for temporal gain). However, this could not cancel out the work of the Spirit. The celebration of the Lord's Supper was a high point for Rev. Elshout—not only because Tom and Meta were seated at the Lord's Table, but especially because it affirmed that the Spirit's work encompasses all kindred and nations.

Rev. Elshout earned the trust of the team and the population. Even though Tom Moerdyk was officially the team leader, Rev. Elshout lovingly gave direction to the ministry. Tom not only relied upon him as his father-in-law but also as his spiritual father. His life had been radically changed under his preaching in Kalamazoo. When the Elshout family moved to Kalamazoo, Tom had just returned from his engagement in the Vietnam War. Having been assigned to be a supply clerk, he had never been called upon to fight on the frontlines. For years Tom had been employed in the construction company of his grandfather, Thomas Moerdyk, Sr. His employment enabled him to finance his pursuit of a degree in agriculture. It also enabled him to assist with the construction of the new parsonage in Kalamazoo.

Meta was not the first member of the family whom he befriended, for he had also been close to Bart and Frits for some time already. Particularly among the young people, the preaching of Rev. Elshout fell as seed in well-prepared soil. Among them was a group of friends who read spiritual books and dialogued about them. Rev. Elshout answered their questions—also Tom's questions. It was therefore not surprising that a bond developed between him and his pastor—a bond that came to good stead here on the mission field.

Rev. Elshout captured the hearts of the Izi people by, among other things, always showing genuine interest in the details of their lives.

Rev. Elshout preached every Lord's Day in Izi. Some churches had already been established, and he would often visit preaching stations in the bush. Frequently, the gospel was being preached to sinners beneath nothing more than a lean-to. Rev. Elshout knew how to reach the hearts of the Izi population by his down-to-earth preaching, in which he even posed questions to his audience. For example, he did so when he spoke of Saul who repeatedly attempted to kill David, fearing that he would replace him. When David had the opportunity to kill Saul, he refused to do so.

Rev. Elshout then asked the village chief whether he would have done likewise. He responded, "I would have let him go the first time, but the second time I would have killed him."

Everyone in the audience reacted by laughing and agreeing with him. This occasion afforded Rev. Elshout the opportunity of explaining that the Lord has different standards, and that David demonstrated that he feared the Lord when he did not kill Saul.

Using such practical applications, he would bind the Word of God upon their consciences. In addition, his instruction in the Bible School was practical and simple, and he used many examples from daily life. Although he could heartily laugh with the people of Izi, he was also very compassionate toward them in circumstances of grief and sorrow. He was and remained himself in all circumstances, and he was first and foremost a Christian. Everyone heard that—but, above all, they could observe it.

After the Elshout family returned to the Netherlands in December, Rev. Elshout returned to Izi by himself and resided with Tom and Meta. After three months, Mrs. Elshout joined him again for a quarter of a year. During the final quarter of that same year, he again labored by himself due to the fact that his wife remained in Slikkerveer.

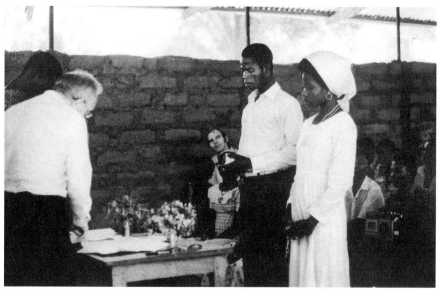

Rev. Elshout had just confirmed the marriage of Moses and Martina Ewogu.
Later, Moses would also be ordained as a minister of the gospel.

As a fruit of their conversion to Christianity, the people of Izi asked Rev. Elshout whether he would also sanction their marriages ecclesiastically. He did not object to that at all, and it would frequently happen during the Sunday worship service that a couple promised in his presence that they would be faithful to each other and to the Lord. This was a milestone in a culture that really had no issue with polygamy and adultery.

An even more remarkable event occurred when two people suffering from epilepsy stood before him. The woman was in the final stage of her pregnancy. In Izi, epilepsy was considered a curse—similar to leprosy among many nationalities. This occasion afforded Rev. Elshout the opportunity of emphasizing in his sermon that the Lord also has compassion on castaways. When vows had to be exchanged, the man responded with an emphatic "yes." However, when the woman was asked whether she would take this man to be her husband, she responded just as emphatically by saying, "No."

Briefly, Rev. Elshout remained silent, not knowing what he should do, for he had never experienced anything like this before. Then he smiled and began to ask the woman some questions. She did not quite know how to explain herself, but finally she said that her husband did not provide her with proper clothing. Rev. Elshout then used the opportunity to explain that our external appearance is not the main issue. The state of our heart is of primary importance. He used such occasions to articulate and apply the gospel. The marriage was confirmed, and the baby was born that night.

There was joy in 1980 when the Bible School students received their diploma.

In the same boat: Babysitting

Rev. Elshout felt compassion for the people who were sitting in the rear of the church. There was a designated bench for all who were subject to church discipline—for instance, for adultery. It was the so-called backseat or the sinner's bench. After having sat there for a period of time, and having shown evidence of sorrow and contrition, a person would then be permitted to make confession of guilt. The church of Izi deemed this procedure very important for the education and training her members.

Rev. Elshout found it difficult to accept this practice. Are we not all sinners, and does such a practice have any educational value? Although the Nigerian church had at one point dispensed with the backseat, the "western" implementation of church discipline did not appeal to the population. It was not even recognized as an exercise of discipline, and the church therefore reinstated the backseat. This event taught Rev. Elshout to respect the local culture. Once he understood that, he invested much time, however, in training office-bearers to make clear to them that church discipline is medicinal rather than punitive.

Another problem manifested itself. In Nigeria, it was common for men to have several wives. Should such polygamous men become believers, however, may they then be baptized, given the fact that polygamy is contrary to God's Word? Should such men then be required to dismiss their wives? This dismissal would precipitate serious problems and would almost compel such women to become prostitutes. This situation could not possibly be condoned. Furthermore, such men had been lawfully married to their wives prior to their conversion. This realization compelled the mission team to advise the Nigerian church to baptize such men.

However, the Nigerian Reformed Church decided not to baptize such men, for polygamy is sinful. As understandable as such a decision was, it also created a problem. The older men in particular had lived polygamous lives, which would prevent them from being baptized and from becoming professing members of the church. Since, however, the growing majority of baptized and confessing members were young people, their view prevailed in the church. However, beyond the boundaries of the church, the older men were still the ones who called the shots in their community. Rev. Elshout also supported the idea that polygamists who had become believers should indeed be baptized. Although he observed these developments with concern, he nevertheless decided to acquiesce in the decision of the Nigerian Reformed Church (NRC).

Church services were held in simple, yet solidly constructed church buildings. The Word is being proclaimed here.

CHAPTER 18

Covenant Faithfulness Toward Zoetermeer

"Come, hear, all ye that fear the Lord, while I with grateful heart record what God has done for me" (Psalter 175:3—Psalm 66). The robust singing of this psalm, as it were, enveloped the pulpit. Rev. Elshout felt himself to be so small, yet so richly blessed. Today he was privileged to commemorate his twenty-fifth ministerial anniversary. The Lord had cared for and sustained him during that entire period! How manifold had his labors been in the service of God's kingdom! He had been privileged to proclaim God's Word in Europe, Africa, America, and Australia. God is a God, even of the ends of the earth. Would there be anyone who was more conscious of this truth than he? He was back in Slikkerveer for a brief period, and soon he would return to Izi. God's Word was also present there—even literally. The New Testament had been translated and printed in the Izi language. Funds were needed for the dissemination of God's Word in Izi; therefore, rather than receiving presents, Rev. Elshout requested that all gifts be designated for the "Elshout Fund."

The little church in Agbaja (Izi)
Rev. and Mrs. Elshout were so desirous to have the recently published New Testament in the Izi language distributed as widely as possible, that all monies deposited in the "Elshout Fund" are designated to subsidize the purchase of Bibles.

His anniversary was a gracious gift rather than something he deserved —only because God had been faithful as He had promised—only because of "what God has done for me." He reflected on what had transpired on the day that he commemorated his twentieth anniversary—exactly five years ago. What an impressive moment, and what an overwhelming day it had been! The reading of 1 Corinthians 1:30 shed light upon his entire life: "But of him are ye in Christ Jesus, who of God is made unto us wisdom, and righteousness, and sanctification, and redemption." Although he had been a minister of the gospel for twenty years, he keenly felt himself to be void of true wisdom, righteousness, and holiness—as a hopelessly lost, guilty, and miserable sinner. "But God, who is rich in mercy, for his great love wherewith he loved [him], even when [he was] dead in sins, hath quickened [him] together with Christ" (Eph. 2:4-5). All that Arie Elshout received and experienced in his life had proceeded from the overflowing Fountain of good: a loving and electing God. From thence proceeded the inexpressible Gift in Christ "unto...wisdom, and righteousness, and sanctification, and redemption." From thence proceeded his union with Christ by faith, so that out of Him he might receive divine "wisdom, and righteousness, and sanctification, and redemption," not only for his personal life and his official labors, but also for the future.

At this moment, he felt what the psalmist felt: He was drinking of the river of His pleasures (Psa. 36:8). He relished and adored the love of God the Father, God the Son, and God the Holy Ghost. He was at a loss to comprehend this love: grace for him, a poor sinner! How could he appropriately praise and magnify Him who had taken him by the right hand? He again had a heartfelt desire, for as long as he would live, to proclaim God's Word anywhere and everywhere to whomever would be willing to hear him—and even to those unwilling to hear him. "Come, hear, all ye that fear the Lord."

Rev. Elshout selected Isaiah 28:23-29 as the text for his anniversary sermon. This passage speaks of a farmer who works in his field and is instructed by God as to how he may secure a fruitful harvest. It also illustrates how the Lord equips His servants to labor in their field; that is, in His blood-bought church. His God instructed him as to how this harvest is to be achieved, "for this also cometh forth from the LORD of hosts, which is wonderful in counsel, and excellent in working" (v. 29).

At the end of the service, Rev. De Gier addressed Rev. Elshout on behalf of his colleagues and also gave him a present. In a striking way, Rev. De Gier summarized the life and ministry of his brother. He stated that Rev. Elshout has been a man of the rearguard who never sought a position of prominence. He had never shown much interest in the politics and major assemblies of the church. Instead, he had always shown concern for people—not prominent people, but rather the insignificant, weak, and elderly among them. Rev. De Gier emphasized that this concern was a good thing. He referenced Israel's wilderness journey during which Amalek chose to attack from the rear. Thus there must be men in the rearguard of the army, men who would resist such attackers. The Lord also calls men to that task and equips them for it. Rev. Elshout deemed it to be an extraordinary privilege to serve in the army's rearguard where the weak who are so vulnerable are to be found, and among whom the enemy seeks to inflict many casualties, as Amalek did toward Israel. Again, it was

On behalf of the ministers, Rev. K. De Gier presented an anniversary gift to Rev. Elshout.

powerfully impressed upon Rev. Elshout that he was called to minister to the poor and needy and to save their souls (Psa. 72:12-13).

"Come, for all things are ready." Rev. Elshout had difficulty hiding his emotions when he saw that his daughter Elfriede could no longer decline the invitation to partake of the Lord's Supper—to be seated at the Table of the Covenant. Not only was the Lord rendering his ministry fruitful in the congregation of Slikkerveer, but also among his children. What an impressive moment it was! Meta was home on furlough from Nigeria with her family, and Nellie spent the weekend at home. Rev. Elshout was therefore privileged to administer the Lord's Supper also to his wife and daughters. He could say, "Who am I, O Lord GOD? And what is my house, that thou hast brought me hitherto?" What abundant reason to be amazed!

Not only was the Lord working in the hearts of family members, but some of these family members were also privileged to labor in the Lord's service. Meta and Tom were engaged in Nigeria, Frits served as elder in Zaandam, and Bart was an elder and Christian school principal in Franklin Lakes, New Jersey. Arie was employed by the Mission Committee of the

Reformed Congregations as administrator. On three continents, members of the Elshout family were engaged in the extension and preservation of God's kingdom.

On March 25, 1982, Rev. Elshout preached his farewell sermon in Slikkerveer. The Lord had shown him another way. Zoetermeer, a congregation in disarray, needed him. His heart was not won over because he had compassion on the congregation of Zoetermeer, but rather, because the Lord was moved with compassion toward the congregation. The moment Rev. Elshout received the call, it was crystal clear to him that he had to accept the call, and he did so immediately. He accepted the call the same day the call letter arrived in Slikkerveer.

On March 31, 1982, he was installed by the moderator (counselor), Rev. M. Golverdingen. The opening psalter was a song of thanksgiving:

> *When priests and prophets called on God,*
> *He their petitions heard.*
> (Psalter 265:3—Psalm 99).

Without having prior knowledge, Rev. M. Golverdingen installed his brother in the ministry by expounding a text that was of great significance for Rev. Elshout.

The text for the installation service was Zechariah 4:6, "Not by might, nor by power, but by my spirit, saith the LORD of hosts." Rev. Elshout was convinced that the choice of this text was not accidental. Forty years earlier, this text had played an important role in his life when he struggled greatly with his call to the ministry. The Lord had then encouraged him with this text. The minister sensed that it now pleased the Lord to do so again. Although Rev. Golverdingen had no prior knowledge of the personal significance of this text, the Lord knew so all the more.

The congregation of Zoetermeer was divided and in disarray. Her minister, Rev. H. Rijksen, failed morally and had to be deposed. This circumstance precipitated a party spirit in the congregation, resulting in the display of intense emotions that resulted even in physical altercations. Part of the congregation sided with the minister and dismissed all allegations as slander. When, however, the allegations proved to be true, this segment of the membership was indignant, believing that the minister had not been treated fairly. A peaceable resolution no longer appeared possible, and many left the congregation to affiliate with another denomination.

Rev. Elshout knew that this would not be an easy task for him. Much distrust had to be overcome, and much skepticism had to be removed in this divided and wounded congregation. The minister did not have to undertake this task in his own strength, however. His sole calling was to labor diligently, and the Spirit of the Lord would undertake and bring about healing.

~

Prior to leaving Slikkerveer, the ministerial couple first went to New Zealand for a four-week period to serve a small congregation of Dutch immigrants. Arrangements for this visit had already been made prior to accepting the call of Zoetermeer.

From the many conversations Rev. Elshout had with these Dutch New Zealanders, it became evident that many of them had departed from their native country to escape the yoke of religion. Their intent had been to abandon the church and to establish a new life apart from God. Although they succeeded in abandoning the religion of their native land, the God of their native land was also the God of New Zealand. He was also able to find them there and return them to the preaching of His Word.

Then there was a phone call from the Netherlands. Rev. Driessen, one of Rev. Elshout's former catechism students, had accepted the call to Slikkerveer. What joy there was, for also in this way the Lord showed His loving care! He had called Rev. Elshout to Zoetermeer, but He also cared for the congregation he had left behind. Yet, Rev. and Mrs. Elshout looked at each other with concern. This meant that they would soon have to vacate the parsonage in Slikkerveer. Although they would be prepared to do so, the parsonage in Zoetermeer was still occupied. The deposed minister refused to vacate the parsonage, and the consistory believed it had no other choice but to initiate litigation.

So often they had had to deal with housing issues during their lifetime. Time and again, however, the Lord had given deliverance. Wouldn't matters also work out this time? A temporary solution was found. Rev. Driessen was still living in the parsonage of Moerkapelle, and he invited the Elshout couple to move in with them. The remodeling of the parsonage of Slikkerveer could then proceed as planned. Once this was finished, the Driessen family would be able to move in, and Rev. Elshout would be able to stay in Moerkapelle.

The parsonage of Zoetermeer, located at 2 Kennemerland

By this time, the Elshout couple was alone, for their youngest son Chris had married Simone de Graaf and was living in Hoogvliet. Unexpectedly, the parsonage in Zoetermeer was vacated when Rev. Rijksen accepted the call of the Reformed congregation of Raamsdonkveer.[29]

An atmosphere of systemic distrust prevailed in Zoetermeer. What is truth, and who was still speaking the truth? As Rev. Elshout reflected on this dilemma, he thought, "How can I ever build a bridge between a damaged past and a new future?" Many people found it impossible to listen to the preaching without any prejudice and bias. Many therefore did not benefit from the spiritual nourishment that was set before them.

One male member of the congregation was recalcitrant and hostile. The minister who had now come to Zoetermeer could not amount to anything. He deemed his preaching to be superficial and his message void of content. It was obvious to him that this minister had not been sent by God. The minister must have imagined that it was God's direction and perhaps considered moving to Zoetermeer to be rather advantageous.

Then the man became ill—seriously ill. His life was hanging by a thin thread. Rev. Elshout came to his bedside, but it was difficult to have a

---

[29]A congregation of the Dutch state church—the original and historic Reformed church of the Netherlands

conversation. He tried to pray, but it had no effect. The minister returned home with a troubled heart.

This man recovered, however, and returned to church. Then the Word became efficacious. He began to listen with different ears, thinking at first that the minister was preaching differently. Increasingly, however, he came to understand that God was confronting him with his sin. Having been a spiritually proud man, he was now being humbled and brought to an end of himself. The Lord was transforming a lion into a lamb, and his life changed radically. Even his children hardly recognized their father. Having been a rather difficult and moody man, one who always had something to say about everybody, he now became a mild man who considered himself to be at fault. He was learning to despair of self, and he was beginning to look for life outside of himself. The critic had become a beggar.

Again, he became ill and needed to be hospitalized. Once more, the minister was sitting at his bedside. The man told him about his concerns, and about that for which his heart yearned. He told him about his having taken refuge to the Mediator between God and man, the Lord Jesus. He told him how the Word of God and the preaching led him to put his hope in Him alone—and also how much inward strife this had caused. It was a delightful visit, for the Lord was present.

Unexpectedly, he was in church on Sunday. The doctors had given him permission to go home for a few days, and he felt good enough to attend

The church building of the (Netherlands) Reformed Congregation of Zoetermeer

the preaching of God's Word. How astonished and joyful he was! The sermon dovetailed with his life, thoughts, and desires. "Who is this that cometh up from the wilderness, leaning upon her beloved? I raised thee up under the apple tree: there thy mother brought thee forth: there she brought thee forth that bare thee. Set me as a seal upon thine heart, as a seal upon thine arm: for love is strong as death; jealousy is cruel as the grave: the coals thereof are coals of fire, which hath a most vehement flame. Many waters cannot quench love, neither can the floods drown it: if a man would give all the substance of his house for love, it would utterly be contemned" (Song of Sol. 8:5-7).

Some people did not appreciate this sermon, and they let the minister know that in a rather blunt and crass manner. He lost sleep over it, felt discouraged, left his bed, and poured out his heart before the Lord. It was all to no avail. He then read Judges 7, where Gideon was encouraged by the words of a Midianite. Yet the Word had no impact on the minister. What was he doing here in this congregation? Why had the Lord sent him here when his presence was not having any effect after all?

That same week, however, he sat at the bedside of this man who began to tell what the Lord had done to his soul. Precisely during that sermon, light arose for him. The Lord used that sermon and achieved glorious things with it. The sermon that had only a negative impact on some proved to be food and drink for this man.

Rev. Elshout was well aware of the fact that the Lord Himself needed to intervene in the congregation of Zoetermeer. This occurred indeed, but in an entirely different way than anyone would have thought. A number of children were born in the congregation with health issues. One of them was even diagnosed with a very malignant form of leukemia. The specialists in the Academic Hospital in Leiden had never before encountered such an aggressive form and were at their wits' end. Although chemotherapy could possibly have some effect, the probability of success was only one percent. It also remained to be seen what the devastating side effects of chemotherapy would be. The doctors anticipated that the child would suffer a great deal, and the parents had to make a decision as to whether they should proceed with the treatment.

This dilemma brought them to the door of the parsonage. After having listened to and dialogued with them, exploring what the way forward would be, Rev. Elshout finally advised that the treatment should be administered to the child, hoping upon God alone for whom nothing is too hard.

Before the treatment was initiated, the child was permitted to come home on Sunday. It was decided that the baby would be baptized that day, and thus there was an unanticipated baptism service. The congregation held its breath when the terminally ill child was carried in. The tension was palpable, and everyone sensed the weightiness of the moment—not because the salvation of this child was contingent on baptism, but because both the child and the congregation stood here before the countenance of God under such special circumstances. Rev. Elshout chose his text accordingly: "They looked unto him, and were lightened: and their faces were not ashamed" (Psa. 34:5).

The weeks following were filled with tension. The entire congregation was supportive and engaged in prayer. The many prayer droplets merged together into a rushing stream. It reunited the divided congregation. The Lord did not put the congregation to shame, for a favorable turning of the tide became evident. Even the hospital staff members were speaking of a divine miracle. The child was treated for a lengthy period until the doctors were convinced that malignant cells were no longer present in the child's blood. The child grew up prosperously, and many deemed this event to be a token of the covenant faithfulness of a Triune God who had not forgotten the congregation of Zoetermeer. This change had been achieved neither by might nor by power, but by God's Spirit. It comforted the minister and gave him new courage to continue to engage in the often difficult task of being a minister of the gospel, a fisher of men.

Too much was happening at once. Mrs. Elshout was stressed out and exhausted. Then the phone call came that Meta was on her way with her three children. She needed to come to Holland for a medical evaluation and further treatment of a serious bout with hepatitis. It was possible that her liver would never function fully again. Exhausted and yellow from the liver ailment, she arrived in the Netherlands. Medical tests also confirmed that a rather serious gynecological issue would require extensive surgical intervention, which occurred shortly thereafter. During the first few months, her family lived in the parsonage of Zoetermeer.

Elfriede also became ill and needed medical care. Although she, too, was obviously welcome in the parsonage, these months proved to be very demanding. Only after Meta moved into the parsonage of Moerkapelle, and Elfriede was admitted into the hospital, did the ministerial couple have some breathing room. Although they remained concerned about their children, Dad and Mom Elshout were no longer responsible for their immediate care. Meta improved gradually, Elfriede also improved somewhat, and Mrs. Elshout was able to get back on her feet. In his sermons, Rev. Elshout would frequently use the illustration of a goat on a leash—something that could often be observed in the Slikkerveer region.

It illustrates how God leads His children by keeping them on a short leash—not to make them miserable, but rather for their benefit. They were also being kept on a short leash. And yet, they thanked the Lord for it, for time and again He would deliver, care, protect, and help. They lacked nothing.

A family portrait taken at the occasion of the 40th wedding anniversary of
Rev. and Mrs. Elshout

All the pathways of Jehovah
Speak of truth and mercies pure
(Psalter 415:5—Psalm 25)

I shall not die but live before Him,
And all His mighty works declare,
That all may joyfully adore Him
Who in His lovingkindness share.
(Psalter 427:3—Psalm 118).

The ties with America remained intact. When Bart was accepted to labor as an evangelist in Denver, Colorado, Rev. Elshout went to New Jersey to install his son as an evangelist-elder of the Franklin Lakes congregation. These were some precious weeks for Bart, as well as for his father and mother. The young evangelist leaned upon his dad who assisted him with helpful counsel. At a time like this, the distance separating them was intensely felt: he was in Denver and his father in the Netherlands. That did not lessen their intimate contact in any way. In response to all the questions Bart had regarding his life, his father unceasingly pointed him to the omniscience of God. Time and again, Bart was impressed by the steadfast and childlike confidence his father and mother had that the Lord was not only acquainted with their lives, but that He would also care for them.

> *But those that trust Jehovah,*
> *His mercy shall surround*
> (Psalter 84:2—Psalm 32).

Repeatedly, his father would say, "Son, I also do not understand certain things, but of one thing I am certain: God makes no mistakes—also not in your life."

Traveling was not a burden for Rev. Elshout—that is, as long as somehow it was connected to the proclamation of the gospel and could be coordinated with his work in the congregation of Zoetermeer. His love and primary commitment were there.

They had saved some money monthly. They faithfully continued to do so, being hopeful that a cherished wish might be fulfilled: a visit to Israel, the Promised Land. That moment arrived in October 1985. The money they had saved was not sufficient. Unexpectedly, however, a sum of money became available of which they had been ignorant until now. The

Mrs. Elshout roaming the streets of the old city of Jerusalem

government of Germany informed Mrs. Elshout that she had a legitimate claim to her over-payment of social security taxes. A lump sum was deposited into her account. The Lord knows how to open doors unexpectedly and to lead His children in surprising ways to bless them. The ministerial couple viewed all of this in that light.

Their journey proved to be an in-depth discovery concerning the contents of the Word of God. Rev. Elshout had often preached about the Sea of Galilee, and now he was sailing upon it. He had preached about the demon-possessed man of Gadara, and now he was walking through these hills. He had preached about the wedding in Cana, and now he entered the church built upon the location where water had been changed into wine. He had preached about Nazareth and Nain, and now he was able to visit these places—and about Capernaum, being able to see that not one stone had been left upon the other. It made a deep impression upon him. They walked the Via Dolorosa where Jesus, weighed down by the cross, bore the sins of His people. They visited Golgotha, the location of the cross, and a hill that still visibly resembles a human skull. It was the place where nearly two thousand years earlier it had resounded, "It is finished"—also for Arie Elshout and Elfriede Melzian.

There was no time left to visit the Garden of the Tomb. In hindsight, Rev. Elshout was convinced, however, that the Lord had purposed that this location should also be visited. On their way back, the car sputtered and broke down, and Rev. Elshout grumbled. Thus they were stranded due to mechanical failure. It became evident, however, that they were stranded in front of the entrance to the Garden of the Tomb, and it proved to be a good opportunity to visit this location. It made a deep impression to be at the location where, according to Christian tradition, the Lord Jesus had been buried; where the angels had descended to remove the stone; and where the deceased Savior arose by His own power. A few American and English Christians were in the garden, and they began to sing John Newton's song,

"Amazing Grace, how sweet the sound,
That saved a wretch like me!"

How true were the words recorded at the exit of the grave: "He is not here! He is risen!" At this moment, the risen Christ prepared a heavenly blessing for two insignificant human beings who had found life in Him, and who in all simplicity had devoted their lives to His service.

Less than two years later, they were again airborne—this time to America. From there, their journey would continue to New Zealand, where Rev.

Elshout would again engage in the ministry of Word and sacrament. The consistory of Zoetermeer had given its approval, and preparations for this journey had been made. The American congregations heard of these plans, and the Mission Committee there asked him also to visit Australia where a group of American members gathered for worship in the town of Wollongong (near Melbourne). They too were in need of pastoral care.

In Denver, Rev. Elshout baptized the second child of Bart and Joan. How different had life's journey been than Bart had ever anticipated! While attending Western Michigan University in Kalamazoo, he heard from a professor that the world would cease to exist shortly after 1971. It had shaken him up, and he believed that he would never have children. His father had then said, however, that God reigns, and not man. The world will not end one second before God has accomplished His purposes. Now the sign and seal of the covenant was bestowed upon little Sarah Joan.

During the evening service, the minister and his wife had the privilege of listening to their son. It was a moving moment for him. Again, the Lord proved to be true to His Word. Rev. Elshout was so convinced that the moment would arrive that Bart would also proclaim the Word of God. This belief was challenged, however, by a disappointment in 1980. Bart was not admitted by the Curatorium as a student for the ministry. What an incomprehensible way this was—not only for Bart, but also for his father!

Rev. Elshout seated in the study of his son Bart in Littleton (a Denver suburb), Colorado

All came now into focus for Rev. Elshout. What a fool he had been! Psalm 145 had certainly spoken volumes to him: "He will fulfil the desire of them that fear him" (v. 19). He knew that he would not close his eyes in death before he would have seen and heard that Bart also would be engaged as a messenger of God's Word. It appeared, however, that this way had been cut off. Yet that was not the case; it only turned out differently than he had imagined. Here his son was now proclaiming the Word of God, albeit as an elder-evangelist. His ministry also matched exactly what is written in Ephesians 4:11: "And he gave some, apostles; and some, prophets; and some, evangelists; and some, pastors and teachers." This is by no means a hierarchical order, but rather a practical and logical order of ministers of the gospel and gospel ministries. The one is not superior to the other, for they are all equally engaged in promoting the coming of God's kingdom.

Of one thing he was now certain: Bart was precisely where he should be, for the Lord was pleased to use him as a missionary minister of His Word. God had fulfilled his promise, and there was a song in the minister's heart:

> *Thy mercy and Thy truth, O Lord,*
> *Transcend the lofty sky,*
> *Thy judgments are a mighty deep,*
> *And as the mountains high.*
> (Psalter 94:1—Psalm 32).

It was a strange sensation. The world is round. Compared to the Netherlands, New Zealand is on the other side of the globe. Consequently, there are two ways you can fly there. In 1982, Rev. Elshout flew via Rome, Bahrein, and Singapore to New Zealand. Now he was arriving from the other side, via Colorado and Honolulu. It was a delight for him that he was privileged to serve the small congregation led by Elder Groen. He engaged in many conversations with members of the congregation, and the experiences of his personal and ministerial life enable him to give advice to many. Time and again, his down-to-earth and common sense approach would yield answers to questions and solve problems.

His journey then took him to Australia. He was warmly received by this small congregation. The people told him that they were already familiar with him—not because they had already met him, but because they had already heard him. Tapes with English sermons by Rev. Elshout had been mailed from America to Australia. By now these tapes had been worn out, and the "Aussies" were delighted that they could not only personally meet the minister but more importantly because they could now hear him.

The return journey also went via America, and once more the children who lived there were not overlooked. On October 31, 1986, the airplane carrying the ministerial couple landed at Schiphol. During a period of several weeks, they had flown more than 30,000 miles. Not only had they been enriched by many experiences, but they were also gladdened by receiving another grandchild, for little Maarten had been born into the family of Arie and Marjan.

Holding little Sarah, daughter of Bart & Joan, at the
Denver Airport, before embarking on their return journey
to the Netherlands (1987)

CHAPTER 19

A Step Back

Rev. Elshout was tossing and turning in his bed. He couldn't fall asleep. Once more he had received a call from Scheveningen. To be perfectly honest, he was very pleased with it. After a period of nearly twenty years, the congregation he had served from 1961 until 1967 once more desired him to be her pastor—a matter that amazed him. He was comforted by the trust and desire expressed in the call extended by this congregation. Although he so often struggled with doubt and strife, this call again ministered comfort to him. The Lord silenced the voices of all who inwardly assaulted him.

He was very much inclined to accept this call, but only if it also were the Lord's will and His way. In a simple and childlike manner, he laid this matter before the Lord. Although he did not dare to ask whether he was permitted to accept this call, he did ask whether the Lord would show him the way. He even asked that the Lord would not delay in answering him, for he knew that a lengthy period of uncertainty would result in a significant elevation of his blood pressure. Thus he agonized, prayed, and asked for light.

His mind drifted toward John 4, which stated that the Lord Jesus was compelled to go through Samaria. Rather than Jesus choosing this way, He was directed by His Father to do so. Had this also not been his experience as a minister? In 1966, he had felt very much at home in Scheveningen, and his work was being blessed. Then the letter from Artesia was deposited in his mailbox—an entirely unexpected, and actually an unwelcome event. He had to go, however, and he went. His seven-year ministry in America had been blessed in spite of the fact that there had been much that he had to either learn or unlearn. Often the way of God's providence had led him to foreign lands, and they were all "Samarias": America, Nigeria, New Zealand, Australia, and the Netherlands.

Quietly, Rev. Elshout reflected on all this. He was privileged, so to speak, to look at the reverse side of God's embroidery, the side on which His determinate counsel becomes visible, where all stitches and threads suddenly display a clear pattern and end in God's honor and glory, as well as man's salvation. Quietly, he sang,

With endless thanks, O Lord—Father, Son, and Holy Spirit—to Thee,
Thy wondrous works will I proclaim.
(Psalter 145:6—Psalm 52)

Rev. Elshout was convinced that the work that prompted his being released from Scheveningen in 1966 had been completed, and that he was now permitted to return to this congregation—now at a somewhat slower pace, for he was nearly sixty-five years of age. Though he was still healthy, it was evident that he was getting older. This fact was affirmed for him by John 4:37, "And herein is that saying true, One soweth, and another reapeth." He had sown in America, Canada, Africa, the far southeastern corner of the world, Slikkerveer, and Zoetermeer. This sowing also included all the plowing that preceded it. Another would now reap.

When he began his ministry in Zoetermeer in 1982, he arrived in a congregation that was very unsettled, resembling a ship that was about to perish in the waves. The Lord blessed his work, and this congregation could now again function as all other (Netherlands) Reformed Congregations in the land. His healing ministry had been completed—not by might, not by power, but by God's Spirit.

During that night, Rev. Elshout, so to speak, terminated his work in Zoetermeer and accepted the call from Scheveningen. He did not have to think long about his farewell text: "And herein is that saying true, One soweth, and another reapeth" (John 4:37).

On January 1, 1987, he communicated his acceptance by phone to Scheveningen. The current pastor, Rev. R. Kattenberg, had accepted the call from Arnhem, and he rejoiced in this news for many reasons. Not only would he depart from his congregation knowing that she would be cared for, but it also reassured him that he had made the correct decision. Rev. Kattenberg had agonized over this call and had asked the Lord to affirm that his decision to leave Scheveningen had been the correct one. He had now received this affirmation in a surprising manner. On January 4, 1987, he preached his farewell sermon in the congregation.

The parsonage in which Rev. Kattenberg resided, located at the Frankenslag, was sold. This home was too large for the Elshout couple. The search for another home led to the so-called Belgian sector of Scheveningen,[30] where a few condominiums were for sale. Although Rev. Elshout felt this arrangement to be suitable, Mrs. Elshout preferred a ground-level residence. They couldn't quite resolve this dilemma, and they agreed that they would leave the final decision with the consistory committee. So often the word of this hymn had been affirmed in their lives:

---

[30]All streets in this section of Scheveningen are named after Belgian cities; hence the designation "Het Belgisch Park"—the Belgian sector.

Do not permit me to chart my own course,
For even if I could, I would not dare.
How erroneous my choice would be
If Thou wouldest leave the choice to me.
Deal with me as a child
That cannot find the way on his own.

In the end, there was but one condominium that was satisfactory to the consistory: 2d Leuvensestraat. The purchase was made.

The parsonage located at 2d Leuvensestreet

When Rev. Elshout preached his farewell sermon to the congregation of Zoetermeer, he stated that there had been difficult times and disappointments, but there had also been times of joy, including that unity in the congregation had been restored. Oh, no, this restoration by no means was to be credited to him, for it was God who had bestowed His blessing. He said, "If you received a blessing during these years, give thanks to the Lord. If you did not receive a blessing under my ministry, ask the Lord to bless the use of other means of grace."

He then used an example by which he had previously comforted his daughter Elfriede during trying times: "How many sparrows are there in comparison to one nightingale? As to my preaching, I would have loved to have been a nightingale. However, in His wisdom the Lord has given us more sparrows than nightingales."

~

During this busy time of saying good-bye and moving, a permit was issued for the construction of a Reformed psychiatric hospital, modeled after Pine Rest Hospital in Grand Rapids, Michigan. Rev. Elshout was one of the driving forces behind this project, and he was therefore among the most grateful for the issuance of this permit. When he had to be hospitalized in 1972, he thought that his ministry had come to an end, his life would never be normal again, and he would be consumed by mental illness and a relentless sense of guilt. However, the Lord had brought him up out of a horrible pit, out of the miry clay, set his feet upon a rock, and established his goings (Psalm 40:2-3). Not only had He put a new song in his mouth, but He had also given him a new task. He was called upon to be a pastor for the mentally afflicted—sometimes directly, and sometimes indirectly. He needed to write articles and books to extend a helping hand to others. He needed to become a member of the Committee for Family and Geriatric Affairs and would become its chairman. He viewed these matters as tasks to which the Lord had called him, tasks for which he had had to be enrolled in a very difficult and demanding "training institute."

There had been negotiations with some members of the Liberated Reformed Churches,[31] resulting in the filing of a formal request to the government for permission to establish a Reformed psychiatric hospital. Although their individual support bases were small, the bundling of resources made such an initiative more likely to succeed. There were deliberations to be made, barriers to be dismantled, parameters to be formulated, and one would have to be of one mind in order to proceed.

This cooperative venture was expanded by including people from the National Reformed Church, the Free Reformed Churches, and the Reformed Denominations rooted in the Secession of 1834.[32] Although the theological differences were unmistakable, there was more that united them regarding this venture than that which separated them. A growing number of individuals recognized that there was a common interest.

There were, however, many setbacks. Applications were denied, and permits were not granted. Yet, little by little there was some progress—until, in 1984, the Department of Health granted official permission to initiate the provision of psychiatric care that would have a distinct Reformed identity.

---

[31]A sister denomination of the Canadian Reformed and American Reformed Churches
[32]The first schism in the historic Reformed Church of the Netherlands (De Nederlands Hervormde Kerk)

Fundraising efforts by the two Reformed daily newspapers generated the needed publicity for this undertaking. Until recently, there had been a taboo in conservative Reformed circles regarding mental illness. However, this initiative not only resulted in more openness, but there was also the growing awareness that this was a calling for the (Netherlands) Reformed churches. Rev. Elshout's books remained popular, for thousands of copies had already been sold—to his utter amazement.

Within weeks, both newspapers raised more than one million guilders, and this amount was more than enough to pay for the initial construction phase. To the amazement of many professionals, this culminated in the issuance of a permit. Although the concept of a Reformed psychiatric hospital was neither in line with the objectives of the Ministry of Health nor with the prevailing views regarding mental care, the Lord reigned. He inclined hearts, and a Reformed psychiatric hospital became a reality.

~

Many visitors were entering and leaving the Fellowship Hall of the (Netherlands) Reformed Congregation of Scheveningen. From every corner of the nation, people had come to congratulate Rev. Elshout on his 65th birthday. Delegates and friends from the various congregations he had served were present. He was amazed that so many people had come to express their best wishes, realizing at the same time that he knew them all. He had visited them in the hospital when their children had been born and when their loved ones were dying. He had visited their homes in times of trial and concern, but he had also been there during days of joy. He remembered that he had married a couple and that another couple had made public profession of faith. One woman had suffered much in her marriage, and another man had lost his wife at a young age after she had suffered much for a long time. How many tears had been shed! Happily, there were also tears of joy, but they were in the minority. "Yet is their strength labour and sorrow" (Psa. 90:10), and Rev. Elshout observed its affirmation at this moment. He was therefore all the more amazed. The Lord had been pleased to spare him for sixty-five years. In spite of all the riddles and trials that had been his portion, he had never lacked anything. He was now permitted, during his sojourn between the cradle and the grave, to experience this milestone. There was a song within his heart:

To Thee, O God, we render thanks,
To Thee give thanks sincere,
Because Thy wondrous works declare
That Thou art ever near.
(Psalter 206:1—Psalm 75)

Many people responded to his interview in the Reformed daily newspaper (*Reformatorisch Dagblad*). He had shared how he felt himself to be as a horse that had been permitted to return to the stable of the congregation of Scheveningen. "I believe that the Lord, by the call from Scheveningen, has concluded a period in which He had a special task for me. Will this be my last congregation? Yes, I believe so."

During this interview, the stressful time of his breakdown in Kalamazoo, that included his time in Pine Rest Mental Hospital, was obviously also addressed. To the question as to whether his illness had impacted his preaching, he responded without hesitation, saying, "Yes, indeed! I have become milder and more nuanced in my assessment of all that transpires in the world. Have I become more gospel-centered? No, I cannot say that. I do believe, however, that I have become more free in proclaiming the riches of the gospel."

Something concerned Rev. Elshout greatly. There was so much work to be done in the congregations. More importantly, however, the gospel had to be preached, both in his own nation and beyond. To achieve this goal, there was a great need for ministers. Many ministers, who knew themselves to be called of God, were needed to proclaim the gospel as servants of their Master, Jesus Christ—that is, to invite sinners to Christ and to cast the net of the gospel into the large sea of humanity so that the net would be filled, His house would be filled, and His kingdom would come in its fullness.

Rev. Elshout knew that many men were wrestling with the question whether it was God's will that they should also labor in His vineyard. It was a question that could not be answered with a simple "yes" or "no." Having laid this matter prayerfully before the Lord they then, after some time, believed to have received an affirmative answer.

They would then—at times joyfully, yet often also groaning within— visit their consistories to request an attestation to be examined by the Curatorium of the Theological Seminary. That was the church-orderly way stipulated by the General Synod of the (Netherlands) Reformed Congregations. Rev. Elshout knew from experience how much anxiety there could be for those who requested such an attestation. How readily people can err in processing such applications, for also then the heart can be so deceitful! It grieved him that so many were turned away by the Curatorium. These men had received an attest from their consistories that evidently were convinced that these men had been called by the Lord and were being thrust forth by Him. Were all these men mistaken, and were all these consistories and their moderators mistaken?

Rev. Elshout therefore questioned the procedure followed by the Curatorium. No, he certainly did not question the sincerity and longing of the curators to do that which was pleasing to the Lord. He realized how difficult the work of the curators was—yes, that it was a superhuman task. He certainly did not wish to challenge that. He recognized that not a single decision was made outside the realm of God's providence. However, all that transpires does not automatically bear the stamp of God's approval.

At the General Synod of 1986, Rev. Elshout was present as a delegate. He proposed that a committee be appointed to which both the Curatorium, as well as the consistories and their moderators, could appeal "in certain explicit and carefully defined circumstances." Such a committee—he preferred not to call it a Committee of Appeal—would then function as a sort of mediation venue that could open the possibility of admitting those who had been turned down. The General Synod did not support this proposal. The status quo would be maintained.

With a rod and a staff, Arie and Elfriede had crossed the Jordan at the commencement of their marriage, now already forty-five years ago. Although there had been mountain peaks and valleys, the Lord had always led them, renewed their strength, and been their help and their salvation. The tokens of His favor had been countless. Rev. Elshout realized that there were no merits in him. On the contrary, in so many ways, he still resembled a lion, and there was yet so little resemblance to a lamb.

The celebration of the 45th wedding anniversary of Rev. and Mrs. Elshout (1990)

He realized that a progressive understanding that we need the Lord Jesus Christ unto divine wisdom, righteousness, sanctification, and complete redemption can be acquired only in a way in which we repeatedly have to die to ourselves. Time and again there would be no other option for him but to take refuge in Him. Such was the way in which Christ received the honor, and he prospered spiritually—and others with him, and sometimes by means of him.

He knew himself to be so blessed—not because of the best wishes received, the loving concern shown, and the gifts given. Instead, they were privileged, above all things, to focus upon God's covenantal promises as articulated in Psalm 128. The blessing of the Lord did make them rich— truly rich. The Lord gave them eight children, and together they were privileged to hold

Rev. Elshout on the balcony of their residence at 2d Leuvensestraat in Scheveningen— his last home here on earth

twenty-six grandchildren in their arms. The Lord fulfilled His promises. How often they had been comforted by Psalm 113:9: "He maketh the barren woman to keep house, and to be a joyful mother of children!" Soli Deo gloria!

CHAPTER 20

The End of the Journey

Traveling to America had become a matter of routine. At least once a year, Rev. Elshout and his wife would visit this country in order to sustain the relationships with their children and grandchildren. During July 1991, they were visiting Bart. Little Sarah was nearly five years old, an age when grandfathers read books to their grandchildren and have childlike, yet profound conversations with them.

Bart and Sarah bidding a final farewell at Newark Airport, New Jersey—
probably on July 22, 1991, merely a few weeks prior to Rev. Elshout's sudden
decease on August 10

His conversations with Bart, however, were of a different nature, albeit that their focus was one and the same: God is a God of the covenant—a covenant that He shall remember throughout the generations and all eternity. That covenant is steadfast and secure in the Mediator of the Covenant. Rev. Elshout stated: "My hope is that I may once lay my head on that pillow."

He was deeply concerned about the congregations of North America. Dr. Joel Beeke had just been suspended as a theological teacher, and

Student James Greendyk was not declared callable by the churches. His studies were extended by a year. Rev. Elshout knew what the consequences could be of such measures. He also knew what profound rifts these decisions could cause within the churches and within families. Internal alienation became all the more evident, and the determination to remain united was decreasing. He astutely observed how similar the situation was to what had occurred in the Netherlands between the years of 1950 and 1956. As was true then, also now there was much mutual distrust. When Rev. Elshout preached on 1 Corinthians 14:1, "Follow after charity," in the Netherlands Reformed Congregation of Franklin Lakes, New Jersey, an elder implied that he had chosen this text purposely in light of current ecclesiastical developments. Although Rev.

During his last visit to Canada, Rev. Elshout took this picture and wrote on its backside: July 1991—"They that wait upon the LORD shall renew their strength; they shall mount up with wings as eagles; they shall run, and not be weary; and they shall walk, and not faint" (Isa. 40:31). During this final North-American journey, he preached about this text in several congregations, and this picture was for him a visible affirmation of this truth.

Elshout, by way of his date book, could readily prove the contrary, it grieved him that this response was evidence of rising tensions.

～

Tensions (though of a different nature) were also rising on the mission field in Nigeria, where in 1988 the Nigerian Reformed Church had officially been constituted. There was difference of opinion regarding the position of office-bearers, the role of ecclesiastical authority, and the role of this new denomination in the Nigeria of 1991—a medley of various churches and groups that had united themselves within the Tekan.[33] These tensions were also reflected in the relationship between the Mission Board and the local mission team. The visitation, early in 1991, by delegates from the Netherlands succeeded only partially in relieving

---

[33]TEKAN is an umbrella organization of Nigerian churches that grew out of the various SUM-ministries. By way of this organization, these churches engage in various cooperative ventures, and they also unitedly communicate with the Nigerian government.

This picture was taken when Rev. and Mrs. Elshout visited Tom and Meta in Lynden, Washington, during July 1991.

some of these tensions. Someone was needed who would be trusted by all parties involved, and who, whenever necessary, would have the authority to admonish and give direction. Given their direct involvement, members of the Mission Board could not be asked to carry out this task, much less someone from the team.

The Mission Board then approached Rev. Elshout. Ten years earlier, he had been privileged to labor with blessing in Izi, and he still maintained good relations with many in Izi. Present church leaders were Rev. Elshout's former Bible School students, and they now viewed him as a father figure. The Mission Board very much desired that Rev. Elshout would travel to Izi for a few months to provide further training, consultation, and advice, and also be there as a pastoral confidante for the members of the team. Rev. Elshout looked up against this task, but he also wanted to serve the church in Izi.

The fact that he had not yet been forgotten was evident a year earlier when his son Arie visited Izi as the Mission Board's administrator. There he met Amos, the leader of the local congregation. When Arie introduced himself, the Nigerian young man asked, "Are you related to the minister who came here with his wife ten years ago?"

Arie replied, "That is my father."

Amos exclaimed with surprise, "What, is my father also your father?" God had used Rev. Elshout to touch the heart of Amos, resulting in an unbreakable bond with the minister.

The team in Izi reported that they were pleased with the proposal that Rev. Elshout and his wife would come for a period of time. The medical staff expressed concern, however. In addition to the proposal to have Rev. and Mrs. Elshout reside in Izi for a few months, the Mission Board also considered sending an older couple to do technical work, and there were several older family members of mission workers who were planning to visit Nigeria. The medical team wrote to the Mission Board, as well as to all involved, that they needed to consider that medical care in Nigeria was very limited in its scope, and that the medical team did not dare to assume responsibility for the increased presence of older people on the mission field. The team advised these travelers to reconsider their plans in light of this fact. The couple that had been scheduled to engage in technical work cancelled their trip. Rev. and Mrs. Elshout thoroughly reassessed the situation, and Rev. Elshout decided that he would not travel to Nigeria under these circumstances.

In 1990, a reunion was held of all who had been engaged as mission workers in Izi.

That was not according to the wishes of the Mission Board, however. The Board proposed that Rev. Elshout would travel by himself, but then only for a short period, and after undergoing a thorough medical examination.

Rev. Elshout agreed to this proposal. He informed the members of the Board, however, that if his preliminary examination for being in the tropics would yield matters of concern, he would view it as a heavenly directive that he was presently not being called to be of help in Izi. The examination did not yield any matters of concern. On the contrary, the internist congratulated Rev. Elshout: "You are sixty-eight years old, and yet you are so healthy...."

Having returned to the Netherlands from North-America, Rev. Elshout departed shortly thereafter for Nigeria.

Circumstances in Izi were similar to those in the worldwide church. The notion that leadership merely consists of being in charge and making decisions is all too common. The recognition that leaders are called to servanthood is far less common. Although one may have received a theological education and may be trusted by either the congregation or the classis, one nevertheless remains a servant. Rev. Elshout's intention was to address this matter in Izi. His briefcase therefore contained a series of sermons about the "I am" texts of the gospel of John. The imitation of Christ and the implications of being His servant are of essential importance for the church and her office-bearers. He was planning to conduct Bible studies with office-bearers as well as with students, and he would also leave copies of his sermon notes in Izi.

On Sunday, August 4, 1991, he preached about Lord's Day 44 of the Heidelberg Catechism during the afternoon service in Scheveningen. At the end of the sermon, he said his farewell to the congregation:

> If next Sunday I may be privileged again to preach in Izi, I neither will nor can preach anything else than I have done here—albeit that it will obviously be done in a different language. The same message I have proclaimed here I must also proclaim there. There will absolutely be no difference. Irrespective of whether we live in the Netherlands or Izi, we must all be converted in the very same manner. When God blesses the preaching, the proclamation of law and gospel will bring forth fruits worthy of repentance. We cannot effect this

transformation. We cannot effect this in ourselves, but we also cannot effect it in others; therefore we all are and remain utterly dependent upon the grace of God and the operation of the Holy Spirit.

You might possibly reply, "Are those ministers not capable of doing this work themselves? Why does someone from the Netherlands have to go there?" Let me be brief: Someone from the Netherlands needs to go there because even in Izi, the holiest of men have but a small beginning of this new obedience. We must make that journey from the Netherlands not as people who are better than the local people, for we all are cut from the same cloth. Instead, we go there to give them much needed practical and scriptural guidance.

The Nigerian church rejoiced in the arrival of Rev. Elshout. They already had prepared a wish list for him. Perhaps Rev. Elshout could instruct them regarding the preparation of sermons, communication with students of the Theological School, the study of Scripture in preparation for the Christmas sermons of that year, administration of the Lord's Supper, and officiating at weddings. They also had many questions regarding the tasks of evangelists and the administration of church discipline. There was more than enough work, and Rev. Elshout was therefore received with open arms.

Saying good-bye to each other at the Schiphol Airport was not easy. For two people whose lives had become so intertwined and who were so intensely involved in each other's lives, it became increasingly difficult to part. Arie Elshout embraced his wife, wiped away her tears, and said, "Elfriede, remember 'whether we live therefore, or die, we are the Lord's'" (Rom. 14:8b). He turned toward his brother-in-law and sister-in-law[34] who had accompanied them to Schiphol, saying, "Comfort Elfriede." He then entered the gateway and progressed toward the airplane.

On Wednesday, August 7, Rev. Elshout arrived in Lagos, the Nigerian capital. The next day, he travelled to Abakaliki, the capital of Ebonyi-State, the province in which the Izi region was located. He was received warmly by Teunis and Jenny Rijneveld. As he surveyed the living room, he saw the photographs of Mom and Dad Rijneveld from Mijdrecht. As a theological student, he had visited them several times, and later, when he resided in Utrecht, he had done so as moderator. Since then, both parents had passed away. "If only they could have known that I am now privileged to lodge with you," he remarked.

They settled in their chairs, and Rev. Elshout was very talkative. He told them how much he had looked up against this journey, and that it

---

[34]Gerhard and Irmgard Veit (nee Melzian) from Braunschweig, Germany

was such a disappointment for him that, after careful consideration, his wife could not accompany him. Not only did he tell them that this had caused him much strife but also how the Lord had inclined his heart when Rev. D. Hakkenberg, addressing the annual Mission Conference in the Netherlands, spoke about the text, "Whether we live, we live unto the Lord; and whether we die, we die unto the Lord: whether we live therefore, or die, we are the Lord's" (Rom. 14:8). This text took away all obstacles for him, and he promised the Lord that he would go to Nigeria. He knew that Teunis had a strong affinity for the youth ministry of the church in which he (Rev. Elshout) had been actively involved for many years. He recounted how at the recent annual Youth Day of the Senior Youth Societies, Rev. C. Harinck had spoken about Psalm 91—about having a Refuge and Dwelling Place.

The evening rushed by, and Teunis asked Rev. Elshout to conclude their visit with prayer. It was his delight to do so, and he read Psalm 145: "I will extol thee, my God, O king; and I will bless thy name for ever and ever. Every day will I bless thee; and I will praise thy name for ever and ever" (vv. 1-2).

Rev. Elshout and Rev. Iziogo
The last conversation between two brothers in the ministry—
The focus of their conversation: The Lord reigns, also over the evil that befalls us.
This is also the very last picture taken before Rev. Elshout's
sudden translation into glory.

On Friday, Teunis accompanied the minister to Onuenyim, the central location of the Izi mission compound. There he would lodge with Adrie and Nellie de Visser. During the day, he visited the parsonage of Rev.

Iziogo. He spoke with him about current challenges within the Nigerian Reformed Church. He also spoke with him about his recent journey to the United States where there was also much reason for concern. He asked his fellow pastor to intercede, particularly for the American congregations.

Rev. Elshout was asked whether he was willing to greet the preachers and evangelists during the weekly sermon preparation. He was obviously prepared to do so. Would he also be willing to preach in Onuenyim on the next Lord's Day? Rev. Elshout readily agreed to do so. During his previous tenures, he had been privileged to do much work there, and he felt at home in that congregation.

During the afternoon, there was a reunion with many acquaintances. Many preachers still remembered Rev. Elshout, and some of the evangelists had not forgotten him. Rev. Elshout spoke passionately to the preachers about the necessity of first submitting yourself to the Word before you can speak to others about the Word with edification.

The sun rose early on that particular Saturday. Many people were already engaged in their daily tasks, for when the sun would be at its zenith, it would be too warm and humid to do anything. Adrie de Vissser was not present, for he had stayed overnight in the Igede region. During breakfast, Matteo de Visser, an intern, walked in. His motorcycle had broken down the previous evening. Perhaps Adrie, being a technician, would know how to resolve this difficulty.

This circumstance initiated a conversation between the intern and the minister about what the Bible has to say about animals. Matteo was enrolled in a course about animal husbandry, and the daily morning devotions pertained to that subject. The lives of animals have a purpose. The Lord cares for them, and as stewards, we must fully grasp our task in that regard. Rev. Elshout told him how he had once made reference to animals in a sermon about the sixth commandment.

After breakfast, Rev. Elshout took a walk on the compound. He was amazed to see how well the bushes and trees had grown since his last visit. He engaged in conversation with Joseph Nwogbala, Moses, the workshop mechanic, and Rex from the Igede region.

Matteo explained the operation of the water tank to him, and Rev. Elshout responded by saying that all laws of nature are in one way or another applicable to spiritual life. Analogies abound everywhere that are useful for preaching or that dovetail with spiritual life. He said to Matteo, "A minister must have a broad field of interest. This will make it easy for him to have conversations with people and then add a spiritual dimension to the conversation. For example, Rev. Koster knows how to converse with dairy farmers, for they recognize in him someone who knows what he is talking about. Rev. Verhagen was once asked to give his opinion about a rooster. There must not be too much of a dichotomy between spiritual and non-spiritual matters—as is often the case in the Netherlands."

He patted Matteo on the shoulder and walked back to the De Visser residence in order to enjoy a cup of coffee. Nellie made the causal remark, "Hopefully, Adrie will not stay away too long."

Rev. Elshout responded very faintly. Nellie became alarmed when she looked at him, for he had become exceedingly pale, and his breathing sounded as if he were snoring. As a medical professional, she reacted resolutely. She immediately opened the minister's shirt and took his pulse. Nellie perceived and understood that this was more than a mere fainting spell, and she immediately proceeded to revive him. She was alone, however. She prayed aloud, cried out for help from above, and several times cried loudly for help. The minister's distress was only of short duration, and Nellie concluded that attempts to resuscitate him no longer made any sense. Rev. Elshout had departed this temporal life and had entered into eternity. "I will extol thee, my God, O king; and I will bless thy name for ever and ever. Every day will I bless thee; and I will praise thy name for ever and ever" (Psa. 145:1-2).

In dismay, Nellie walked to the home of Ad de Pater. Fortunately, he was home, and he immediately accompanied her. Together, they placed Rev. Elshout's body on a bed and they then proceeded to inform Rev. Iziogo.

∽

With a generous gesture, Mrs. Elshout opened the door to Frits and Nellie who had just returned from their vacation. She always found it delightful to be surrounded by her children. She wanted to quickly make a cup of coffee—something that would obviously appeal to them. Frits and Nellie's demeanor was very somber, however, and they said, "Let us first sit down."

Irmgard, Mrs. Elshout's sister, and her husband Gerhardt were still visiting. When everyone was seated, Frits said, "Mother, the Mission Office has been notified that something has happened to Dad. It is not good news." Carefully, he told Mrs. Elshout that her husband was no longer alive. It hardly sank in for Mrs. Elshout, and for a long time everyone stared straight ahead. They were numb and dismayed. After about half an hour, Mrs. Elshout was the first one to speak: "We must inform others and the family before they hear this from others."

∽

Many arrangements needed to be made. First, the other children were informed. Whoever could do so, traveled to Scheveningen at once. As this was not possible for Bart and Meta, they immediately booked flights. The first matter of concern was to transport the body to the Netherlands as quickly as possible. This would enable Mrs. Elshout and her children to yet see his body, and in so doing bid him farewell. Arie, being employed by the Mission Office, would be the point man to make all these arrangements.

The Sunday immediately following Rev. Elshout's decease, consistory members of the entire Izi region are on their way to a service in Onurnyimu.

The body of Rev. Elshout was lovingly cared for by Nellie de Visser, Elsbeth Bosch, and Rev. Iziogo. They would have to depart for Enugu as quickly as possible, however, to secure refrigeration for the body. Nigerians customarily bury their dead on the day of death, or sometimes the day after. The local climate made it impossible to display the body for several consecutive days. Without refrigeration, arrangements for transportation to the Netherlands could not even be initiated, and the body would then have to be buried in Nigeria. This concern became a matter of prayer for the family, the mission workers, and the church of Izi.

Upon arrival in Enugu, refrigeration appeared to be unavailable. Teunis Rijneveld was thoroughly acquainted with Nigerian customs, however, and he kept on talking until a space was made available. Then there appeared to be no room in the cargo section of the airplane that would fly to Amsterdam. Once more phone calls were made, and everyone deliberated. Politely and yet firmly, they pressed their case. Everyone was convinced that the Lord again made room. "Them that honor me I will honor" (1 Sam. 2:30). The Heidelberg Catechism confesses that God's children are the property of Christ in both body and soul. The bodies of all God's children have also been purchased with the precious blood of Christ. Would He therefore not provide for this body? The Lord was faithful to His promises.

On Thursday, August 15, 1991, the body of Rev. Elshout, placed in a simple wooden Nigerian casket, arrived in Amsterdam. The widow and her children decided that they would not avail themselves of a different casket. This casket was most fitting for Arie Elshout. In Ridderkerk, the widow and her children were yet able to bid their husband and father farewell. The funeral would take place on Saturday, August 17, 1991.

Strict regulations must be observed when the body of a deceased person is to be transported by airplane. Following these stipulations also required extra time in preparing Rev. Elshout's coffin for transport to the Netherlands.

Even the local population assembled in large numbers to pay their last respects
to a minister who had captured their heart.

Grieving and stunned members of the mission team gather around
Rev. Elshout's coffin.

CHAPTER 21
"And He Was Not; for God Took Him"

The church building of the (Netherlands) Reformed Congregation of Zoetermeer was filled—so full that there was no room for even one more person. A great number of people had come to pay their last respects to Rev. Elshout. "Thou givest glory, truth, and grace" (Psalter 421:6— Psalm 84). Rev. Elshout had been privileged to experience grace during his life, grace for the chief of sinners as he deemed himself to be. He had found grace in the blood of the Lamb; he had received grace to follow the Author and Finisher of his faith; and he had received grace to put himself in the background for the sake of God's kingdom. Rather than harboring bitterness about the maligning of his preaching, he had also received grace to lay it at the feet of the One who had sent him. Finally, he had received grace to rest solely upon the Word of God and to leave everything else for what it was, saying, "I feel as free as a bird in the air."

Visitation by delegates of the Dutch Mission Board in 1979
From left to right: Rev. Elshout, Rev. J.J. van Eckeveld, and Rev. D. Hakkenberg

In addition to bestowing His grace, however, the Lord also honors his servants—in this life, as well as after their departure. He did so first of all by translating the saved sinner, Arie Elshout, into glory, saying, "Come, ye blessed of my Father, inherit the kingdom prepared for you from the foundation of the world" (Mat. 25:34). He also did so by way of a funeral that made it so evident that the child of a King was being brought to his final resting place. The honor bestowed upon such a royal child is a derived honor, for the Lord brings honor to Himself by causing it to be reflected upon His children.

Such was the manner in which the body of Rev. Arie Elshout was committed to the grave in anticipation of the eternal enjoyment of glory in both body and soul. On the day of the resurrection, when his soul and body will be reunited, he will perfectly and eternally magnify His God.

The memorial service, conducted by Rev. D. Rietdijk, was preceded by three addresses. Rev. J.J. van Eckeveld spoke on behalf of the Mission Board. He focused on the many unanswered questions. "Why did Rev. Elshout have to travel to Izi, only to die two days after his arrival? Yet the Lord makes no mistakes. If we truly may believe that, we will find peace in submitting to God's ways."

Rev. van Eckeveld briefly spoke about Rev. Elshout's commitment to mission work:

From 1959 until 1967, he was a member of the Mission Board, serving also as its treasurer. In 1966, he made his first trip to Nigeria as a board member, enabling him for the first time to observe this missionary endeavor with his own eyes. Although he had to vacate his position as a member of the Mission Board upon his departure to America in 1967, he was also privileged to serve in that capacity on the other side of the ocean.

During the years of 1979 and 1980, he was personally engaged in mission work in the Izi region. He was frequently privileged to preach God's Word in one of the churches. We have personally been present when he did so. As a result, a bond was forged between him and the young church of Izi. This bond prompted him whole-heartedly to make himself available once more to minister there for several weeks. Now he has come home, but not because he was a minister. Oh, he was indeed a minister of the Word of God with heart and soul, and he once told me what a wonder it was to him that he had been privileged to proclaim God's Word on five different continents!

One cannot die as a minister, however. When Aaron died, he first had to dispense with his high-priestly garments. One can be saved only as a naked sinner through the blood of the Lamb. That required the removal of his ministerial garments. Brother Elshout was deeply conscious of that fact. In 1979, brother Hakkenberg and I had unforgettable conversations with him in Izi. The three of us were residing in the guesthouse close to the Onyim River, and then what lived in his heart became so evident.

It is so true what Rev. Elshout wrote after the decease of his brother in the ministry, Rev. A. Vergunst: "He has entered into the rest that remains for the people of God. Let us not begrudge him the enjoyment of that rest, for the Lord will not permit His people to remain on this earth one second longer than is absolutely necessary. Christ yearns to have His congregation where He is".

That does not mean, however, that we do not miss him. Yet, the God of Arie Elshout remains the same. We are reminded of the cry of Elisha when Elijah was taken up, 'Where is the God of Elijah?' Children and grandchildren, may that also be your desire, saying, 'Where is the God of our father and our grandfather? Where is the God of my beloved husband?' He is able to comfort you more than men will be able to do.

Rev. K. U. Iziogo, the Nigerian pastor, first read Psalm 121, and then spoke:

All the people of Izi so much desire to be present personally, but that is obviously not possible. We are grateful that the Mission Board has made it possible for me to be present this morning as a representative of the church in Izi.

Rev. Elshout was the first minister from the Netherlands to serve in Izi. That was approximately eleven years ago. When he came to Izi, he took the initial steps in developing an organized ecclesiastical structure, doing so by appointing a committee that would oversee the formation of such an orderly structure in Izi. With God's blessing, this committee organized consistories, and ultimately a classis was constituted. Ever since his initial visit, his heart was always drawn to Izi. Since his heart burned with love for God's sheep there, he felt compelled to return to Izi on the ninth of August. Man proposes, and God disposes. How much we wish that he would still be present with us! I know from experience what this means for the family, for in 1982, my own father passed away. In 1987, Mr. Hielke Visser[35] was taken away by the Lord, and on the seventh of January

---

[35]Mr. Hielke Visser was a member of the NRC Mission Team in Izi. In 1987, he died tragically in a car accident.

of this year the Lord also took our own child from us. The Lord is, however, the One who reigns over all things.

During Rev. Iziogo's last conversation with Rev. Elshout, the Dutch pastor directed his attention to Psalm 121, which states that the Lord also governs the evil that befalls us. The Lord has not promised His children that no evil shall come upon them when He calls them to follow Him, but rather, that He is the One who governs all things, no matter what may transpire.

The Nigerian pastor exhorted the family to lift up their eyes unto the Lord, "for only there will you be able to find your help and comfort. The Lord Jesus has laid down His life for His own sheep. Then we can also read in Psalm 121 that the Lord is the One who shall preserve your soul."

Elder M. Pronk, elder of the Scheveningen congregation, considered it a privilege that Rev. Elshout had been their pastor. Divided over two periods, he served as pastor in this fishing village for nearly ten years.

I know that in 1987 it did not take him long to conclude that he would return to Scheveningen. There was a special bond with our congregation. Scheveningen was, so to speak, his home base to which he returned after many wanderings abroad. I am reminded of his inaugural text in 1987, a text that is also referenced in the obituary notice, namely, 2 Peter 1:13: "Yea, I think it meet, as long as I am in this tabernacle, to stir you up by putting you in remembrance." He then referred to it as his mandate—as the commission of His Sender for the time at hand. And the Lord had decreed that this time frame would consist of four years and four months. When that moment arrived, his task had been completed.

In light of his sudden departure, the text following his inaugural text is extraordinarily significant. Verse thirteen is not a complete sentence, for it ends with a semicolon. The sentence continues in verse 14. There Peter says, "Knowing that shortly I must put off this my tabernacle, even as our Lord Jesus Christ hath shewed me." Peter thereby adds a great measure of urgency to his words—to his exhortation. He knew that he would not be able to labor much longer, and thus without delay he engaged in that which he was still able to achieve. Did Rev. Elshout have a premonition that he was approaching the end of his earthly journey? We do not know. We do know, however, that it was his wish that Scheveningen would be his last congregation.

Elder Pronk reminded Mrs. Elshout of the extraordinary circumstances that culminated in their marriage. He also spoke of its remarkable conclusion.

Elder Pronk stated that it was for the second time that a pastor of the Scheveningen congregation had passed away suddenly. In 1960, Rev. J.W. Kersten had also suddenly exchanged time for eternity. He was certain that their labors, as well as the labors of other pastors who had served the Scheveningen congregation, were not in vain in the Lord.

Elder Pronk described Rev. Elshout as a man who knew how to combine gravity and humor. With a twinkle in his eyes and with kindness, he knew how to address problem areas. Precisely because of the manner in which he did so, people were generally inclined to listen to him.

Rev. D. Rietdijk, the moderator of Scheveningen, but also a friend of Rev. Elshout, proclaimed God's Word from Genesis 5:24b, "...and he was not; for God took him." He highlighted the abruptness of what had transpired: "He was not." What a shock! Without uttering a word, without a deathbed, without a final farewell, and without dealing with the struggle that typifies the end of life, it suddenly became reality that Enoch "was not."

Life is but a handbreadth—not the breadth of five fingers, but rather, the thickness of a hand. There is but one step between us and death. A painful absence will then become a reality. People will miss the people whom God has given them.

It caught Rev. Rietdijk's attention that Rev. Joel R. Beeke, who had written on behalf of the American churches, stated that not only the

Rev. Iziogo and Mr. Ad de Pater accompanied the body of Rev. Elshout on its return journey to the Netherlands. Here, together with Mrs. Elshout, they are sitting in the living room of the parsonage in Scheveningen.

words of Rev. Elshout commanded respect, but also his walk. He was a man who was upright and honest in his walk. Rev. Rietdijk continued:

> What a testimony he has left us by way of his walk! What a privilege it is when you may say of your father that his walk was truly an extension of the words he spoke. To walk as one of the children of light is pure grace.

"For God took him." These words unveil to us the hands of God that took Enoch away—hands that have also taken Rev. Arie Elshout away. Remember that these hands are the hands of a Father!

Tenderly and lovingly he has been taken away. We may say that, so to speak, he did not see death. Although Christ's hands are caring and loving hands, please remember that they are also pierced hands, for Rev. Elshout has not been taken away and taken up because he worked so much and preached so much or because he has been a minister for thirty-six years. No one will enter heaven as either a minister or an elder. Only lost sinners will enter heaven who have been washed in the blood of the Lamb by virtue of these pierced hands. Only such sinners will arrive there, sinners who have been sanctified and renewed by the Holy Spirit, whom God has led through this life in ways they did not know and upon paths that were past finding out.

In Genesis 5, we hear the repetitive refrain, "and he died." Yet, in the midst of all these mortal men, Enoch stands as a witness—as a witness that in a dying world God has a people whom He has purposed to be the recipients of life. In the midst of the old pre-flood world, Enoch was symbolic of the life that has been secured in Christ. If you were to ask, "Where did the Lord take Enoch?" then the author of Hebrews provides us with the answer, "God had translated him: for before his translation he had this testimony, that he pleased God" (Heb. 11:5).

If you were to ask, "To which place has our minister gone?" the answer is, "Your minister has gone home." Last week he departed from home to go home. From the land in which he sojourned, he has journeyed to his Father's eternal home where he may eternally behold the King. He has been translated into glory on the basis of the merits of His Lord and Master, "which was dead, and is alive" (Rev. 2:8b).

Elfriede, Arie has gone home! If you could only see for a moment how he may now worship his King before His throne, then you would not wish him back for one minute. On the contrary, our most earnest desire would then be that which the Apostle Paul expressed, saying, "…having a desire to depart, and to be with Christ; which is far better" (Phil. 1:23). Children, your father has come home!

Congregation of Scheveningen, your minister may now be engaged in a worship service that will never end. He may eternally magnify God. Do not forget his spoken word, and do not forget his walk. Consider the end of his conversation (Heb. 13:7). Perhaps you respond: "What is there to be considered?" We may consider that God took him away, and God translated him.

"Mark the perfect man, and behold the upright: for the end of that man is peace" (Psa. 37:37)—eternal and never-ending peace. There will never be any interruption, for this peace has been purchased and secured by the blood of the Lamb, resulting in his being forever with the Lord. Let this comfort you, and may your meditation upon this be sweet. Let us seek that peace, saying with the psalmist, "With my whole heart have I sought thee" (Psa. 119:10a).

Family and friends then traveled from Zoetermeer to the Eik en Duinen Cemetery in The Hague. At intersections, police officers were directing the flow of traffic to make sure that the exceptionally long funeral procession would have the right-of-way. At the cemetery, the body of Rev. Arie Elshout was committed to the grave. Christ Himself rested in a grave and thereby sanctified it.

The journey to the cemetery "Oud Eyk en Duinen" in The Hague

The gravesite was surrounded by children and grandchildren. Rev. C. Harinck spoke on behalf of the ministers of the (Netherlands) Reformed Congregations—and especially as a friend. He spoke of the strong bond of love that was evident in Rev. Elshout's family:

It was a bond that, irrespective of trials and circumstances, had grown stronger during the years. The family has therefore lost more in him than just a father.

As ministers we have also lost much. We have lost a beloved brother and friend who was always loving and upright in his interaction with us, and who, especially in difficult circumstances, was compassionate, supportive, and ready to give advice.

The certainty of the glory that may now be his portion is in the first place not rooted in either his own testimony or his blameless walk, but rather, in the Word of the Lord: "He that…believeth on him that sent me, hath everlasting life, and shall not come into condemnation" (John 5:24). His hope was founded upon the Word of the God which declares in the gospel that whoever looks unto the crucified Jesus and believes in Him shall not perish but have eternal life. What a struggle it was before he had learned that lesson! Frequently, he thought that eternal life would be for those who bettered themselves, or for those who wept heartfelt tears about their transgressions and sinful way of life. Then again he thought that salvation was for those whose conviction of sin was sufficiently deep and who were convinced of their sins and deep misery. He frequently spoke to me about this struggle.

When I told him that there was so much of the world that I had to leave behind, and how painful my parting with all of this had been, he replied, "But I had to die to religion." God thereby taught him to seek his salvation in Christ, and the wonder of the unconditional justification of the ungodly purely by faith in Christ became a reality for him. He no longer sought to be saved by self-improvement—not even by weeping and praying, but by faith.

What was true of Paul can also be said of Rev. Elshout: "Without were fightings, within were fears" (2 Cor. 7:5). There was a thorn in his flesh, the messenger of Satan to buffet him (2 Cor. 12:7b). He was subjected to trials, however, so that he would be able to comfort those who are being tried. He was thus led in the way of trials. I experienced this firsthand when I served as a pastor in America, for there we became intimately acquainted with each other. How he was then subjected to "fightings and fears!" How Satan then buffeted him, saying, "You are not a called servant, for you would then be far more esteemed by the people! You do not possess the grace of God, for then it would not have become so dark in your heart. You are not one of God's elect, for do you think that God would subject His beloved people to such darkness and such cross-providences?" Added to this was his unanswered petition that the thorn be removed from his flesh.

Last but not least, he was burdened by his concern for the churches. How troubled he was when the church did not fare well—especially when people were disingenuous toward one another, when people sought to promote themselves and did not hesitate to step on others to achieve their goals! God thus led him in a way of many trials. However, God's wisdom in all of this was that he was enabled to comfort others with the comforts with which God comforted him. It was not until later that he comprehended this truth, and then acknowledged and thanked God for having led him in this way. The fruits thereof are to be observed until this day.

Words of sympathy and comfort—What tender memories of their time in America were there for Mrs. Elshout and Rev. and Mrs. Harinck.

Rev. Harinck then had a special word for the grandchildren from America who hardly knew any Dutch. He addressed them in English, expressing his wish that they might ask the Lord: "Lord, give me that blessed portion; give me that portion of my grandpa, that portion of the children of God."

On behalf of his mother, brothers, and sisters, Bart Elshout expressed his gratitude to the speakers. He had a special word of thanks, however, for the mission team of Izi:

> ...for the special love with which you have surrounded our father prior to and following his death. We were touched by the manner in which you cared for his body following his death. While giving thanks to the Lord for all this, we also wish to express our heartfelt gratitude for your extraordinary commitment that has made it possible to have this funeral here in the Netherlands.

> Thus the life of our beloved father has come to an end. In God's sovereign wisdom, He has put a period behind his life. I fully concur with that which Rev. Harinck has articulated so clearly, namely, the profound impact our father has had on our lives. Together with our beloved mother, he exemplified for us the fear of the Lord. Since the days of our youth, they lovingly urged us to seek the Lord and to seek a refuge for our soul in the Lord Jesus and His mediatorial work. Since our childhood, we have sensed that he fervently loved the God whom he served.

> Frequently he would end his prayers at the table with the words, "for Thy covenant's sake." Because of that covenant that is eternally secure in the Son of God's good pleasure, he may now eternally "joy in [his] God as ne'er before, faith's victory achieving" (Psalter 420:2—Psalm 68). With the entire redeemed multitude, he may now eternally jubilate that which is expressed in Psalter 197:2 (Psalm 72).

At Bart's request, this psalm was sung by all who were present. It was a fitting conclusion to the funeral and the conclusion of his father's earthly journey. It expresses the worship in which Arie Elshout may now be engaged in heaven:

> *And blessed be His glorious Name*
> *To all eternity;*
> *The whole earth let His glory fill.*
> *Amen: So let it be!*

Rev. Arie Elshout

A sinner saved by grace, and a minister of the gospel
who was privileged to preach Christ and Him crucified
on five continents—and thus to the ends of the earth.

(A picture taken during his visit to Australia)

Grave of Rev. and Mrs. Elshout

Cemetery "Oud Eyk en Duinen"
The Hague, the Netherlands

Here lies buried
until the day of the resurrection
our beloved husband,
father, and grandfather

ARIE ELSHOUT

Minister of the
(Netherlands) Reformed Congregations

Rotterdam Izi, Nigeria
January 20, 1923 August 10, 1991

and
our loving and caring mother,
Oma, and great-grandmother

ELFRIEDE IRMGARD ILSE
ELSHOUT-MELZIAN

Rothenfelde, Germany
December 15, 1922

Zwijndrecht, the Netherlands
September 24, 2013

Whether we live therefore, or die, we are the Lord's.
Romans 14:8c

But the LORD is my defence; and my God is the rock of my refuge.
Psalm 94:22

Appendices

Two Sermons by Rev. A. Elshout

Jesus or Barabbas

A PASSION SERMON BY REV. A. ELSHOUT

~

Scripture reading: Luke 23:13-25

Psalters:
231:1,3
157:1,2,4,5
83:1
292:1,2,5

~

You can find the portion of Scripture on which we wish to meditate in the Gospel of Luke, chapter 23:13-25. We will read once more verses 24-25: "And Pilate gave sentence that it should be as they required. And he released unto them him that for sedition and murder was cast into prison, whom they had desired; but he delivered Jesus to their will."

This passage speaks of *The Suffering of the Lord Jesus in the Courtroom of Pilate.*

We will consider the following three thoughts:

       1. A Benefactor scourged
       2. A Redeemer sentenced to death
       3. An evildoer released

1. A Benefactor scourged

Congregation, as Benefactor, Jesus had always done good. He had kept the law of God perfectly. This Benefactor, having always loved God above all and His neighbor as Himself, was deemed worthy of being scourged. What a dreadful humiliation that must have been for the Lord Jesus! Day and night He had been actively engaged as Savior and Mediator in meriting salvation for lost children of Adam and in making payment for their debts. He had been laboring to secure life for a people subject to death and damnation.

What a great Benefactor He was! He had healed so many sick people from their diseases! How many He had delivered, even from death! He had fully lived up to what had been prophesied about Him in Psalm 72, namely, that He would deliver the needy when they cried. How many wayward sinners He had taught the way of salvation, leading them in the way of righteousness! How very evident His goodness had been when He declared that, upon believing in His Name and trusting in His work, forgiveness of sins would both be possible and certain.

Never before had there been a Benefactor like Him! He fully answered to the purpose for which God created mankind. His conduct conformed exactly to the purpose for which His Father had sent Him into the world. His tender mercies and lovingkindnesses had been ever of old (Ps. 25). Yet, how was He rewarded for all the good He had done? He received nothing but hate and scorn in return. He had to experience what so many before and after Him have experienced, namely, that ingratitude is the world's reward.

How intense His suffering must have been when He was treated as an evildoer, as the worst criminal! The vilest slander proceeded from the mouths of His accusers. The chief priests, as well as many of the people, demanded His execution. His innocence was of no avail to Him. They cried out, "Crucify Him, crucify Him," treating Him as if He were the worst criminal imaginable. Pilate had investigated their accusations but had found Jesus to be not guilty as charged. He then sent Him to Herod to let him investigate the whole matter as well, and Herod also had to admit that Jesus had done nothing that made Him worthy of the death penalty.

When Jesus returned to Pilate, the entire crowd (stirred up by the chief priests) cried out, "Crucify Him, crucify Him!" It was clear: He had to die! How immense the suffering of the Savior must have been in light of this verdict! How intensely it must have pained His heart and soul! After all, He was as human as you and I are! He always had treated the people well. He had been laboring for their salvation day and night and then to receive such treatment!

They demanded His death because they loved darkness rather than light. They did not want Him to be King over them. They had no use for His doctrine. They loathed the kind of life He had lived, even though His life had been in full harmony with the will of God.

The people who had gathered were fully aware that there were two possible options: either their own self (their old man) had to be crucified, or Jesus had to be crucified! It was one of the two. They fully sensed what was at stake here! Submission to the teachings of the Lord Jesus would mean a perpetual crucifixion of self, and thus of one's own pride. It meant that they would have to humble themselves before God as contrite sinners, and that was something they were unwilling to do! His teachings not only demanded a perpetual crucifixion of their pride, but also a crucifixion of the lusts of the flesh. The teachings of the Lord Jesus cut so deeply into that which our flesh and blood so much desire. His teachings cut so deeply into our sinful selves. Given the two options, their choice was: He must be crucified! They preferred that choice above crucifying their own sinful flesh.

Perhaps you reply: "How perverse—how perverse indeed! How could they treat this Benefactor in this manner, saying, 'Crucify Him. Away with Him!'?"

Have you ever seen your own image in the mirror that was just held before you? Did you ever see yourself as you truly are? Have you not seen yourself among those who said: "Let Him be crucified instead of me being crucified because I don't want Him to rule over me?"

Congregation, the confession of these people is ultimately to be found in the inner recesses of all of our hearts. Is there anyone among us who desires to be crucified? Who desires the crucifixion of his own ego, his own pride, his own lusts, and his own strength? Who is inclined to crucify that "old man" deep within us? Let us be honest, boys and girls. Do you desire to have such a King rule your heart and life?

You may possibly have experienced this dilemma already in your life. You do not necessarily have to be old for that to be the case. Boys and girls can also have this experience. Such will indeed be the case when God, by His mighty grace, has intervened in our lives. Apart from that, however, we will indeed seek to safeguard our sinful selves. We don't want to be laid low and die to everything that is of the world and of self. We will oppose this with all our might! One person will show this opposition more blatantly and carnally than another person, whereas someone else may do so more hypocritically. One thing is certain, however: We will resist!

That, in fact, is precisely what the people did when they cried out: "Crucify Him, crucify Him!" Obviously, some people in the crowd yelled these words because they were stirred up to do so. They didn't really know what they were doing. They later realized what they had actually done, and then they smote upon their breasts as they returned home.

Have we ever smitten upon our breast as they did? We read of the publican in the parable that he smote upon his breast, saying: "O God be merciful to me, a sinner." If we would but briefly look at ourselves in the mirror of the sufferings of Jesus, we would detect the same sins in our hearts and lives as we detect in the lives of those who desired the death of this Benefactor. Oh, congregation, how often did you and I behave ungratefully toward God in response to all the blessings He has bestowed upon us? We may have thanked God with our lips, but was our gratitude visible in our lives? Is our life a living sacrifice unto God? Do our lives bear witness to the fact that we no longer live unto ourselves, but rather unto the Lord? How regrettable it is that we too have chosen so often in favor of our sinful lusts rather than letting Jesus be King over us!

Pilate sought to get out of this predicament strategically. He came up with the idea of presenting a duo to the people: Barabbas or Jesus. What a duo! Has there ever been a more humiliating duo than this one? The other party of this duo, Barabbas, was truly a lawbreaker. He was a real criminal! Today we would probably have called him a terrorist. He was truly a menace to society. He truly deserved the death penalty to which he had been sentenced! The other party of this duo, Jesus, was innocence personified. How the Savior must have suffered from having been nominated for this duo! The Benefactor versus the criminal! Goodness par excellence versus the embodiment of evil! Such were the parties of this duo. Could anything be more humiliating for the Savior than this duo?

Nevertheless, the golden thread of God's plan is woven throughout the fabric of this ungodliness and injustice. It was God's plan of salvation to save evildoers by means of a Savior who only did that which was good. His perfect benevolence also included His being obedient even unto His death on the cross. How extraordinary is the mystery of redemption embodied in this fact! God has made Him to be sin who knew no sin, so that sinners can be justified and be made heirs of eternal life (2 Cor. 5:21). Pilate had surely counted on the Benefactor Jesus to have been chosen. He was mistaken, however, because Barabbas was chosen.

In his address to the Jews on Pentecost, the Apostle Peter accused the Jews of having denied Christ when He stood before Pilate—when they desired the release of a murderer. They had cried out: "Release Barabbas and let Jesus be crucified!"

Congregation, here we observe the climax of wickedness and ungodliness. What grief was inflicted upon Him who had never done anything else but soothe pain and grief! What we are capable of doing under certain circumstances is astonishing indeed! How often have we too made choices in our lives that were blatantly evil! We had better not throw the stones that we were thinking of casting at all those ungodly people who made such a dreadful choice.

Is it not true that you and I also have frequently made choices that were diametrically opposed to God's will? How often did we make sinful choices in our conduct toward our civil government? How often did we make evil choices when we decided to gratify our sinful lusts and desires at all costs? How often we have permitted ourselves to be tempted and seduced to commit sin in given circumstances and we later asked ourselves in agony: "What have I done? How could I have done this?" How often it happens in our present age that people are encouraged to sacrifice innocent life by having an abortion in order to eliminate inconvenient circumstances!

How many, throughout the ages, have been stirred up to commit the most heinous crimes! I am then thinking of the awful crimes that have been committed in support of national-socialism, communism, or any other ideology. We all know what happened in Auschwitz and other concentration camps. No, we had better not throw any stones at others, for if the circumstances are suitable, we all are capable of doing heinous things if God does not refrain us.

Prior to releasing Barabbas, Pilate first tried to change the opinion of the crowd by permitting Jesus to be scourged. He gave his men orders to batter the body of Jesus with a whip. Such a whip or scourge consisted of leather strips in which metal pellets were wrapped. They lacerated the body of the Lord Jesus with that scourge, causing deep wounds.

How terrible that was! What terrible injustice! He was subjected to a judicial scourging, even though the investigation had clearly shown that He had done nothing worthy of scourging. Pilate was hopeful that this action might soften the hearts of the people.

After the scourging, Pilate led the Lord Jesus outside and he said to the crowd, "Behold the Man!" Congregation, what a sight that must have been! Behold the Man! There He stood with His bleeding body, crowned with a crown of thorns that caused blood to ooze from his pores. Behold the Man! Pilate was hoping that this sight of Him would have moved the hearts of the crowd to say, "Let Him go!" That did not happen, however. On the contrary! They preferred Barabbas. Their choice remained unchanged!

How enormous must have been the pain inflicted by this scourging, and how inexpressibly must Christ have suffered in His soul! Suffering injustice is also a dreadful experience for us, isn't it? When that happens to us verbally, it can already feel as if we are being pierced with swords. If we are also abused physically, it would be a horrifying experience for us.

Nevertheless, this Benefactor had to be scourged so that there might be a people who would learn to stammer the words recorded in Isaiah 53:5, "…and with His stripes we are healed." They have learned to acknowledge before God that they were deserving of such a scourging. Therefore, when God does indeed chastise them, they have to acknowledge before Him that they are worthy of much more than that!

In Hebrews 12, we can read that God will chastise every son or daughter that He receives. There may be a time in our lives that the Lord will indeed scourge our souls, reminding us of our offences and indicting us for our many sins and iniquities. When that happens, we may have to go through a period of time when our soul must experience God's displeasure. It can also happen that external circumstances function as a scourge. Oh, how very painful can God's scourgings be when He chastens us!

We must, however, always bear in mind that these chastisements are of a totally different nature than the chastisements Jesus had to endure. He endured these scourgings as a judicial punishment, whereas the chastisements administered by God to bring sinners to Himself proceed from His saving love. God will chasten those whom He loves to make them partakers of His holiness—so that by His stripes they may be healed. In Psalm 103:3-4, we read of His healing grace: "Who healeth all thy diseases; who redeemeth thy life from destruction; who crowneth thee with lovingkindness and tender mercies."

He was crowned with a crown of thorns, and sinners are crowned with kindness and tender mercies. What a difference! We are worthy of those thorns. How astonishing: He bearing the crown of thorns, and sinners the crown of honor! How is that possible? That is possible only because of God's eternal and sovereign good pleasure! God unveils His good pleasure to us in directing and permitting the scourging of His Son. He permitted the scourging of His Son so that sinners could be kissed with the kiss of His friendship. Only because of the oppressive suffering of His Son is He able to offer us His love and friendship. He will also manifest His friendship toward us in times of sorrow and affliction. The Benefactor was scourged so that transgressors could be blessed.

Congregation, however dreadful this scourging may have been, it was nevertheless not sufficient. For the salvation of sinners, more than just a scourging was needed. The Redeemer had to be sentenced to death! That brings us to our second thought:

2. A Redeemer sentenced to death

The crowd that demanded His death was not to be satisfied with His scourging. Pilate ended up caving in to their desire that He had to die. The scourging Christ had received did not suffice for them.

However, that scourging also did not suffice for God. It had been decreed that Jesus would die this violent death on the cross. His death had already been foreshadowed in the Old Testament by means of all the sacrificial animals that died a substitutionary death so that guilty sinners could be acquitted and live.

When, at last, Pilate sentenced the Lord Jesus to death, he did not just do so as a private person. Instead, he did so as the representative of the government to whom God had given the sword to execute justice in punishing evildoers. As our catechism points out, Jesus suffered under Pontius Pilate as judge. The execution to which Jesus was sentenced was therefore a judicial one. To be executed is the most dreadful, disgraceful, and shameful thing to which a person can be subjected. However, if we were to be executed while absolutely innocent, it would also be the most grievous thing that could happen! How deeply this must have grieved the Lord Jesus! He would be executed as a perfectly innocent person.

In addition to that, the death on the cross was accursed of God. And yet, all of this happened by God's direction. Even though Pilate and the chief priests were and remain fully accountable for their criminal acts, it all happened by God's direction that the Savior, by virtue of this death sentence, would fully satisfy God's justice. God's justice demands, without any exception, the death of the sinner. Since death is the penalty for the commission of sin, Jesus had to undergo all of this suffering.

Modern theologians try to persuade us that God did not really want the Lord Jesus to suffer. They try to tell us that His suffering was actually a most wretched mistake. Congregation, that is absolutely untrue! We can read in Isaiah 53 that it was God's will that all our iniquities would be laid upon Him. That does, however, not mean that all who collaborated to have Christ executed were not fully accountable for their wicked deeds. Although God is not the author of injustice, He nevertheless overrules it toward the accomplishment of His predetermined purpose. We always are and remain fully responsible for our sins!

Jesus was sentenced to death to lay the foundation for the just acquittal of sinners. Salvation is not only a matter of mercy but also of justice. Not only was there an exercise of justice toward Jesus, but also toward all who are comprehended in Him as the Head of the covenant of grace. They are saved because God's justice has been satisfied. Thus, salvation is not only a matter of mercy but also of satisfied justice. Christ, having been subjected to death for all that belong to Him, is the absolute warranty that their guilt will never again have to be absolved in God's judgment. That guilt has been fully absolved: "Thy pardoning grace has made us free, And covered our iniquity."

Congregation, God will see to it that there will always be a people who will savingly understand and experience that salvation is as much a matter of grace as it is a matter of justice. Justice was executed toward the Lord Jesus who merited salvation, and mercy is bestowed upon those who as evildoers are entirely deserving of eternal damnation.

This brings us to our third thought:

3. An evildoer released

Congregation, for a moment let us imagine ourselves to be in the prison cell where Barabbas was locked away. He had already been sentenced to death because of his crime. He was sitting in his prison cell, waiting for the moment of his execution. What would have been on Barabbas's mind as he was sitting in his cell? Did he sit there in the same spirit as Manasseh? We know that Manasseh came to the acknowledgement that the Lord was God while in his prison cell. Would Barabbas, just like Manasseh, have bowed before God in his prison cell? Would he perhaps have cried out repentantly, "Against thee, thee only, have I sinned, and done this evil in thy sight: that thou mightest be justified when thou speakest, and be clear when thou judges." (Psa. 51:4)?

We don't know whether Barabbas was thus disposed in his cell. We do know, however, what happens in the life of those whom the Lord is preparing for the revelation that He delights in mercy, and that judgment is His strange work. In order to value the fact that God's wrath has been quenched, something needs to happen in our life. What then needs to happen? God, by His Word and Spirit, must confront us with our sin and its consequences. He will convince us that we have grievously transgressed all His commandments, that we have kept none of them, and that we are inclined toward all evil. That has to happen at least once, but it is even better if that happens more often.

For some, it takes years before they come to that point, but for others, it does not take that long. God's ways vary significantly in that regard. In the life of one person, such conviction is accompanied by much anguish, whereas in the life of someone else, there may not be that much anguish. However different such experiences may be, one thing is certain: it is not a very pleasant experience for our flesh and blood. It will be an unsettling experience when God establishes His court of justice in our conscience and summons us before His omniscience. Sinners will then begin to understand the words of the poet in Ps. 142:4, "Refuge failed me; no man cared for my soul."

When God truly converts someone, He erects His court of justice in the conscience, and the following accusers will be present: the law of God, the Prince of darkness, and one's own conscience. He or she will then have to admit: "Lord, it is true that in Thy judgment Thou art just, and in Thy sentence right." We will then be in a spiritual prison cell, and we will be unable to escape. Congregation, at this point the distinction between a true conversion and that of a hypocrite will be evident. There are many people who, in their distress, have succeeded in delivering themselves by means of their own reasoning and conclusions. Perhaps they were set at liberty by the persuasive arguments of others. One thing is certain, however: they were able to liberate themselves. They were able to deliver themselves by their self-manufactured faith, by their own good works, and by their manifold religious activities. Thus they presumed to have found peace for their soul.

When the Lord works in our hearts and lives, however, it will be different. When it pleases the Lord to grant us the knowledge of this blessed acquittal secured by the mediation of the Lord Jesus, we will be unable to deliver ourselves. When God's Spirit works in our hearts, we will experience that even our best works are unacceptable to God. The Lord thereby will make us willing to humble ourselves before Him in true repentance. When we are made willing to humble ourselves before God, we will acquiesce in our just damnation. I am hereby not implying that it will be a matter of indifference to them whether they are saved. Not at all, but by saying "amen" to their damnation, they, to use the language of the Bible, "shall accept of the punishment of their iniquity" (Lev. 26:43)—or as expressed by the psalmist, "Lord, in Thy judgement Thou art just, and in Thy sentence right!" (Psalter 143:2—Psalm 51).

As he sat in his prison cell, Barabbas was ignorant of what was happening outside the jail. Jesus was being delivered to be crucified, and Barabbas would subsequently be set free. To be set free meant that he could never again be held accountable for his crimes. His freedom was secured by a legal verdict! However, Barabbas did not yet know about this decision.

Congregation, just try to imagine Barabbas sitting in his cell and hearing approaching footsteps that stopped right in front of his door. What else could Barabbas have thought other than: "Now they are coming to get me for my execution!" However, as the door was opened, somebody told him to get out! Then they told him that he was a free man! How amazed Barabbas must have been! Had he really been acquitted? Had his right to live been restored? He certainly must have asked: "How is that possible?" They must have told him that he had been acquitted for Jesus' sake!

The Heidelberg Catechism rightly links Pilate's judicial sentence to the acquittal and salvation of sinners. Lord's Day 15 answers the question, "Why did He suffer under Pontius Pilate as judge?" by saying, "that He, being innocent, and yet condemned by a temporal judge, might thereby free us from the severe judgement of God to which we were exposed." When it pleases the Lord to bestow upon His people the comfort of this acquittal, He frequently directs the circumstances of their lives in such a way that they will wholeheartedly say "Amen" to the verdict of God's law, namely, that they are worthy of death.

Precisely then it pleases the Lord to use the gospel of a condemned Mediator to direct their attention to that one offering by which He, from eternity, has perfected them that are sanctified. He will reveal to them that this is an Offering without blemish. In so doing, He will reveal to them the value of Christ's condemnation as the basis for the acquittal of ungodly sinners. When that happens, the heart will be enlarged, and the soul filled with joy.

Oh, what joy and enlargement of heart is experienced when one may perceive that salvation is possible without God's justice being compromised in any way! When that possibility is unveiled to us, there will already be a measure of assurance embedded in it. That assurance is not contingent upon anything to be found in men, but instead, is rooted in the faithfulness of the Lord and the power of the blood of Christ that cleanses from all sins. Such will be the effect of faith in the hearts of those who penitently take refuge to the blood of the Lord Jesus that speaks better things than the blood of Abel. They will then experience an enlargement of heart that will prompt those penitents to join us in singing: "Come, let us voice our jubilation, and triumph in the grace supplied" (Psalter 427:6—Psalm 118).

What a transformation there will then be! What a miracle! "As heaven is high above the earth, so great His mercy proves; as far from us as east from west, He all our sin removes" (Psalter 277:8—Psalm 103).

How glorious a salvation it is indeed to be pardoned for Jesus's sake and to secure a right to eternal life—a salvation secured by God's promises! All of these blessings issue forth from the Lord Jesus having been obedient even unto death, even the death of the cross! Let us sing together about that salvation by way of Psalter 83:1 (Psalm 32):

How blest is he whose trespass
Hath freely been forgiv'n,
Whose sin is wholly covered
Before the sight of heav'n.
Blest he to whom Jehovah
Imputeth not his sin,
Who hath a guileless spirit,
Whose heart is true within.

Congregation, blest is he to whom Jehovah imputeth not his sin. Did you hear that? God could justly declare us all guilty, and yet He will justly acquit sinners as the fruit of Jesus having been judicially sentenced. Even though Pilate's actions were so perverse from our vantage point, Christ nevertheless received the death penalty justly by way of a judicial verdict.

Blessed is he to whom Jehovah imputeth not his sin. Throughout the ages, there have been many people who have been privileged to experience that God justly acquitted them for Jesus's sake. How many there have been who were privileged to experience that God gave witness of this blessing in their hearts! What a salvation, and what adoration, worship, and joy this blessing engendered! One cannot actually express its effect in words. You must have experienced it in order to be able to understand it.

What a wonder it is that sinners may indeed experience this acquittal, and that you may also experience it! Perhaps you will reply that this acquittal is laid away only for God's people. That is true. However, even though you may still be unconverted, the day may come that you will also truly become a child of God. Granted, He cried out, "It is accomplished!" only for His elect. But you may very well be one of them. Although you may presently still be unconverted, that does not mean that it will never happen. Oh, seek the Lord's countenance, for He delights in being sought by sinners.

Blessed is he to whom Jehovah imputeth not his sin. What sort of people are they? Are they good people—lovely and obedient people? No, congregation, there is only one adjective that is fitting here: they are ungodly people. We could also say: "Blessed are the ungodly to whom Jehovah imputeth not his sin." Evildoers and transgressors of all God's commandments are acquitted. What a wide open door is set before us here! This is possible only because of the blood of the Savior. Even if the whole world were to avail itself of the efficacy of His mediatorial work, there would be more than enough!

I also have a word for you who have never been troubled because of your sins. Humble yourself before the Lord and beseech Him to be gracious to you for Jesus's sake. Ask Him also to work in your heart and life.

Perhaps you reply, "I don't really feel like it. I absolutely do not desire to be troubled because of my sins. I want to be happy!"

Oh yes, I know that. You need to know, however, that there can be true happiness only after having been troubled. This is how God has worked and has taught His people throughout the ages.

God will give joy after sorrow. The measure in which we will experience that sorrow is not to be determined by us. I am certain, however, that all who have been saved know of a time in their lives when they have bowed before God as humble penitents. They all have acknowledged that they were worthy of eternal death, and that He would have done them no injustice if He would have cast them away forever. All who are yet to be saved will experience some of that conviction in their hearts. In saying that, I am by no means implying that the depth and length of such convictions is to be determined by us. On the contrary!

Having said that, however, we must have some experiential acquaintance with being inwardly inclined to humble ourselves before God, so that we will accept the punishment of our iniquity (Lev. 26:43). The Lord is pleased to use such inner conviction to make us receptive and grateful for the substitutionary and mediatorial ministry of Christ. The Lord's Supper form expresses it in striking terms: "Whereas you otherwise would have suffered eternal death, I have given My body to the death of the cross and shed My blood for you."

How shall we ever learn to value this truth if we have never been persuaded inwardly that we are worthy of eternal death? Congregation, I am not making the case here for the experience of gloom and doom, but rather that you would experience these matters with clarity. Humbly beseech the Lord to grant you this needed clarity. When He does so, we will not only humbly and wholeheartedly bow before Him, but we will also adore the sovereign good pleasure of the Lord in sending His Son to die on the cross. We will then begin to marvel that He, in spite of Pilate's miscarriage of justice, has been pleased to forge the foundation upon which sinners can and will be legally acquitted. We shall then honor God for all His wondrous doings, and we will worship Him as recorded in Psalter 292:1 (Psalm 107):

> *Praise the Lord, for he is good,*
> *For His mercies ever sure,*
> *From eternity have stood,*
> *To eternity endure.*
> *Let His ransomed people raise,*
> *Songs to their Redeemer's praise!*

Amen.

APPENDIX TWO

The Slaying of the Children of Bethlehem
A SERMON BY REV. A. ELSHOUT

∽

Scripture reading: Matthew 2

Psalters:
268:1,4
425:4,5
439:1
15:1,2,3

∽

In Jeremiah 31:17, we read: "There is hope in thine end, saith the Lord, that thy children shall come again to their own border." Under what circumstances were these words spoken? This question is answered in verse 15: "Thus saith the LORD; A voice was heard in Ramah, lamentation, and bitter weeping; Rachel weeping for her children refused to be comforted for her children, because they were not."

By way of the prophet Jeremiah, the Lord said to the weeping Rachel: "Refrain thy voice from weeping, and thine eyes from tears: for thy work shall be rewarded, saith the LORD; and they shall come again from the land of the enemy." Then the words follow in which the Lord communicates that in the end there is hope for her children.

The children of Israel found themselves in very dire circumstances when these words were spoken, for they had been led into captivity. They are referred to here as the children of Rachel, one of Jacob's wives. When these words were spoken, the oppressive sway of the enemy was so great that it appeared as if the children of Rachel would never return from their captivity. Their sins had brought them into bondage to their enemy, and their situation appeared to be hopeless. Therefore Rachel wept and refused to be comforted. How readily we can understand her reaction!

As we reflect on the dark times in which we are living today, we see many similarities with the historical context in which Jeremiah spoke these words. Would we also not weep when we reflect on the age in which we, our children, and our grandchildren are currently living—times that are both fearful and dark?

Worst of all, however, is the fact that we and our children are conceived and born in sin, and therefore are children of wrath. This is not merely a hollow phrase, but indeed stark reality! When we focus on that reality, who would not weep? As we look toward the future, what shall then become of our children and grandchildren? We are truly living in the land of the shadow of death, and thus we lie in the midst of death.

Therefore, what a blessing it is that until this very day the Lord, in the sacrament of holy baptism, visually signifies and seals the identical truth He commissioned Jeremiah to proclaim centuries ago: *There is hope for your children.*

Was there any expectation from man's side? Absolutely not! That expectation originates in God. You might ask, "What then is the basis for this hope?" This basis will become clear when you read the entire chapter of Jeremiah 31. Only for His covenant's sake and His Name's sake is there hope or expectation for the children of the congregation. That expectation does not imply that our children are better or different than others. There is but one reason: There is a covenant rooted in eternity, in the Council of Peace, in the Lord's good pleasure. Therefore, and therefore *alone*, there is hope for our children. That expectation proceeds solely from the fact that the Son of God engaged His heart to be a Surety to save men who lie in the midst of death (Jer. 30:21b).

He redeems and saves them by His Word and Spirit on the basis of Christ's mediatorial work. His atoning blood, signified by the water of baptism, is the sole foundation for the expectation we may have for our children. The water of baptism directs us to the blood of Christ that cleanses from all sins (1 John 1:8).

That blood will be efficacious even until the last generation. However dark our times may be; however true it may be that our children lie in the midst of death; yet, there is hope for our children. That which is impossible with men is possible with God—all because of His eternal covenant of grace!

> *Jehovah's truth will stand forever,*
> *His covenant-bonds He will not sever."*
> (Psalter 425:5—Psalm 105)

In light of this truth, we wish to reflect on the history recorded in the chapter that has been read: Matthew 2. You can find the text to be expounded in verses 16 through 18. There we read as follows: "Then Herod, when he saw that he was mocked of the wise men, was exceeding wroth, and sent forth, and slew all the children that were in Bethlehem, and in all the coasts thereof, from two years old and under, according to the time which he had diligently inquired of the wise men. Then was fulfilled that which was spoken by Jeremy the prophet, saying, 'In Rama was there a voice heard, lamentation and weeping, and great mourning, Rachel weeping for her children and would not be comforted, because they are not.'"

These words speak of *The Slaying of the Children of Bethlehem.*

We will consider the following three thoughts:

      1. Who perpetrated this slaying
      2. Who escaped this slaying
      3. Who perished in this slaying

1. Who perpetrated this slaying

Not everyone rejoiced in the news reverberating throughout the land of Israel, namely, that the King of the Jews had been born. One person, King Herod, was not at all happy when he heard about the birth of the King of the Jews. The wise men from the East had communicated this news to the citizens of Jerusalem. Upon their arrival, they had asked: "Where is He that is born King of the Jews?" King Herod was neither a Jew by birth, nor had he been born as a king. The Roman emperor had installed him as his vassal. The annals of history refer to this king Herod as "Herod the Great". This name was given to him in light of his having commissioned many important building projects. One of these large (or great) projects was the expansion and enhancement of the post-exilic temple. Herod had enlarged this second temple immensely. It took them forty-six years to complete it. However, he undoubtedly also "earned" this title due to being an evil monster. Herod literally walked over dead bodies. He slew several of his own sons, for he viewed them as being a threat to his throne. When he heard about the birth of a Jewish King, *the* King of the Jews, he trembled.

His throne was being challenged! He summoned the scribes to inquire of them as to the exact location where this King would be born. They replied, "But thou, Bethlehem Ephratah, though thou be little among the thousands of Judah, yet out of thee shall he come forth unto me that is to be ruler in Israel; whose goings forth have been from of old, from everlasting" (Micah 5:2).

We know what Herod did—this sly fox and horrible monster! How applicable to him are the words of Psalter 93:4 (Psalm 36):

While on his bed his thought he gives
To planning wickedness;
He sets himself in evil ways,
He shuns not to transgress.

He sent the wise men from the East to Bethlehem to have them investigate whether the King of the Jews had indeed been born there. He gave them the following instructions: "If it is indeed true, please come back to tell me, for I also wish to worship Him." What a hypocrite he was! He had no intention whatsoever of worshiping this Child. His real intention was to pierce the heart of this Child with a sword—that is, if this Child had indeed been born. What an abominable man he was!

One could say that Herod exemplified man at his very worst. He was a man who fully manifested his innate depravity. The root of such depravity is to be found in the heart of every man, for by nature we are all inclined to hate God and our neighbor. What a blessing that not every human being fully manifests the depravity that dwells within!

When the wise men from the East did not return, however, Herod was outraged. He then gave the satanic and horrendous order to slay all the children who were two years old or younger in Bethlehem and its surrounding region.

What sin had these parents and children committed? What sin had these children committed to justify the commission of such a horrible crime? Absolutely nothing! Oh, what a horrendous miscarriage of justice this was! Herod would not get away with this deed, for the angels witnessed it. The children he killed were covenant children of whom the Lord Jesus said in Matthew 18:10, "For I say unto you, that in heaven their angels do always behold the face of My Father which is in heaven." We believe that, for His covenant's sake, the children of the congregation are the special objects of the Lord's care.

Herod ruthlessly murdered these children. Not only had the angels witnessed it, but the Lord, their covenantal Father, also witnessed what happened, and His retribution would soon follow. Not long after this sacrilege, Herod would die a most wretched death (Acts 12:23).

Had Herod been victorious in executing this mass murder? Was it perhaps a victory for Satan? Satan indeed had a vested interest in having all the children of Bethlehem who were two years old and younger killed. The newborn Child, the King of the Jews, was also one of the intended victims. Did he thereby score a victory after all? Not at all! God intervened, and this Child escaped Herod's infanticide. This leads us to our second thought:

2. Who escaped this slaying

Congregation, the Son of Man was no longer present when the massacre of these children was executed. The Son of God was no longer in Bethlehem, for He was now in Egypt. God safeguarded His Word and His Son!

If we examine this drama in Bethlehem only superficially, our faith in God's providence will be severely tested. How severely it was tested for the people of Bethlehem! Was God aware of what happened there? Why did He permit this massacre to be executed? What purpose did these tragic and trying circumstances serve?

If presently we also find ourselves involved in similar trying circumstances, how different our experience would then be! It would differ greatly from such times when we are only peripherally affected by them. How dreadful it must have been to lose one's children and grandchildren in such a horrible fashion!

How severely the faith of these parents in God's providence must have been tried! They must have asked themselves: "Is it really true that nothing happens apart from His will?" How could all of this have taken place? How could God have permitted this to happen? How many fathers and mothers, and how many grandparents, have already cried out in utter despair: "O Lord, how can all this be? I don't understand it!" How immense can the riddles and the ensuing sorrow be!

Although many of life's riddles will never be solved, some of them will. Do you know when this will transpire? When we may view such circumstances in light of God's Word—when the Lord lets His Word shine as a light into a dark place. That Word also sheds light on the tragedy in Bethlehem. We will then discern that what happened there was also a fulfillment of scriptural prophecy.

Congregation, how do you view the Scriptures? Somebody once put it this way: "The Scriptures, the Bible, are the inspired minutes of the Counsel of Peace—the minutes of God's sovereign decrees. When we permit the light of the Scriptures to illuminate this massacre in Bethlehem, we will evaluate it very differently. However dreadful this event was, yet it was a fulfillment of prophecy: "Then was fulfilled that which was spoken by Jeremy the prophet, saying: In Rama was there a voice heard, lamentation, and weeping, and great mourning, Rachel weeping for her children, and would not be comforted, because they are not" (Matt. 2:17-18).

Even more importantly, there was more than one prophecy that had to be fulfilled. The prophet Hosea had prophesied: "Out of Egypt have I called My Son" (Mat. 2:15; cf. Hos. 11:1). This prophecy also had to be fulfilled. Since Herod sought to kill the Child, God commanded Joseph and Mary to flee to Egypt. If they would have stayed in Bethlehem, how could He have called His Son out of Egypt? Do you now see that God reigns after all? Whatever riddles there may be, and whatever may happen, God reigns!

No, the Lord does not always exempt His church and His people from all evil. However, He will overrule it to achieve a specific and predetermined objective. It is neither the Devil who reigns, nor even Herod nor ultimately Caesar Augustus! God reigns! God so overrules evil that it must even work together for good. In the end, all things must be subservient to fulfill His Word, to the comfort and salvation of His people and the punishment of the ungodly.

There was One who escaped this massacre: the Son of God! Oh, yes, He would ultimately also die due to a murderous execution, for that which Caiaphas and Pilate would inflict on Him would be nothing less than murder. Christ would indeed die at the hands of murderers—but at God's time. That was not to happen in Bethlehem, but instead on Golgotha. There He would die on the accursed cross!

From a human perspective, the Son of God would also die due to a grievous miscarriage of justice. Yet, He had to die to accomplish redemption and merit salvation by way of His active and passive (= suffering) obedience from cradle to cross. His blood would have to be shed in order to secure reconciliation on the basis of satisfaction. That needed to happen in order to secure salvation for sinners such as you and me— for sinners such as our children and grandchildren. To achieve that, the Son of God had to die—but not in Bethlehem. That had to take place on Golgotha.

When this tragic massacre occurred in Bethlehem, no one was able to evaluate this event in light of the Scriptures. That was impossible. A proper evaluation of this event could occur only at a much later date. Only after the Holy Spirit had been poured out, did He lead all writers of the Bible into all the truth. When that happened, an extraordinary transformation took place.

When it pleases the Holy Spirit to shed His light over the entire trajectory of the life of the Lord Jesus, all things will prove to have been an exact fulfillment of everything that had been foretold. We will then perceive it to be in full agreement with the "minutes of the Council of Peace."

This still takes place today when it pleases the Lord to shed light on so many perplexing circumstances in the lives of His children. A well-known illustration can help us grasp this truth. If you look at a the wrong side of a piece of embroidery, you will not be able see a logical pattern connecting all the threads. Instead, it will appear to be a chaotic intermingling of threads. However, after turning over this piece of embroidery, we will observe the most beautiful scenes. We will then discover that such scenes were embroidered according to a very precise pattern.

At times, the Lord is still pleased to do so in the lives of His children. Reverently speaking, He will show them the other side of the cloth! Then riddles will be solved that no man could ever solve. Everything will then fit perfectly. If we then may be led to understand it "afterwards" (John 13:7), we cannot but marvel and worship. Prior to such a moment, we may have lamented like Asaph, "How doth God know? and is there knowledge in the most High?" (Psa. 73:11). We may then have said, "God does everything wrong! If there is indeed a God, He is doing everything wrong!" Perhaps we were reluctant to say this (a healthy reluctance!), but we have thought it nevertheless! If, however, the Lord "afterwards" sheds His light on it, He will have made all things well!

We read of Jacob that he said near the end of his life: "Bury me with my fathers in the cave that is in the field of Ephron the Hittite…there I buried Leah" (Gen. 49:29-31). His entire life he had struggled with the fact that he had received Leah as his wife. According to Jacob, the Lord had done it all wrong. However, what the Lord had done was right, and what Jacob had done was wrong! Jacob thought that all these things were against him, but he was mistaken. Later he would discover that it all had to work together for good (Rom. 8:28-29).

Congregation, I believe that eternity will not be long enough for God's children when He will show them that all things had to work together for good. Then they will finally understand that all things did work together for their salvation and in fulfillment of the "minutes of the Counsel of Peace." Eternity will for God's children not be an experience of idleness. Then it will be seen and adored that all things transpired according to God's holy will.

Before considering our third thought, we will first sing Psalter 439:1 (Psalm 73):

> *O Israel's God, how good Thou art*
> *To all the true and pure of heart!*
> *Though paths of saints are fraught with evil,*
> *Thou showest favor to Thy people.*
> *While faith sank low, I hardly knew*
> *That Thou art Israel's Keeper true;*
> *When in my grief I nurtured doubt,*
> *I well-nigh slipped from ways devout.*

3. Who perished in this slaying

It does not require too much imagination to recognize how immense the sorrow must have been in Bethlehem! We don't know how many children were involved, but it must have been a considerable group.

Rachel weeps over her children because they are not. Perhaps you are wondering what the connection is between Rachel and Bethlehem. It is a very significant one! When Rachel was about to give birth to her second son, Jacob and his family were in the vicinity of Bethlehem. We know that Rachel died shortly after she gave birth to her second child, and Jacob also buried her there. Until today, her grave is still located between Rama and Bethlehem. The people who lived in that region were therefore designated as "the children of Rachel." Long after Rachel had died, the prophet Jeremiah referred to them by the same name, saying, "Rachel weeps over her children."

We can thus say that the children who perished in Bethlehem were Rachel's children. Rachel, as Jacob's second wife, was also a mother in Israel. The children who perished were therefore covenant children. The seed of God's Church perished in Bethlehem! These covenant children were in and of themselves as sinful as all other children.

Yet, in Psalm 8:2, we read, "Out of the mouth of babes and sucklings hast Thou ordained strength." Thus, God will be praised and worshiped out of the mouth of sucklings!

In the Canons of Dort, chapter 1, article 17, our fathers have spoken about the children of the church. There we read: "Since we are to judge of the will of God from His Word which testifies that the children of believers are holy, not by nature, but in virtue of the covenant of grace, in which they, together with the parents, are comprehended, godly parents have no reason to doubt of the election and salvation of their children whom it pleaseth God to call out of this life in their infancy."

This article confronts the claims of the Remonstrants. What did they claim? They claimed that if one teaches that no one will be saved on the basis of foreseen faith, good works, and conversion, and if one thus teaches that we can be saved by faith only, you are thereby condemning all of your little children, for they are incapable of exercising faith.

Our fathers very firmly rejected that accusation. They responded that it is entirely untrue that we are condemning our little children. On the contrary, there is hope for our children when they die very young. That expectation is not based on anything to be found in either the parents or the grandparents. Our hope for children who die is not based on that at all! Our fathers replied that there is a covenant of grace, of which baptism is a sign and a seal.

The administration of baptism is neither a mere formality, a ritual, nor a mere ecclesiastical transaction. Baptism is of far greater significance than many people think. I recognize that there are many people who overestimate baptism as administered to little children—as if baptism yields salvation to those who receive it, thus making it equivalent to regeneration. That is by no means the case! That is heresy! Those who teach this error are deceiving themselves and others.

The true meaning of baptism has been clearly articulated by our fathers in the form for the administration of Holy Baptism. It is a sign and a seal of God's covenant!

God said to Abraham: "I will establish My covenant between Me and thee and thy seed...to be a God unto thee, and to thy seed after thee" (Gen. 17:7). God communicates that exact same promise to His church until this day.

"There is hope for your children." Jeremiah already said this many centuries ago. When Jeremiah uttered these words on behalf of the Lord, Rachel was weeping for her children because they were not. They were captives in Babel. How would they ever return? It was impossible!

Under these circumstances, the Lord spoke to Rachel, saying, "Refrain thy voice from weeping. They shall return!" Did they all come back? No, they did not all come back, yet a core element of the nation did return. We can read in the Bible how this return did indeed transpire. The Lord watched over these children who lived in exile.

There is also hope for the children of our day. There is hope for children who either are growing up or have grown up under the ministry of God's Word. From God's perspective, there is expectation, for Jehovah's truth will stand forever, and His covenant-bonds He will not sever.

Many years ago, when I had liberty to testify of my faith and hope regarding this truth, an old child of God said to me: "Can you always go forward believing that?"

I responded by saying to her: "Regretfully, I do not. But I also have a question for you: Can you always go forward in your unbelief? Then it became very silent. I did not say anything, and neither did she.

What a blessing it is when we no longer have anything to say, and when we let the Word of God speak for itself! There must come such a moment in our lives. What a blessing it is when we come to an end with all our reasoning—with all of our "Yes, but...statements"! What a blessing it is when we may surrender to the Word of God when it is preached and sealed by the sacraments! May the truth that "God be true, but every man a liar" (Rom 3:4), sink so deeply into our hearts that we are totally finished with our reasoning. Oh, what a blessing it is when that happens time and again!

Congregation, even today there is hope for our children and our off-spring. As I have grown older, I have seen with my own eyes and heard with my own ears that God is true to His own Word—also these words! He will build and sustain His church from the children of the congregation.

Is that true for all the children of the congregation? No! In that respect, we clearly see the demarcation of God's sovereignty. Also for the children of the congregation it is true: "Therefore hath he mercy on whom He will have mercy, and whom He will He hardeneth" (Rom. 9:18). He will treat no one unjustly. If it is well, we will humbly admit that. If He were never to look upon any of our children, He would not be doing us any injustice.

But…God's truth shall stand forever! There is hope for our children growing up under the ministry of God's Word. Sunday after Sunday they may be the recipients of this ministration. Either in Sunday school or catechism class, or in school, they will come into contact with the Word of God, and that will not fail to bear fruit.

Perhaps you will ask: "But how about those who are no longer attending church and have said, 'I no longer want to have anything to do with this,'" who have rejected everything that is related to God and His service and have trampled upon their upbringing?"

There is hope for them too! Throughout the years, there have been so many who have turned their backs upon everything. Sometimes you meet them at the other end of the world—people who have left their country because they wanted to rid themselves of religion. In any event, they wanted to rid themselves of the religion of their parents and of the life of faith to which they were exposed in their upbringing. They wanted to part with this at all costs. Away with it! Immigration to New Zealand or Australia was the solution for them. At least you are then far away at the other end of the world where no one can either see or find you.

There was an elder in one of my former congregations who left the Netherlands for that same reason. When he was about nineteen years old, he decided to part with the religion of his God-fearing parents. Most of all, he wanted to part with God Himself. He decided to emigrate, taking his journey into a far country. When he finally arrived in New York and disembarked from the ship, a man standing at the end of the gangway approached him. He said to him: "Boy, oh boy, have you also come to America? Well, you know, boy, the same God who lives in the Netherlands is the same God who lives here." These were the first words that were spoken to him when he came ashore! When his God-fearing mother could not stop him and had to let him go, she did the only thing she could do: bend her knees and beg the Lord if He would be merciful to her son. And...he had barely arrived on the other side and set foot on the soil of that new country, when, unasked, he heard these words: "The same God of the Netherlands is here too." Although he had turned his back upon God, God did not let him go. Later on, he served as an elder for many years. Who would have expected that?

There is hope—also for our young people who have left us! Many have done so, perhaps thousands of them. I have no idea where they are. Parents and grandparents, there is, however, one comfort: God knows where they are!

His truth will stand forever,
His covenant-bonds He will not sever!

God would not be unjust if He would not be merciful to a single one of them. That would be just indeed! We cannot make a single claim to the contrary. Nevertheless, He will pursue them for His Name's sake! None for whom Christ shed His precious blood will be plucked out of the hands of this blessed Savior. I once read that—and I believe it to be true—if there will be one thing on the last day that will give God's children reason to be eternally amazed and joyful, it will be that they are there themselves. For them that will obviously be the greatest miracle of all. However, they will also be amazed and joyful when they shall witness what has become of their seed! That which they never dared to anticipate—that which they never dared to either hope for or witness during their lifetime—they will then witness. Then their children and grandchildren will be among the redeemed. They will then see those who belonged to the seed of the church.

I know of someone who during his youth caused his father much grief. His sinful conduct, humanly speaking, significantly contributed to the premature death of his God-fearing father, whose hair had turned grey from sorrow. After his father had passed away, the Lord conquered the young man's heart. As did the prodigal son, he too came to himself. He could no longer go to his human father and ask him for forgiveness. Happily, he could come to the heavenly Father who is ready to forgive for Jesus's sake (Psa. 86:5). He was privileged to experience what so many have experienced throughout the ages:

But when I owned my trespass,
My sin hid not from Thee,
When I confessed transgression,
Then Thou forgavest me"
(Psalter 83:2—Psalm 32)

This prompted him to say, "When the last day arrives, my father will witness two miracles. The first miracle will be that he himself is there. However, he will then also see me, such a beast, and that will be an even greater miracle!"

There is hope for our children. There is also hope for the slain children of Bethlehem. We do not know with certainty whether they were all saved. We may believe, however, that a number of these children have been saved—perhaps all of them.

Do you know what the well-known and highly esteemed Theodore Vander Groe says regarding this hope in his exposition of the Heidelberg Catechism? He writes that he believes with confidence that all baptized small children who die in infancy shall be saved. Wilhelmus à Brakel believed this as well.

The authors of the Canons of Dort have provided us background information in which they documented all that transpired during the Synod of Dort. In this supportive documentation are recorded the opinions and sentiments of the various delegates. It is noted that some delegates emphasized that also regarding little children we must submit to the decree of God's election and reprobation. The Synod of Dort did indeed fully endorse that conclusion. However, they also recorded in the Canons of Dort (Head I, Art. 17) that parents whose children have died in infancy—believing parents who are members of the congregation of the Lord—should not doubt the salvation of their children who die in infancy. They should not consider it to be incumbent upon them to do so.

How many a parent has already been comforted by the words of this article of the Canons of Dort! How many of them have indeed found comfort in the Word of the Lord, "Out of the mouth of babes and sucklings hast Thou ordained strength" (Psa. 8:2)!

Congregation, such is indeed the message proclaimed to us by way of the dreadful massacre of the children of Bethlehem. What a blessing it is that God's Word sheds light upon this murder of infants! There is hope for your children!

That expectation also is part and parcel of the essential meaning of the birth of Christ. There is hope, for the Christ Child has been born! "For unto us a child is born, unto us a son is given: and the government shall be upon His shoulder: and His Name shall be called Wonderful, Counselor, The mighty God, The everlasting Father, The Prince of Peace" (Isa. 9:6).

Amen.